Authoring a Life

*A*uthoring a *L*ife

A WOMAN'S SURVIVAL IN AND THROUGH LITERARY STUDIES

BRENDA DALY

State University of New York Press

Published by
State University of New York Press, Albany

For information, address State University of New York Press,
State University Plaza, Albany, NY 12246

Production by Bernadine Dawes • Marketing by Patrick Durocher

Library of Congress Cataloging-in-Publication Data

Daly, Brenda   1941–
    Authoring a life : a woman's survival in and through literary
studies / Brenda Daly.
        p. cm.
    Includes bibliographical references and index.
    ISBN 0-7914-3679-9 (hc : alk. paper). – ISBN 0-7914-3680-2 (pbk.
: alk. paper)
    1. Incest victims–Rehabilitation. 2. Bibliotherapy.
3. Autobiography–Therapeutic use. 4. Incest in literature.
I. Title.
RC560.I53D35   1998
616.85'83606–dc21   97–45988
                                                                CIP

    10 9 8 7 6 5 4 3 2 1

For all my sisters

CONTENTS

PREFACE

In my last phone conversation with my mother—she died while *Authoring a Life* was in production—she asked me, again, why her two youngest daughters did not call her. I reminded her, as I had in the past, that my sisters had been sexually abused. "Not Darcy!" she answered immediately, adding, "Once I caught your father with Darcy in his arms, and I said, 'Where are you going with that girl?' and he stopped." In this remarkable admission—she had never before acknowledged having observed my father in the act of sexually abusing a daughter—I could hear my mother's fantasy: that she could say, with authority, "Stop," and my father would stop. But the terrible truth was that my mother had not stopped my father: the abuse began with my older sister in 1947, when she was only seven, and continued until 1968, when my youngest sister left home at age sixteen. Following my reiteration of this truth, my mother was silent; then, as so often happened, she changed the subject. Her roses were beautiful, she said, and her tomatoes were ripening nicely. She had almost completed quilts for two great-grandchildren. Having long ago accepted her habit of denial, I allowed my mother to change the topic. As always, I said in closing, "I love you, Mom." "I love you, too," she answered. I wasn't sure how to interpret my mother's silence the following Sunday because it was her turn to call me that week. However, based on past experience, I knew that her silence could last for a long time: once, in the mid-1970s, she had not spoken to me for two years.

Her silence on Sunday, August 17th, might mean only that she was sleeping—she was aging and arthritic—but it might also mean that she was punishing me. Perhaps, I speculated, she didn't wish to talk to me because I had again reminded her—when prompted by the persistent question, Why didn't her daughters call?—that my sisters had been sexually abused. Did she remember, I asked, how she had run away when in 1983, my sisters, Una Fay and Che Che, had asked her to meet with them to talk about the abuse? My mother had answered, "I wasn't ready then. I know more about incest now from reading and watching television. I am ready now." I was hopeful but cautious: did she, at last, feel ready to talk with my sisters about their feelings of violation and betrayal? I recalled the loving letter my sisters had written her in 1983: they longed for our mother's acknowledgment of their abuse, as well as for a mother-daughter reconciliation. Understanding that my mother would be afraid and guilty, they had generously offered her the power to choose a therapist-mediator. Now, tragically, before a reconciliation could take place, our mother had died. When I called her that Sunday in August, her body had already lain on the kitchen floor for two days. This time her silence was final.

While my mother was alive, she had often used "the silent treatment," as her children called it, as a method of punishment. Perhaps because, like so many women, she had been silenced herself, she knew its terrible power. Since I feared her long silences, I wondered, as I wrote *Authoring a Life,* how my mother would respond if I invited her to read it. On the one hand, I wanted her to read my book—she was my ideal reader, the reader I most wanted to hear me. I wanted her to understand that, although she was not to blame for what my father did, she could take action against child abuse, not alone, but with other women. I wanted her to know about feminists such as Florence Rush and Louise Armstrong who had spoken out against the sexual abuse of children. On the other hand, I feared that my mother, whose views of the family came from the religious and political right, would resist my feminist analysis of child sexual abuse. If she read *Authoring a Life,* I surmised, she would probably subject me, once again, to the silent treatment. Although the loss of my mother's love would be a terrible price to pay for writing this book, I had decided—for the sake of my sisters and myself–that the terrible truth of father-daughter incest must once again be told. What is this "truth"?

Here, in my view, is the crux of the problem–the problem of truth, authority, authorship. Who has the authority to claim to speak "the truth"–or even "a truth"? When I write about father-daughter incest, I know that my credibility–my authority–will be challenged, and not only by those who wish to deny or ignore its reality, but also by those who view autobiography as a form of fiction. Since the lives of my sisters–all my sisters– are at stake, I do not view the debate over the status of autobiography as a strictly literary matter. If we are to change an educational system which taught my mother that "father knows best" even if it meant sacrificing her daughters, an educational system that treated my sisters as second-class citizens or even prisoners, an educational system that has historically failed to acknowledge women's voices and texts, we must address the political issue of authorial "truth." While acknowledging that memories may be unreliable–for example, when I relate a conversation, my words may sometimes be inexact–I insist on one truth: that my sisters and I are survivors of father-daughter incest. My sisters, all of whom have read the manuscript of *Authoring a Life,* support this claim. Even though their views of father-daughter incest may differ from mine–just as their experiences were more severe than mine–we also agree that our father's incestuous acts, along with our mother's denial of the abuse, came close to destroying our family.

However, since the death of our mother, some wounds have begun to heal. As Darcy says, "Since our mother's death the embracing of one another that you and I have experienced has been a great comfort to me." I agree, with all my heart. When she says, "I am sorry that our family dysfunction did not allow me to be there for you as a sister," I answer, "I am sorry too." It means a great deal to me that, after reading *Authoring a Life,* Darcy responded, "I love and respect you for the work that you have done and continue to do, both personally and in your literary field. It is always a risk for a victim to speak the truth, but one I have found to be quite healing and therefore worth taking." Since our mother's death, Darcy and I have committed ourselves to resolving our conflicts openly rather than withdrawing in silence. She says, "I too have learned outside our family that there are some relationships which are capable of resolving conflict." As each of us has begun to learn the other's "truth," the other's story, Darcy comments, "You and I have walked different but, in some ways, similar paths for our survival and recovery from incest." Each of us, through this sharing of stories, is supportive of the other's efforts to author her own life.

ACKNOWLEDGMENTS

I would like to acknowledge the support of Linda Alcoff, Dorothy Allison, Chester Anderson, David Bleich, Lynn Z. Bloom, Charlotte and David Bruner, Susan Carlson, Stephan Daly, Andrea Dern, Louise De Salvo, Elizabeth E. Flynn, Diane Freedman, Olivia Frey, Shirley Nelson Garner, Laura Gray, Lee Hadley, Arlene Halldorson, Ann Barger Hebert, Marianne Hirsch, Roseanne Hoefel, Carol Holly, Carole Kazmierski, Fern Kupfer, Angela Larson, Che Che Luckine, Debra Marquart, Toni McNaron, Theresa McCormick, Michael Mendelson, Sidney Morris, Joyce Carol Oates, Sharon O'Brien, Lois Patton, Steve Pett, Derionne Pollard, Laurin Porter, Susan Porterfield, Laura Armstrong Randolph, Maureen Reddy, Martha Roth, Una Fay Rystedt, Christina Sanchez, Elaine Showalter, Jane Smiley, Kathy Sotol, John Solensten, Madelon Sprengnether, Jane Tompkins, Roberta Vann, Faye Whitaker, Karl Woelz, Susan Woods, Suzanne Zilber, and Frances Zauhar.

Thanks also to those who granted permission to reprint all or portions of previously published essays: to *The Children's Literature Association Quarterly* for "Father-Daughter Incest in Hadley Irwin's *Abby, My Love*" (1992); to *Hurricane Alice: A Feminist Review* for "I VIVIDLY REMEMBER, pretty well" (1983); and to Duke University Press for "My Friend Joyce Carol Oates" from *The Intimate Critique*, eds. Diane Freedman, Olivia Frey, and Frances Murphy Zauhar (1992).

CHAPTER 1

Death of the Author, Birth of an Author

What we need, instead of a theory of the death of the author,

is a new concept of authorship that does not naively assert

that the writer is an originating genius.

−Cheryl Wall

The architectonic activity of authorship, which is the building

of a text, parallels the activity of human

existence, which is the building of a self.

−Clark and Holquist

Only a feeling person can grasp the way an empty

theory may function as a means to power, for he or she will

not be intimidated by incomprehensibility.

−Alice Miller

WHEN MY FATHER DIED IN 1976, I was thirty-five years old, but I had not yet become the person I wanted to be. A survivor of childhood sexual abuse, I suffered from shame and self-doubt so severe that my imagination had been constricted and my professional development impeded. As a young woman, I had, with fear and trembling, managed to become a high school English teacher, but I hadn't dared dream of becoming an author. Yet for victims of trauma, the act of authoring is an essential step in the recovery process: in order to reconstruct meaningful lives, they must put their traumatic experiences into narrative form. It is a task that, as Judith Lewis Herman says, "challenges an ordinary person to become a theologian, a philosopher, and a jurist" (*Trauma and Recovery* 178). It is also a task that creates a painful double-bind for the victim: as a result of her violation, she cannot imagine herself the author of her life, but in order to recover a sense of agency she must tell the story of her traumatic experience(s), complete with accompanying affect. Until she is capable of this act of narration, a victim may unconsciously constrict her imagination, as well as her life, in order to feel safe. In short, recovery is primarily, though not exclusively, a linguistic event, an act of authorship by which a woman transforms her victim-self into her ideal-self.

When I began a doctoral program shortly after my father's death, I didn't understand any of these things. Indeed, because

3

my father had abused my sisters much more severely, I didn't identify myself as an incest victim. Furthermore, I had not yet fully recognized that my mind–my intelligence and imagination– had been constricted by listening, fearfully, night after night, as my older sister struggled against my father's sexual advances. I now understand that, as a result of this fearful listening, I have suffered for years not only from "learned helplessness," but also from what Judith Lewis Herman calls "witness guilt." This guilt inhibited me, time after time, from imagining myself an author: what right did I have to claim a life in language, to become an author, when my sister had been denied authority over her own body? How could I go forward without her? How could I claim the power–the power to be heard–which she had been denied? In part because of my guilt, in part because of my shame, I dared not think of myself as an author at the time I began a doctoral program. I thought of myself primarily as an insightful reader who might become a professor and who might one day publish literary criticism. Gradually, however, with the encouragement of feminist professors at the University of Minnesota, I began to entertain the possibility that–if I had the courage to break my silence about childhood sexual abuse–I might become part of a community of feminist women, women who dared to write and speak with authority.

Unfortunately, because I was a graduate student when I finally recognized myself as a survivor of incest, I could not take the time to find a feminist therapist. Given my age and poor financial situation–I had filed for divorce after my first year of graduate work–my first priority was to finish my degree and find a job. After completing my course work and dissertation in 1984, I took a low-paying lectureship while continuing to seek a tenure-line job. When I moved in 1986 to take a one-year teaching position, I came close to a nervous breakdown: I felt that my plot had run out. With each new challenge, old fears of abandonment and self-doubt intensified. I knew that if, by some miracle, I actually found a tenure-line position, I would have to move again. Having already lost my family, my home, and my community, I wasn't sure I could sustain any further losses. During the final year of my job search, I managed to survive by imagining myself a water lily which, though it might appear to float freely on the water's surface, is actually anchored securely, by invisible roots, in the mud. In 1987, when I finally found a tenure-line job, I considered myself reasonably safe. However, since I could achieve tenure only by speaking and writing effectively, I faced yet another challenge: imagining myself as someone who could speak, in the classroom and at conferences, and write with genuine (not feigned) authority.

Ironically, during the very years I was struggling to imagine myself an author, I learned that, according to Michel Foucault and Roland Barthes, "the author" was dead. Initially, since it appeared that neither of these theorists could help me to write with authority, I resisted their views of language, just as I resisted the views of French feminists such as Helene Cixous, Luce Irigaray, and Julia Kristeva. To imagine my mind as having been invaded by the Father was a concept of language that I abhorred, undoubtedly because it paralleled too closely my experience of sexual invasion by the father. At the same time, I began to suspect that my anxieties about language—the pervasive self-doubt that inhibited my ability to speak and write with confidence—originated in my childhood experience of abuse and helplessness. The poisonous lesson of my childhood was that I could speak, I even could cry out, but no one would hear me, no one would listen. In what sense, then, did I possess language? What was the point of speaking and writing if no one listened? At the same time, I wanted, more than anything else, to be heard and believed. If I told the story of how my sisters had been sexually molested as children, I wanted people to believe that they had not fantasized this abuse, nor had they desired it. But who was I to challenge the Bible and Sigmund

Freud? As told in the Biblical story, Lot's daughters seduced him; they initiated the incest. I also knew from reading Freud–who concluded that his patients had fantasized paternal sexual abuse–that psychiatrists did not believe women patients who told them they had been sexually abused by their fathers.[1]

What I needed most–to examine the debilitating effects of paternal sexual abuse on a woman's ability to use language, to read, write, speak, and listen–was authority. It is difficult for women to claim such linguistic authority, according to some feminist theorists, because language is governed by the Law of the Father. Under this Law, women may speak, but their voices are ventriloquated; therefore, women must invent a new language. Without this new language, without a "mother tongue," women could not speak or write their own desires. Since my own mother had almost no linguistic authority–she couldn't discipline her children without threatening, "Wait until your father comes home!"–I was skeptical of this notion of a mother tongue. My skepticism was intensified by that fact that during the 1950s, if my mother had tried to tell health-care authorities that her husband was sexually abusing her daughters, she might not have found anyone to believe her.[2] It was not until the early 1970s that feminists such as Florence Rush began to challenge Freud's view of father-daughter incest. And not until the late 1960s did women writers–such as Maya Angelou and Joyce Carol Oates–begin to tell the incest story from the daughter's perspective. So far as I know, the story has never yet been told from a maternal perspective.[3] Even though mothers clearly possess linguistic ability–in fact, they are more likely than fathers to teach children to speak–they have rarely had authority over public discourses, such as religion, law, history, education, politics.

Yet I have come to believe, with Mikhail Bakhtin, that "we must all, perforce, become authors."[4] As Nancy Miller and Cheryl Wall argue, the "death of the Author" does not work for women because it "prematurely forecloses the question of identity for them" (Miller, "Changing the Subject" 106; quoted in Wall 556). Women's relationship to language differs from that of men: while sons assume they have a "natural" right to authority, a right to authorship, women have been taught that their rightful inheritance is maternal silence. Therefore, if it is true that "the author" is dead, I prefer to imagine that it is the father-author, the author who demanded silence from his victimized daughters, who has died. If this god-the-father-author is truly dead, it might then be possible for feminists, at long last, to redefine the act of authorship. Women have been engaged in this struggle, as I came to learn, for centuries. For example, in the eighteenth century, according to Susan Lanser in *Fictions of Authority*, women novelists began to redefine authorship as a communal rather than an individual act; yet so pervasive is the notion of individual authorship that narratologists have had no term for communal authorship. Unfortunately, until I began a doctoral program in feminist studies of literature, I knew nothing about women's struggle to redefine authorship because, as an undergraduate in the 1960s, I hadn't studied any women writers.

Like most women of my generation, I had been miseducated—denied knowledge of literary foremothers such as Edith Wharton or Virginia Woolf—while taught to revere male writers. As a result, while I thought of myself as a reader, I couldn't imagine myself a writer. It was not until after the death of my father in 1976 that I declared, with newfound audacity, that Joyce Carol Oates, a contemporary woman novelist, deserved as much critical attention as Shakespeare, Twain, or Joyce. It was very important for me to finally claim the right to study the fiction of a brilliant woman writer, in particular a woman whose fiction illustrates Phyllis Chesler's point that father-daughter incest functions as a paradigm of the imbalance of power in heterosexual relationships.[5] In Oates's fiction men who marry women half their age—as, for example, the wealthy Mr. Revere does in *A Garden of Earthly Delights*–are located on a continuum with those men who, like my father, take their own daughters as their wives. Because Oates's novels provided a feminist analysis of father-daughter incest, her fiction spoke for me before I could speak for myself. While some women refuse to read Oates because her characters are "frightening" (Juhasz 272), I am attracted to her fiction for exactly this reason: it enables me to confront the darkness. Oates's fiction provided me with a safe space–a therapeutic space–in which to imagine and understand frightening characters and events, some of them evocative of my nightmare childhood. Reading a woman writer taught me the power, not only of reading, but also of writing. That is why, once the women's movement taught me to think big–to think that I too might become an author–I was determined to write about the fiction of Joyce Carol Oates. My dissertation would be a rough sketch of this project; when I achieved a tenure-line position I would write the book. It was the boldest dream I had ever dreamt.

But by 1987, the year I finally found a job, the symptoms of my traumatic past had become almost overwhelming: when I spoke in public, I would black out, and when I wrote, I could produce words only after waging a painful struggle against my own increasingly rigid body. My recovery began when I began to explore, through an analysis of this physical symptom, my paralyzing fear of speaking and writing. Even before seeing a therapist, I suspected that this fear was rooted in a childhood myth, a myth that had provided me with at least the illusion of safety: if I were perfectly obedient, if I lay perfectly still, my father would not notice me. I would be safe from his sexual attentions. I hypothesized, as a child, that my father had abused my sister because she was "bad"–by which I meant that she was daring, a risk-taker. I would be safe, then, as long as I was "good." Once, in fact, when my father chastised me for a minor infraction of his law–I had come home a few minutes late from a date—my fright was so great that I fainted. To my surprise, my disappearance act so astonished my father—or so I assume—that his anger turned to pity. As I explain in chapter 1 of *Authoring a Life*, I maintained this myth of the "good" girl because only by seeing my sister as a "bad girl" could I believe myself safe. The problem with this defense mechanism is that for years I was alienated from my beloved sister. Another problem, as Herman maintains in *Father-Daughter Incest*, is that such defense mechanisms create enormous amounts of psychic tension which may become manifest in a wide range of self-defeating behaviors.

In my case, it appears that the "good girl" of my childhood (the-self-frozen-in-the-past) tried to control the "bad girl," (the-ideal-self-in-the-present), the transgressive daughter who dared to write and present feminist papers. According to the childhood logic of my unconscious, a woman with the courage to advance a feminist thesis would inspire the father's wrath. As Roberta Culbertson says of a more severely traumatized survivor: "Finally free, she was silenced by her own memory; or more precisely, by the loss of the self who might communicate, by the continuing concomitant bodily reality of her wounding and her memories of it, and by the persistence of a limited survivor self" (173). I (the intellectual I) knew better, but my unconscious—my more limited survivor self—was resisting, armoring itself by way of physical rigidity. My body's resistance to speaking or writing was exacerbating my struggle for academic and personal survival. After years of accumulated stress—divorce, doctoral program, job search, several new jobs and relocations—came the additional stress of earning tenure. In the past—when I heard my father entering the bedroom I shared with my sister—I recall being frozen with fear; now the symptom had returned, as if of its own volition. In response to intrusion," says Ellyn Kaschak, "women do freeze more . . . and also maintain a tenser posture at rest" (48). Stress often triggers physical symptoms, according to Herman, but flash-backs are more likely to occur if the trauma has been repressed. Because the psychic tension between my mind and body mani-fested itself in physical pain, a friend recommended that I see a chiropractor. However, in my state of hyperarousal—a state of "permanent alert, as if the danger might return at any moment," as Herman explains (*Trauma and Recovery* 35)—I could not allow any-one, least of all a man, to touch me.

Instead, for the second time in my life, I sought a woman therapist. In order to feel safe, I had to find a feminist therapist whom I could count on to believe my story. Because Freud—as well as Jung, his famous disciple—had discredited the stories of incest survivors,[6] I feared that even in the 1990s some therapists might not believe me. Their disbelief would seriously impede my recov-ery, and, possibly, cause me further trauma. I knew that I must have a therapist who believed me: it was a matter of personal and professional survival. If I were to earn tenure, I had only a few months in which to overcome my speaker and writer's block. Fortunately, through a feminist network, I was able to find such a therapist, and I began work immediately. Since I recognized that my intellectual "self" could not solve this problem, I deliberately made myself receptive to dreams and images. When an image of a woman-in-the-room emerged, I told my therapist. At once, she said, "Tell me more about her." The woman was sitting in a chair, I responded, in the middle of an empty room. She looked as if she had been abandoned. "What kind of chair?" my therapist asked, "Is it upholstered, for example?" I answered, "It's a plain wooden chair, the kind that the Shakers made—very simple, almost severe." Shakers, she pointed out, practice celibacy. Did this mean, I won-dered, that I was still afraid of sex? Did it mean, perhaps, that I did not wish to produce? One thing was clear: I was resisting linguistic production. These associations prompted recollections of my inner life.

In a jocose-serious voice, I explained my fantasy of an endowed chair: during my search for a tenure-line position, my mother—who had recently inherited farm land and mineral rights—would strike oil and, with her wealth, would endow a university chair. I would occupy this chair and, from this powerful feminist place, help to change the world. Since my reality principle was intact, I knew that such a miraculous mother-rescue would not occur. Finally, when these explorations of the woman-in-the-room appeared to be fruitless, I asked, "Perhaps I should redecorate the room?" "Oh, no," my therapist said, "Get her out of there." I understood, then, that she viewed the woman as stuck inside the empty room. Even though Virginia Woolf, herself a survivor of childhood sexual abuse, had argued that, if a woman wishes to write, she must have a room of her own and an independent income, this room had somehow become a kind of prison. The-woman-in-the-room, I came to understand, was not so much an image of my accomplishments, but an image of constriction, of my attempt to contain fear. As Herman explains in *Trauma and Recovery*, "In an attempt to create some sense of safety and to control their pervasive fear, traumatized people restrict their lives" (46). In fact, the image of the-woman-in-the-room may be a double-memory, an overlay of two moments of transition and stress: one memory from my adolescence, when I was about to leave my father's house to go to college, the other from the time when, as a divorced woman, I left my husband's house to complete my doctoral degree.

Shortly before I left for college in 1959, my father had walked into my bedroom while I was dressing to go out on a date. I was wearing only my slip, but what made the situation even worse was that my father, walking in a trancelike state, was nude. I was paralyzed with fear, but he didn't touch me. When he finally left the room, I returned to what I thought was "normal." Apparently, this traumatic moment—during which I felt vulnerable to paternal

11

attack—had remained frozen in my memory. Because stressful transitions often trigger flashbacks and hyperarousal, I was frozen with fear once again when, more than twenty years later, in 1986, I was about to sell the home I had shared with my husband and son. On this occasion, a therapist—whom I imagined as a mother-surrogate—helped me to overcome my fear long enough to sell my house, move to a nearby city, and take a one-year position as a professor of English. One year later, it was necessary to move again, this time to take a tenure-line job. I felt very much alone. Finally, I had a room and income of my own, but I could not write. Once again, I needed the presence of a maternal figure, someone capable of nonjudgmental listening. Kristeva explains why this is necessary when she says, echoing Melanie Klein, "I think that in the imaginary, maternal continuity is what guarantees identity" (quoted in Glass 22).

With a therapist who acted as maternal presence, I realized that the woman-in-the-room was afraid of moving out, afraid of moving on. At first I despised this frightened woman, but gradually I began to visualize her as a girl still locked inside her father's house, listening to the sounds in the night, frozen with fear. This girl had prayed for her mother's help, but she had not come. Finally, I realized that this child-self would not leave the room as long as I despised her; instead, I must grieve for her. As I searched my memory for farewell rituals, I recalled that on moving days I would always go back for one last look at each empty room. With the security of this ritual, I returned to the woman-in-the room to begin the painful process of letting go of a former self. Suddenly one day, the-woman-in-the-room appeared to me on the page of a large coloring book: as melting crayons flowed out of the room, coloring the yard, I watched the woman emerge from her isolated room. I had not noticed, until that moment, that the-woman-in-the-room had always appeared in static tones of gray. With the grief for this lost self, came the letting go. With the flowing of my tears, my imagination was again in motion. At last, I could envision myself as part of the world, a world in "living" color. Now that these mute but painful memories were integrated into my new "self"–a more fluid narrative self–I felt that I would be able to write again. But could I speak in public? To reassure myself on this point, I transformed the woman-in-the-room into a an invisible maternal presence hovering just above my right shoulder. If I became nervous before presenting a paper, I could call upon this presence to absorb my fear.

Thus, I owe my recovery–a recovery that continues to this day–to a mysterious, moving image: the transformation of an image of a woman alone in a room, abandoned and helpless, into a nurturing maternal presence. I describe it as "mysterious" because, although the image itself is quite ordinary, I do not, even now, fully understand where it came from, or why it began to change. But the image did change, and I know that this moment of metamorphosis–a moment at which the frozen image became fluid–signified my return to health. My frozen self, a constricted identity impairing my ability to function, became part of a more fluid "author-self." I understand this more fluid author-self, not as a "core," but as a self which, though once injured by traumatic experience, is now healed, largely through a narrative process that enabled me to integrate frozen memories (images from the past) into my present life. As long as the affect of earlier traumas were stored as fragments, as suggested by the image of the woman-in-the-room, I could neither write nor overcome an often pervasive sense of helplessness. Happily, with the convergence of image, music, and color, I no longer needed to image my "self" as isolated in a room, frozen into a protective posture; instead, I could imagine myself as ontologically secure enough to venture outside the room and, in time, confident enough to welcome the linguistic flow of writing. According to my own reflective experience, then, Julia Kristeva is right: the subject is fluid, the subject is a process.

In retrospect, I understand that my father's struggle to maintain a unified identity—a dominant "core" of masculinity—made him a monster inside his own family, a monster unable to see his own double or, in Jungian terms, his shadow self. Within the privacy of his own family, his repressed self, his shadow self, emerged. Because my father had not integrated his shadow, it became destructive. Therefore, I found it frightening to claim my own shadow-self, my "bad girl," but once I had accepted her, integrating her with the "good girl," my author-self finally emerged. Through this process I have learned that in order to become an "author"—that is, to develop the courage to risk linguistic self-assertion—it is necessary to put "unspeakable acts" into words. Herman explains why this is so. Normal memory, she says, might be described as "'the action of telling a story,' while traumatic memory, by contrast, is wordless and static" (*Trauma and Recovery* 175). Initially, Herman says, the survivor recounts the trauma "as a series of still snapshots or a silent movie; the role of therapy is to provide the music and words" (175). Probably because my traumatic experiences were not as severe as my sisters'—that is, I was not as repeatedly or aggressively violated as they—it took only a few months of therapy before I experienced the return of words and music, along with, in my case, color.

Since that time, I have come to view the creation of an ideal self and the writing of autobiographical criticism as parallel activities, activities which enable me to claim a sense of agency almost lost to me during my childhood. A survivor must tell her story, Herman explains, because "this work of reconstruction actually transforms the traumatic memory, so that it can be integrated into the survivor's life story" (*Trauma and Recovery* 175). That is why Bakhtin's belief, that "we must all, perforce, become authors" inspired the title of this study. Because Bakhtin's concept of the author assumes a self-in-relationship—one cannot author without a listener or reader—it is congruent with my own experience: without someone to hear my story, without someone willing and able to bear witness, I would not have recovered my capacity for self-authoring. Indeed, one of the most traumatic aspects of paternal rape is that the father, to whom the daughter turns for protection, is deaf to her voice. I reject this paternal notion of authority, along with this notion of authoring. To author a life is, for me, to bear witness, not only to my own trauma, but to the traumas of others. As Dori Laub explains, "Bearing witness to a trauma is, in fact, a process that includes the listener. For the testimonial process to take place, there needs to be a bonding, the intimate and total presence of an *other*–in the position of one who hears. Testimonies are not monologues; they cannot take place in solitude. The witnesses are talking to somebody: to somebody that they have been waiting for for a long time" (Felman and Laub 70–71).

As Ronnie Janoff-Bulman emphasizes, bearing witness is one way that survivors find meaning in their suffering. The question is, Should academic readers be expected to "bear witness"? My answer is a decided yes, but not all academics agree. For example, when I used the phrase "bearing witness" in an autobiographical-critical essay submitted to an academic journal, one reader objected. "Sorry," the report read, "the evangelical language of 'bearing witness' (used twice in this essay) makes me squirmy. Might be because a former chair, a weekend minister, used it in talking about what we do when we go to conferences." Were I still afflicted with shame, I might perceive such criticism as a lack of support, as abandonment. However, my ego is no longer so fragile; furthermore, because I wanted to publish the essay, I tried to determine whether this reader, having found the topic of sexual abuse too emotionally charged, was attacking my prose rather than acknowledging her own discomfort. As I know from experience, survivor stories make listeners uncomfortable. "It is very tempting," as Herman says, "to take the side of the perpetrator. All the perpetrator asks is that the bystander do nothing. . . . The victim, on the contrary, asks the bystander to share the burden of pain. The victim demands action, engagement, and remembering" (*Trauma and Recovery* 7). However, in this instance, the reader's criticism of my prose was not an attempt to avoid engagement or avoid sharing the burden of pain; in fact, she recommended that the journal "pursue" the piece, which she found "provocative."

But this mixed genre has its critics. For example, Daphne Patai argues that the feminist phrase, "the personal is political"– which, as she says, means "making public the long-neglected personal stories of women disrupts the traditional version of masculine culture and challenges the conventional boundaries between public and private life"–has been "reduced to near meaninglessness through sheer overextension" (53). On the contrary, academics have only begun to examine our responses, as readers and writers, to the violations of conventional boundaries between public and private life. Nevertheless, when feminists criticize the use of the personal in academic essays, describing it as self-indulgent, exhibitionistic,[7] or simply irrelevant, I take this criticism seriously. If it is true, as Daphne Patai argues, that autobiographical writing leaves us "with nothing more than a shared awareness that scholarly works do not descend from heaven, but are written by human beings" (53), what have we actually accomplished? For example, when I write about the sexual abuse of children, what difference does it make that I, like many women, have actually experienced such abuse? I understand that, for some readers, personal revelation would actually weaken my argument against male violence since, presumably, I lack the objectivity of a detached observer.

My answer to such charges is this: when Freud decided that his patients were not credible, that they were fantasizing sexual violation by their fathers, women did not have the institutional power–they did not have the public authority–to challenge Freud's conclusions. As a consequence, hysterics were defined as liars and, for years, told to ignore their own experiences to achieve mental health. Freud's lie—which, in a generous mood I call a "mistake"—forced me, while a doctoral student, to read the following theoretical nonsense: "If hysterics lie, they are above all the first victims of a kind of lie or deception. Not that they have been lied to; it is rather as though there existed in the facts themselves a kind of fundamental duplicity for which we would propose the term deceit" (Laplanche 34). What does Laplanche mean by the phrase: "not that they have been lied to"? He does not attempt to clarify the phrase, but instead obfuscates its meaning and confuses his readers. This way of doing theory has had severe consequences for hysterics—that is, for sexually abused women and men. It took the collective power of women, during the second wave of the women's movement, to challenge the damaging Freudian view of father-daughter incest which Laplanche reiterates in this passage. In the meantime, for almost one hundred years, victims of sexual abuse—including my own sister—were victimized by therapists who refused to believe them. Although victims cannot claim unmediated access to our experience—I recognize that patriarchal language shaped my experience and understanding of father-daughter incest for many years—survivors must claim the authority to name and theorize our own experiences.

It is only by developing feminist theories that we can defend women from potentially damaging theories. Regardless of race, as bell hooks argues, women must resist the impulse to leave the theorizing to white men, for theories which have not been tested by the experiences and insights of women can be used to oppress them. James Glass makes this point in *Shattered Selves*. As a result of his study of women suffering from multiple personality disorder—all of whom are victims of paternal sexual abuse—he argues that it is irresponsible for poststructuralists to base their arguments of fragmented identity on textual examples only. While I agree with Glass on this point, I disagree that the only alternative is to return to a concept of a "core" self. Since the concept of a "core" self retains its associations with normative a "masculine" subject, I prefer Julia Kristeva's poststructuralist notion of a "subject in process." Significantly, and despite his commitment to the concept of a core self, Glass found Kristeva's theory of a "subject in process" compatible with humane treatment of women suffering from multiple personality disorder. In my view, because theories of identity–of the self or the subject–have the potential to damage us, women cannot afford to leave such theorizing to men. Yet not all feminists believe that theory has value: Nina Baym states the case against theory in "The Madwoman and Her Languages: Why I Don't Do Feminist Theory," while Laurie Finke argues the case for theory in "The Rhetoric of Marginality: Why I Do Feminist Theory." My position is that we must "do theory," but we must, as Jane Tompkins suggests in "Me and My Shadow," do it differently. Survivors of father-daughter incest must, for example, insist on the right to theorize our own experiences, not by avoiding emotions, but by including them in our analysis.

As Alison Jaggar argues, Western epistemology is "shaped by the belief that emotion should be excluded from the process of attaining knowledge" (lecture cited by Tompkins 123). This belief is, as Tompkins points out, oppressive to women. "Because women in our culture are not simply encouraged but required to be the bearers of emotion, which men are culturally conditioned to repress, an epistemology which excludes emotions from the process of attaining knowledge radically undercuts women's epistemic authority" ("Me and My Shadow" 123).[8] Tompkins explains, "I saw that I had been socialized from birth to feel and act in ways that automatically excluded me from participating in the culture's most valued activities. No wonder I felt so uncomfortable in the postures academic prose forced me to assume; it was like wearing men's jeans" (124). Jaggers' insight also enabled me to understand not only my own discomfort with academic writing but also how my father had developed the capacity to objectify his own children. Because he had been culturally conditioned to repress emotion, he was deaf to the cries of his daughters. Indeed, his authority depended upon such deafness: as a father-author, he could not hear his daughters, nor could he see them as rightful owners of their own bodies. Rather, he had been taught to view them as his property. However, while Tompkins has decided that theory, "at least as it is usually practiced" (122), ought to be avoided, I believe it necessary to continue "wearing men's jeans" (to use Tompkins' simile) while, at the same time, feeling free to take the jeans off and stand "naked" before an academic audience.

Yet some academic readers respond with distaste—even disgust—to the nakedness of personal disclosures in academic writing. But what, exactly, is "good taste"? According to Richard E. Miller, taste is both "a way of being in the world in general, and a way of being in one's body in particular" (271). As Miller points out, we may believe our tastes in writing or art are "natural"—for example, we may react with disgust at "hearing someone discuss a personal tragedy in an academic forum" (271)—but taste is, in fact, something we have been taught. Although Miller argues that taste is largely determined by "one's social class or one's schooling" (271), my experience of near-paralysis during the writing process suggests that taste is also determined by gender training. It would be in very bad "taste," I had been taught, to disclose the trauma of childhood sexual abuse. Nevertheless, as I discovered, I could not make myself heard—I could not write with authority—until I had listened to my own muted body. As Miller suggests, "The writer's response, during the process of composing, might be a site at which to explore the relationship between modes of writing legitimated by the academy and the circulation of cultural capital in our society" (273). From the pain emanating from my body/mind[9] during the composing process, I was forced to acknowledge that I had once been a form of capital, my father's property. This familial lesson, reinforced by lessons at school and in church, had been"scored" deeply into my body/mind. To free myself from this debilitating childhood lesson, I would have to transgress conventions of "good taste."

How, then, would I speak to readers, particularly academic readers? Because mixed-genre writing includes emotions, which the academy has dictated shall be excluded, I have accepted the fact that *Authoring a Life* may offend some readers. At the same time, I am authorized to write in this mixed genre by the example of highly respected members of the contemporary feminist community. Two of the best known and earliest are the poet-critics Adrienne Rich and Susan Griffin; more recently Gloria Anzaldua, Lynne Z. Bloom, Diane Freedman, Jane Gallop, bell hooks, Nancy K. Miller, Sharon O'Brien, Madelon Sprengnether, Jane Tompkins, and many others have also synthesized the autobiographical and theoretical (or critical). Yet, despite numerous successful models of such writing by feminists, my doubts and anxieties continue to surface as I write autobiographical criticism. One reason for my insecurity is that the synthesis of autobiography and theory varies greatly—ranging from Jane Gallop's confessions of uncertainty while reading Lacan to the situational dynamics of television talk shows that often deny the power of theoretical analysis, or expertise, to survivors of sexual violence.[10] At least for a feminist audience, Gallop's revelation of uncertainty makes her authorial stance seem less godlike and more appealing; by contrast, revelations of uncertainty by an unknown incest survivor may automatically disqualify her as an expert on the topic. The status of the speaker, and the context in which she speaks, make all the difference. As a survivor of father-daughter incest, I know how vulnerable one can feel when acknowledging such a history; at the same time, I believe it is important for survivors to claim the right to theorize their experiences in the effort to change a culture in which such violence occurs.

Linda Alcoff and Laura Gray address this very problem in an article called "Survivor Discourse: Transgression or Recuperation?" They use a synthesis of autobiography (they briefly acknowledge the fact that they have been victims of sexual violence) and theory (Foucault corrected by feminist insights) to analyze the problem of confessional modes of discourse, primarily those confessional discourses that involve sexuality—including rape, incest, and sexual assault. After analyzing a variety of discourse situations, including television talk shows, they conclude:

> Our analysis suggests that the formulation of the primary political tactic for survivors should not be a simple incitement to speak out, as this formulation leaves unanalyzed the conditions of speaking and thus makes us too vulnerable to recuperative discursive arrangements. Before we speak we need to look at where the incitement to speak originates, what relations of power and domination may exist between those who incite and those who are asked to speak, as well as to whom the disclosure is directed. (284)

Alcoff and Gray argue that survivors, in their "struggle to maintain autonomy over the conditions of our speaking out if we are to develop its subversive potential" (284), must claim the right of "obstructing the ability of 'experts' to 'police our statements,' to put us in a defensive posture, or to determine the focus and framework of our discourse" (284). This analysis, as well as the work of bell hooks, has helped me to articulate why it is imperative that trauma survivors, along with members of oppressed groups, maintain authority over their own discourse.

As I know from experience, even when the occasion to speak out is provided by feminists, it is difficult for a survivor to strike the right balance between self-disclosure and self-censorship, between autobiography and theory. For example, when I sent an autobiographical-critical essay to Diane Freedman who was editing a collection called *Nexus*, she asked me to revise, omitting some textual references and providing more autobiography. Initially, because this request made me feel as if I were being asked to take off more clothing, I struggled to determine whether, by complying, I would be giving up authority over my own discourse. I finally recognized that Freedman's editorial recommendations would actually improve my essay, for in this case I was trying to hide behind theoretical/textual analysis. It was a strategy for armoring myself against the vulnerability I felt when writing in the confessional mode. As I wrestled with this issue, I determined that for me to speak with authority requires that I speak clothed in theory, whereas to speak strictly autobiographically means to stand naked, defenseless, exposed. This conflict—a conflict with myself, not with Freedman—forced me to acknowledge that I sometimes use theory as armor to protect myself and/or my audience from the embarrassment of emotion.

In *Authoring a Life*, a narrative of my survival in and through literary studies—a chronicle of my struggles to speak and write effectively—I strive to strike a balance between intellect and emotion. In the process, I sometimes encounter the conflicting conventions of genres, in particular, the conventions of autobiography and academic writing. In this way, I demonstrate—even as I tell—the manner in which I have been transformed by language, as well as the ways in which I am attempting to transform myself through language. The subject is fluid, according to Julia Kristeva; the author, as I imagine her, is also fluid, a work-in-progress, a collaborative subject. In chapter 2, "Pretending Not to Know, While Reading in the Dark," I illustrate how such a metamorphosis of the "I" occurs over time, largely through the intervention of the women's movement, but also through the therapy of reading in the dark. Chapter 3, "A Mother-Daughter Story," shifts the focus from fathers to mothers. It also illustrates the process of self-revision: in order to establish myself as a writer in the early 1980s, I had defined myself in opposition to maternal silence and victimization; however, ten years later, while coediting a collection of essays called *Narrating Mothers*, I recognized this oppositional practice–which is common among women writers–as a symptom of the destruction of mother-daughter bond in a patriarchal society. Fortunately, through the feminist emphasis on sisterhood–a sisterhood often in conflict, as I illustrate in chapter 4, "Sisterhood Is Powerful"–I have relearned the importance of developing strong bonds with other women.

Furthermore, because I believe that authorship is a collaborative process–without the women's movement I could not have become author of my life–I argue that survivors of sexual trauma must struggle to create a sense of community, despite our differences. For example, feminists must come to terms with the fact that, despite their successful efforts to transform the literature curriculum in colleges and universities, most junior and senior high school students continue to read the traditional canon. That is why, in chapter 5, "Politics and Pedagogy," I argue that a middle school classroom is an appropriate place to teach father-daughter incest narratives, particularly those designed for young adult readers. Victims of incest should not have to wait until they enter college to read narratives which enact resistance to the violence of father rule. However, chapter 6, "My Father/My Censor," explains why feminist professors may find it difficult to create trusting bonds with women who teach in junior and senior high schools. Curriculum reform in public schools is also hampered by parents who, because of their own desire not to know–their fear of knowledge–resist change. In chapter 7, "The Scarlet Letter I," a student and teacher, survivors of incest, engage in the collaborative process of self-authoring, openly debating how to read and teach stories of childhood sexual abuse. The concluding chapter, "What Do Survivors Need?" argues that teachers of literature must find ways to support young women who are struggling, through their engagement with language, to author their own lives.

CHAPTER 2

Pretending Not to Know, While Reading in the Dark

In order to protect the culprits, the authority figures,
from accusations of their victims, our society,
including professional experts,
stubbornly denies or glosses over and minimizes
the connection between what was endured
in childhood and later symptoms of illness.

—Alice Miller

That women identify less with authorities might be
accounted for by the fact that the authorities they meet
do not include women in their "we."

—Mary Field Belenky et al.

AWAKENING, I FELT A MAN'S HAND rubbing the nipples of my unformed breasts, first one, then the other, in a gentle circular motion. At first, dreamily, I felt only pleasure at being touched in this new way. Once fully awake, however, I stiffened with the sudden realization: my father was in my bed. Or, rather, I was in his bed. "Relax," he whispered, and I obeyed. Perhaps it was my instant obedience that stopped him. I will never know. I remember only that, suddenly, he stopped fondling my not-yet-breasts and held me gently, as a father would, in his shaking arms. Then he carried me back to my child-bed and, miraculously, never again touched me in a sexual way. It is difficult, even as an adult, to make sense of this experience.

When my father told me to "relax," what was his intent? If he imagined me an adult sexual partner, he may have meant I should enjoy the experience of sexual violence. Rapists do assume, or so they say, that their victims enjoy such violations. However, if my father saw me as the child I was, perhaps he meant that I should not fight him. As a child who had been raised to obey my parents, I heard my father's word "relax" as a command (which is why the word *seduction* is not accurate when describing father-daughter incest, even when nonviolent). Yet how does someone relax when ordered to do so? I recall that, at the word *relax,* my body, which was stiff with fear, went limp. However, despite my fear, my body (as if with a will of its own) began, gradually, to feel aroused. I was disoriented by this strange mixture of fear and arousal when, suddenly, to my great relief, my father stopped. Holding me, he seemed to grieve for what he had done. Was the man who stopped the same man who had carried me to his bed? Which man was my father? Was it his love for me that made the man able to stop himself? Such questions, difficult enough for an adult to comprehend, were baffling to me as an eleven year old.[11] Given this complex range of emotions, I can easily understand why some victims repress memories of sexual abuse. However, I did not forget this trauma. Moreover, as I struggle to find a narrative shape for this memory, I recognize that "truth" is a complex issue. Nevertheless, my body retained the memory of my father's touch–how could I have been so violated by such a gentle touch?–even though his motives continue to baffle me.

To further complicate matters, I had, for a number of years, been aware of my father's nocturnal visits to my older sister's side of the bed. She records her first memory of his abuse in the following words:

> I was seven years old. I recall my father gently picking me up from my bed to carry me and then falling back into deep sleep in his arms. My next memory is of awakening in terror. I couldn't breathe and was choking. This heavy man on top of me, I realized, was my father. His thighs clamped against my head, my legs held down by the ankles, and a hard, slimy thing shoved down my throat, and hairy, smelly stuff covering my face. I couldn't breathe, I couldn't yell, I couldn't get away. I was instinctively fighting for my very life. I struggled frantically to free myself. My arms were free. I clawed at the blankets covering us both. I blacked out–whether from lack of oxygen or fright, I don't know. (2–3)

Both my sister and I recall being carried from our beds into his, as if we were meant to take his wife's place, and both of us recall his first touch as gentle. Our accounts differ dramatically from this point on, the greatest difference being that my father's abuse of my sister was more violent and that his abuse of her continued for many years. She says, "I recall waking up in a dreamy, half-sleep feeling intense pleasure I had never experienced before. I awakened with a jolt of shock when I realized my father was manipulating my body with his fingers. I jerked his hand away, conscious of my sister sleeping next to me and the need to be silent. I was about ten years old."

I don't know where my mother was the night my father carried me into his bed, but my sister told me, years later when we finally talked about the abuse, that she was first molested while our mother was in the hospital having a baby. Struggling to make sense of the abuse, my sister concluded, "I had taken my mother's place in their bed and since she wasn't there, I was to assume responsibility for taking care of my father." Why, we wondered, had he continued to abuse her while he had stopped molesting me? Was it because he wanted a partner who would fight him, as my older sister had? Or did my father think of me as belonging, not to him, but to my mother? "She's *my* mother," I reportedly told the strange man I found in my mother's bed one morning. It was 1946, and with the end of the war, my father had finally returned from the navy. Since I had been born in 1941, my mother and sister had been my only family during most of the war years. Perhaps the obvious pleasure my mother took in repeating this story—punctuated with a daughter's bold assertion, "She's *my* mother"—made my father afraid I'd tell my mother what he had done. I shall never know for certain. But I didn't tell my mother. I didn't tell because, as a child, what would I say? I had no words to describe what had happened to me or to my sister, no words for what I felt. Words failed me.

29

By contrast, words did not fail me at school. Once, for example, the teacher praised me for explaining the process of photosynthesis to my classmates. It was a guilty triumph, however, because my explanation was not authentic: I didn't understand the connection between the words I repeated so glibly and the actual process of photosynthesis, which I had never observed. All through grade school, I puzzled over words which did not fit into my mental schema of how the world worked. I recall my confusion, for example, while listening to an excited voice on the radio report that two men were winning great numbers of "boats." The number kept growing until, finally, I could no longer imagine why one man might want so many boats. Eventually, someone explained what "votes" meant in an election for president of the United States. At home, certain things happened that I could not name, while in the wider world, I encountered names for things I had never seen happen: war, elections, photosynthesis. Throughout grade school, my love of words grew, along with my anxiety about using them. When I won the McKenzie County Spelling Bee in the fifth grade, my classmates awarded me a giant chocolate Easter egg. Strange prize: I didn't know how to share it, but I couldn't eat it by myself. Perhaps they bought that egg because they knew we were all about to hatch into the adult world. That year I quickly outgrew the new school clothes my aunt had sewn for me during the summer.

Increasingly, I felt the world, and my consciousness, splitting into two realms: the visible daylight world in which I was smart and "popular" (how I loathe that word), and the invisible night world, an unspoken world associated with dishonesty, shame, guilt, and self-doubt. It was probably the next year, in sixth grade, that I confronted, for the first time, my fear that the night world was somehow visible to others. When Edith Ann held our class's first boy-girl party, I happened to hear about the party, to which I had not been invited. I was struggling with the terrible pain of exclusion when, the day before the party, Edith Ann sent me a note asking that I meet her after school. When we met on the side-walk outside school, she asked me come to her party. She was sorry, she said, that she hadn't invited me. I went to the party, but I understood—from that time forward—that Edith Ann saw me as someone she would prefer to exclude. I wondered: did she know my secret? Some years later I understood that she hadn't guessed my secret; instead, she saw me as her chief competitor, not just for grades, but for boys. I saw myself as at a disadvantage in this com-petition, not because Edith Ann was prettier than I—in fact, I was probably considered "cuter"—but because I knew such a shameful secret. Eventually I would learn that guilty secrets don't show, that what is "inside" can be hidden from what is "outside."

I knew something that others my age did not; nevertheless, I was constantly pretending not to know so that others would see me as a "nice" girl, a "good" girl. In this disavowal of my own knowl-edge, however, I was actually not so different from other adoles-cent girls who, as Carol Gilligan says, "often seem divided from their own knowledge, regularly prefacing their observations by saying, 'I don't know'" (*Making Connections* 14). Part of the problem is that, for a girl, knowledge is often equated with being "bad." Since only "bad" girls know things, especially sexual things, I con-structed a false public persona: I was an "innocent" girl, a "good" girl who was smart but who didn't understand dirty jokes, a girl who took home economics rather than science. I pretended not to know. With the increasing divide between what I knew and what others thought I knew, I began to think of myself as playing a part. Like the protagonist of Hadley Irwin's *Abby, My Love*, a victim of father-daughter incest, I became a "schoolaholic" (see chapter 5). To avoid going home, I tried to participate in as many school activ-ities as possible in order to create a socially acceptable "self." This public persona would, I hoped, compensate for the unacceptable self I was inside. Smiling and cheerful, an "all American girl," I became an honor student (smart but not too smart), a cheerleader (athletic but not in a "masculine" way), a homecoming princess (not a queen, just a princess), coeditor of the student paper (competent but not too competent), and a Thespian (who played only bit parts, never major roles).

Despite my accomplishments, the principal somehow knew I wasn't worthy of going to college. Once, when he came to my home room to invite honor students to interview for college scholarships, he made his opinion of me known. After calling out the names of other honor students, he pointed to me and said, "You might as well come too." His words implied that, although it was a waste of time for someone like me to learn about scholarships, I "might as well come" for an interview since I happened (by some fluke) to be an honor student. What, in fact, did the principal's cruel phrase mean? In retrospect, I understand that, since the principal couldn't possibly have known about my family's shameful secret, he was probably alluding to my family's working-class status. If I had been the daughter of a doctor, he would have thought me deserving of a college education, perhaps even a scholarship. Since many men employed in public schools come from working-class backgrounds, he may have been projecting his own discomfort with his lack of class status onto me. For years I carried the shame of the principal's words, "You might as well come too," not knowing why they made me feel ashamed. Shortly after I had enrolled at the University of North Dakota, the Dean called me to his office to ask why I hadn't applied for a scholarship. I wish I had dared to say, "If you knew my family secret, you would know why I am not worthy of receiving a scholarship." However, what I told him was that my maternal grandfather, a wealthy farmer, was paying my room, board, and tuition.

I maintained my silence about sexual abuse in our family even when, in my junior year, I was invited to participate in a psychological study of students who, despite high scores on entrance examinations, were not achieving according to their ability. How could I tell the researchers that I chose the safety of a B average because it was too dangerous to do otherwise? When I look over my old college notebooks, I recognize myself as a "submissive" learner. I took copious notes in my literature and history courses, and I was adept at giving back these words on examinations. Once the instructor of my American literature class told me that if I wanted to earn an A I would have to go beyond what he had taught me. Had I understood what he meant, I wouldn't have dared try it. What would have happened, I wonder, had he taught even one novel by a woman writer? Recently, as I reread the stories I had written for an undergraduate creative writing class, I could see my struggle not to reveal anything about my personal history while, at the same time, drawing on my own life for story material. One untitled, incomplete story includes the following veiled reference to my father's possessiveness: "The exciting stories of Hamlet, Odysseus, and the other MEN in literature that I read in a college prep course had completely changed my romantic inclinations. Daddy would hardly object to my dates with them. They were secret. I went with them to the library and to the Wooden Steps. It's funny how reading a few books makes places seem different." This story, written in the painfully constricted voice of a "good girl," was never completed.

Like other girls of my era, I had a problem without a name. Only in retrospect, only after the emergence of the feminist movement, has it become possible for me to recognize how the lessons I learned at school and church complemented the lesson I learned at home: that men were in charge of these worlds. Although women might be mothers or teachers, men defined reality, using words to name some things, while not naming other things. Of course, the word *incest* was not used at all. Nor do I recall being assigned to read, either in high school or college, a single story by a woman. Women, as well as people of color, were entirely absent from the literature curriculum. And, although I read a lot—in grade school I won a prize for reading the most books in my class—I did not come across a single story about father-daughter incest. I doubt that in the 1950s such stories, at least for young adults, could be found in either the school or the public library. Today, narratives about father-daughter incest are readily available, including some suitable for young adults such as Maya Angelou's *I Know Why the Caged Bird Sings*, Hadley Irwin's *Abby, My Love*, and Toni Morrison's *The Bluest Eye*.[12] How might my life have changed had I read these stories while in junior high or high school, years when I lay in frozen silence as my sister struggled against my father? At that time, I wasn't aware that my experience was missing from the literature curriculum; nevertheless, I was aware that the men in charge—fathers, ministers, principals, doctors—spoke with authority even when what they said was quite at odds with my reality.

For example, my Lutheran minister informed me, when I was in high school and a member of Luther League, that dancing was "like having intercourse standing up." His voice was filled with disgust, but I wasn't sure then, nor am I sure now, which activity was more disgusting to him: sex or dancing. Since dancing was a source of great pleasure to me—the only way I could express sensuous delight without fear—his words didn't fit my reality. I also hated being forced each Sunday to repeat the liturgy, "I am by nature sinful and unclean." Why, I wondered, was I "unclean"? Alice Miller has an answer to this question; she argues that "the Church's struggle (supposedly an expression of God's will) against children's vitality is renewed daily by training them to be blindly obedient to those in authority and to think of themselves as wicked" (99). Fortunately, despite the cognitive confusion created by my religious training, I was in touch with my feelings. I recognized my anger. I saw the same anger in my aunt, my father's sister, Kari, when, at the funeral of my uncle Ivan, she stood up and shouted at the minister, "That's a lie. That's a damn lie!" Later I heard that the family had put my aunt away in a mad house. Is that what they did to you, I wondered, if you got mad? Undoubtedly, some of the anger I felt toward the church should have been directed toward my father, but it was far too dangerous to be angry with him. After all, he was "the head" of the only family I had.

Since no one ever spoke of what my father did to my sister, the message was clear: women were to bear such abuse in silence. This silence was pervasive through the end of the sixties, at which time one of my younger sisters told me that she too, along with our youngest sister, had been sexually abused by our father. I was horrified. I thought that, once my older sister left home in 1959, the abuse had stopped. I recognized that by not telling anyone about my sister's suffering, I had allowed my younger sisters to become incest victims as well. My guilt intensified. In a desperate need to understand and help my sisters—one of whom still lived at home at the time (1969)—I turned to Sigmund Freud, a name I had encountered some years earlier. But once again, I was betrayed. While reading the "Case History of Dora," I recognized that Freud viewed Dora as the problem, despite the fact that her adulterous father was using his daughter as a sexual pawn.[13] Freud chose to protect the father at the expense of his patient, an adolescent girl. As Alice Miller says in *Thou Shalt Not Be Aware*, "Freud shrank from the reality that was being revealed to him,...allying himself instead with the patriarchal society of which he was a member (322).[14] The lesson was, once again, that daughters are expendable. Where, if not from a therapist, could I find help for my sisters? Freud had proven to be a false father, confirming what I knew already: that no one would listen to me, that women might cry out on the cross of sexual abuse, but no one would acknowledge their suffering.

I learned, at about this time, that when my older sister sought therapy during the 1950s, her psychiatrists responded to her story of abuse by completely avoiding the topic. Undoubtedly, because they had been trained to regard such stories of abuse as lies, these therapists abused my sister a second time. As Dori Laub explains, "If one talks about the trauma without being truly heard or truly listened to, the telling might itself be lived as a return of the trauma—*a reexperiencing of the event itself*" (Felman and Laub 67). My sister's reality was deemed—as I understood from reading Freud—a fantasy, a falsehood. However, my distrust of Freudian-trained therapists was not the only reason I did not seek help for myself in 1969. Having just learned that my two younger sisters had also been sexually abused, I was suffering from what Judith Lewis Hermann calls "witness guilt." In despair, I tried to commit academic suicide: I simply gave up on my dream of earning a doctorate in literary studies. At the very moment I had learned how voiceless—how truly unheard—women are, I gave up on language: I deliberately failed "Introduction to Linguistics." How could my life matter now that I knew that my sisters, like prisoners of war, had continued to suffer repeated trauma during the very years that I, who had escaped from home, was enjoying college? So obvious was my happiness that during my freshmen year a fraternity elected me their "Sally Sunshine." Now I realized, with horror and grief, that while I was playing "Sally Sunshine"—like a perpetually smiling Doris Day—my younger sisters were living a nightmare.

My assumption about my place in the world—especially the belief that my safety depended on my being good—was shattered. Finally I had learned the lesson that my father, my minister, my linguistics professor, and Freud had been teaching me: since men controlled women's bodies and since language belonged to men, I was helpless. As Ronnie Janoff-Bulman explains, "The phenomenon of learned helplessness involves the perception that there is no contingency between one's actions and one's outcomes; nothing one can do will make a difference" (10). If I couldn't help my sisters, how could I go on trying to help myself? Because I had always loved to read, I was slow to accept the lesson that language belonged to men; in fact, a certain kind of reading had sustained me for years—at least since junior high English. While in "General Science," the coach had ordered us to complete meaningless fill-in-the-blank exercises, in literature class, the teacher, a kind and intelligent woman, had introduced us to the stories of Edgar Allen Poe. In Poe's stories I first encountered the darkness, the darkness I was always pretending not to know. Exploring this darkness became, for me, a strategy—a therapy—for emotional, spiritual, and cognitive survival: I knew that something was wrong with a system of good and evil that divided me from my sister, but I couldn't figure it out. From Shakespeare's "Julius Caesar" in grade-ten English through Thackeray's *Vanity Fair* in grade twelve, I kept trying to understand the dark side of human nature—in all its complexity. I hoped this knowledge might protect me while, at the same time, I could love my sister and even, some day, understand why my father did such terrible things. I also feared that, if madness were inherited, I too might be capable of terrible deeds.

I used reading, not as a form of escape, but to discover how to resist such a plummet into darkness. Jean Kennard has given a name, "polar reading," to this kind of imaginative experience—that is, the experience of identifying with characters who stand in for both acceptable and unacceptable aspects of one's identity. Based on psychologist Zoseph Zinker's description of the "dark" and "light," Kennard explains that "one's inner reality consists of both those qualities in one's self that one finds acceptable and those that are unacceptable and therefore hidden and denied" (68). According to Kennard's theory, the habit of reading allowed me to look within and thereby resist censoring the "truth" of my personal experience. Unfortunately, most of the time, with the possible exception of Becky Sharp in Thackeray's *Vanity Fair*, I did not find female figures in male-authored literature very interesting. As a result, I used my intellectual energy to try to understand the violent male heroes, whether Brutus, Hamlet, or Odysseus. In Dostoevksy's *Crime and Punishment*, which I read on my own, I finally encountered characters who embodied aspects of my father's dark side. I am still fascinated by the way Raskolnikov intellectualizes his crime, even daring to publish an essay in which he argues for the criminal's presumed superiority. I believe my father joined the John Birch Society for similar reasons: to rationalize the secret crimes which allowed him to claim "masculine" superiority. The Society's defense of the American constitution against attacks from "the enemy within" gave my father a self-aggrandizing cover-story for his fear of governmental authority.

However, feminist Nina Pelikan Straus provides the best explanation of the similarities between my father and Raskolnikov when she argues that "the murder-of-women and salvation plot of *Crime and Punishment* offers the most concentrated exposure of a young man's experience of violence toward women in relation to the construction of his masculine self" (54). According to Straus's argument, my father, like Raskolnikov, was attempting to confirm his insecure manhood through the dominance of women. In his exploration of the problem of male dominance, Dostoevsky also confronts the problem of the sexual abuse of children, the crime he viewed as "the most fearful" (Straus 64), through Raskolnikov's double, Svidrigalov. (Is this why the novel made such an impression on me?) Given the nature of Svidrigalov's crime, it is fitting that he commits suicide, whereas Raskolnikov, a murderer, confesses his crime and accepts his punishment. There is hope for Raskolnikov, not so much because of his conversion to Christianity, but because of his capacity for sympathy with Sonja. I recall, as an adolescent, finding comfort in the fact that someone as terrible as Roskolnikov could be redeemed by a woman's love: perhaps, then, my father might also be saved. However, as an adult, I recognize that Dostoevsky's conclusion encourages me to feel pity, not only for Raskolnikov, but for my father—a lesson I learned again and again from male writers.

In my Shakespeare class in college, for example, I learned that even a man like Macbeth, a man who killed not only a king but another man's wife and children, deserved my sympathy. Othello too deserved my sympathy, despite the fact that he had killed his innocent wife. In other words, even though Shakespeare's plays gave me an opportunity—not available in other courses—to explore the dark side of human nature, I was also being taught to feel sympathy for men like my father. Learning such sympathy would have been fine if it had been gender balanced; however, I do not recall being asked to read a single novel or play which had, as its central theme, that white men should learn to imagine and sympathize with women or children, regardless of race or class. For that reason—because male-authored narratives teach women to sympathize with men, often at the expense of those they victimize—I view the traditional canon, which is still upheld in most high schools according to Arthur Applebee (1993), as helping to perpetuate male violence. As Judith Fetterley argues, "We suffer today from a national narrative that valorizes violence, that defines masculinity as the production of violence and defines the feminine and the foreign as legitimate recipients of such violence" ("Not in the Least American" 893). As I explain in a later chapter, defenders of the traditional canon, who often identify themselves as conservative Christians defending "family values," also oppose any negative portrayals of parents in works assigned in school.

Tragically, these defenders of the patriarchal family fail to take into consideration that a high number of parents, more often fathers, sexually abuse their children. And although feminists have transformed the literature curriculum at the college and university level, in most high schools, where the traditional canon still prevails, it functions as an impediment to the psychological and intellectual development of survivors. The traditional canon, which valorizes the violent patriarch, makes even more difficult the near-impossible task an incested daughter faces as she struggles to comprehend the contradictory views of the father: the differences between the father she has idealized and the father who has assaulted her. One might assume that an incested daughter would refuse to idealize the father; however, the incestuous father actually "intensifies the need for idealization," according to Janet Jacobs, because "the extent of his control and the threat of his abuse violate the basic needs of trust and security upon which healthy psychological development relies" (34). To preserve at least the illusion of security—without which the child cannot live—the incested daughter must somehow reconcile her dependency on her father, and consequent need to trust him, with the recognition that he is dangerous.

How does the child manage such an impossible task? When she cannot escape the abuse—and children do not know that they can seek protection unless they have been educated about sexual abuse—she accommodates herself to the abusive situation, usually through repression or self-blame. In cases of repression, according to Jacobs, Nazi soldiers or the devil may serve as screen memories, protecting the victim from recognizing her father as her abuser while allowing her to retain her idealized image of him. Jacobs explains: "The demonization of the perpetrator can...be understood as the splitting off of god the father from god the devil, as the former retains the quality of idealization and the latter is attributed with the violence and shame of abuse" (42). Repression of paternal sexual abuse protects a child from unbearable knowledge: that no one can be trusted, that there is, in fact, no safe place. As Jacobs argues, through its denial of incest, society reinforces such distortions, with the tragic result that "the victim's fears and terrors are mislabeled as either the true work of the devil or the psychosis of disturbed women" (42). Young women should not have to wait until they enter college to read narratives which confront, rather than repress, the dark truth of their traumatic experiences.

Probably because I had a healthy caretaker in my early years, during the three or four years that my father was away at war, I did not repress memories of my father's sexual abuse of my sister or me when he returned from the war. I did, however, shift the responsibility from my father to my sister. The reason my father had abused my sister, according to my childhood logic, was that I was my mother's "good girl." Only after I finally struggled free of this conception of good and evil–shattering a cognitive framework that had afforded me the illusion of safety for more than twenty years–did I recognize that this belief was a betrayal of my sister. I find it difficult, even now, to acknowledge that, by defining my sister as "bad," I too had abandoned her. For years, while I lay terrified but untouched beside her, my sister was completely alone in her struggle. Of my father's nocturnal visits to her side of the bed, she writes, "I would struggle as silently as possible to avoid his touching, always aware that I must not cry out and alarm anyone" (4). Why must she not cry out? "My understanding today, " she writes, " is that I had somehow gotten the message there was something wrong with me; that's why my father did this to me. I couldn't be responsible for causing trouble in the family. My mother would hate me even more" (4). Why did my sister think my mother hated her? Why did I not cry out? Since my mother tended to blame my sister and favor me, shouldn't I have been the one to tell the tale of my father's nighttime activities?

Feminist scholars of father-daughter incest, such as Judith Lewis Herman, Janet Jacobs, and others, have helped me to answer these questions and to forgive my child-self. As Elaine Carmen and Patricia Rieker argue, "Victims of physical and sexual abuse are faced with a formidable and complex series of social, emotional, and cognitive tasks in trying to make sense of experiences that threaten bodily integrity and life itself" (quoted in Jacobs 43). To reduce her feelings of helplessness, my sister assumed responsibility for my father's behavior: "There's something wrong with me; that's why my father did this to me." Furthermore, Herman has demonstrated, as Jacobs argues, that the victim's tendency toward self-blame is "reinforced by cultural and religious beliefs that depict women as sexually corrupt and licentious" (43). For victims in religious families, the problem of self-blame is even more severe. Although ours was not an excessively religious family, I now understand why my father chose for his family a conservative wing of the Lutheran church, the Missouri synod, which to this day refuses to allow women to become ministers. Such a church supported my father's misogynist views of women. Even though I was healthy enough to feel angry toward this church, I had no words with which to resist the flesh-hating (woman-hating) phrase, "I am by nature sinful and unclean."

Faced with the complex task of making sense of my life, I tried, through reading, to conduct a private investigation into the dark side of human nature. I knew there was something wrong with the virgin/whore dichotomy–I knew, at some level, that it was wrong to think of my sister as "bad"–but once again, language betrayed me. Because the canon consists almost exclusively of father-son stories, I could not find words–I could not find cognitive frameworks–with which to make sense of my experience. I concluded, finally, that there was something wrong with me, something flawed in my thinking. Feminism would soon change this habit of self-incrimination; however, even in 1968, at the time I learned of my father's abuse of two younger sisters, it was still possible for Northrop Frye to claim in *The Educated Imagination* that "literature belongs to the world *man* constructs, not the world he sees" (my italics 27). Who was I, a female reader with only an undergraduate degree, to doubt the word of so eminent a male critic? Since that time, of course, feminist approaches to the study of literature have enabled me to recognize that Frye's book might have been more accurately entitled *The Miseducated Imagination.* Feminist theory also enabled me to recognize that the romance plot–which Frye calls the "secular scripture"–is often an incest plot. Frye acknowledges that the romance plot–such as the story of

Guinivere who is unfaithful to the father-king—is often accompanied by "the theme of incest, very often father and daughter" (44), but he argues that "this shows us nothing at all about the relation of fiction to reality: what it shows us is that some conventions of story telling are more obsessive than others" (44).

Frye's faulty assumption, that the presence of incest in romance plots has little to do with "reality," is completely at odds with my experience. In fact, the literature curriculum, with its focus on male suffering, mirrors the dynamics of the incestuous family in which the victimized daughter is conditioned to empathize with her abuser. As Jacobs argues, "Nurturing the aggressor...becomes a strategy for constructing a sense of self-worth under conditions of powerlessness" (72). Why do so many women—not just incest survivors—nurture the aggressor? To explain this point, I turn first to an analysis of the nurturing behavior of incested daughters. It may seem unlikely that an incested daughter would sympathize with and nurture her oppressor. However, as Jacobs explains, by caring for the perpetrator the victim reframes the relationship, changing it from a shameful and humiliating experience into a "loving, caring relationship through which the child perceives herself as the valued daughter" (72). Like other incested daughters, my sister managed to preserve some sense of security, as well as some self-esteem, by becoming the emotional caretaker of her abuser. She writes, "I began to separate my father into two people in order to cope: my father, the man that everyone admired and my father, the man in the night who would sometimes go into a trance" (5). At night she clawed at the hands of this father-in-a-trance, but during the day she nurtured the emotional needs of the man "everyone admired," by going "out to dinner [with him], maybe a dance, often places where only adults belonged" (6). She even acted as his "confidante" in an attempt, she says, to "ward off his sexual advances in the middle of the night without punishment" (6).

My sister's effort to protect herself by transforming her rapist-father into her husband-protector may seem bizarre. However, according to Janice Radway, a similar fantasy—that the beautiful heroine (for she must be beautiful) will transform the rapist (often a man old enough her father) into a loving husband—is still a staple of women's romance novels. Today's English majors, most of them well acquainted with feminist approaches to the study of literature, are capable of critiquing this popular genre, but many nonmajors, unacquainted with feminist approaches to literature, have not acquired the critical tools to become resisting readers. It is difficult to generalize about the attitudes of today's young women; however, based on my teaching experiences at Iowa State, where many nonmajors enroll in upper-division literature courses, I would argue that most nonmajors, while intelligent, are not feminist readers: they do not recognize the seductions of popular romance novels. For example, at the outset of a course called "Women, Romance, and the American Novel," many nonmajors favored *The Flame and the Flower* by Kathleen Woodiwiss—a popular romance in which a "Cinderella" Beauty triumphs over the Beast through marriage. By contrast, many English majors have been introduced to feminist theory, and they have also read and discussed *Jane Eyre*, a novel which enacts the "Beauty and the Beast" plot with a feminist twist: Jane (who is not beautiful) rejects the traditional wifely role (nurturing the male aggressor) when, just before she is to wed Rochester (a man old enough to be her father), she leaves him to begin a psychological quest for her "lost" mother and sisters. I would have found great comfort from reading such a narrative in a high school English class, but I was never assigned a work which centered on women—on sisters, for example, or on mothers and daughters.[15]

And unfortunately, neither my sister nor I felt that our mother—who was too timid to make phone calls and rarely left the house—had any power to help us. My sister escaped from home through an early marriage, one year after graduating from high school. While acting the part of my sister's "happy" bridesmaid–I was then a senior in high school–I kept thinking, with desperation, that I must escape from this marriage plot. However, because I knew my parents had no money to send me to college, I became increasingly depressed. I couldn't ask my father for help; in fact, I was terrified to ask him even for a ride anywhere since I feared that, if I were alone in the car with him, he might attack me. As usual, I was more fortunate than my older sister: my maternal grandparents offered to pay for my room, board, and tuition at the University of North Dakota. And I would not be forced to ask my father for a ride because my grandparents decided to drive me to college. I had been rescued–and through my mother's intercession. Why, then, did my mother fail to intercede for my sister? I am not yet sure how to understand the differences between the way my mother treated my sister, her supposed "bad" daughter, and the way she treated me, her supposed "good" daughter.

However, feminist research on how incestuous fathers destroy the mother-daughter bond helps me to at least begin to understand my own experience in relationship to those of my sister and other survivors. One of the most devastating effects of father-daughter incest, as both Herman and Jacobs argue, is the destruction of the mother-daughter bond. Jacobs explains that victims usually blame their mothers for their abuse, rather than their fathers, because they believe their mothers are omnipotent. Since mothers are omnipotent, from the point of view of the child, they should know, without being told, what the father is doing. Without a feminist framework for understanding a mother's lack of structural power in a patriarchal society–that is, her lack of economic, religious, political, or legal power–children assume that their mothers could save them, if only they wished to do so. Another reason that children, like my sisters, do not seek help from their mothers is that, as both Herman and Jacobs emphasize, they are made to feel responsible for holding the family together. In fact, one of my younger sisters told me that when, in an attempt to stop the abuse, she threatened to tell, our father said that, if she told, she would then be responsible for breaking up the family. Another powerful inhibitor for the victim is her fear of exposure, her fear of public shame.

Nevertheless, in *Mothers of Incest Survivors,* Janis Tyler Johnson concludes, as does Jacobs in *Victimized Daughters,* that most mothers—if informed of the sexual abuse—do take steps to protect their daughters. This knowledge contradicts earlier studies of incestuous families which, from a feminist perspective, engage in mother-blaming. These earlier studies, which fail to analyze the imbalance of power between mothers and fathers, frequently describe mothers as colluders, as helpless dependents, or as incest victims themselves. In fact, there is a degree of accuracy in each of these descriptions: my mother did not actively collude with my father, but she did tend to see my older sister more as a competitor than a daughter; she was also extremely dependent, frequently calling on her daughters to "help" her with simple tasks, such as making a phone call or adding up figures; and she seems to have been, at least psychologically, an incest victim herself. To this day, she persists in thinking of herself as a child, even calling herself a "Daddy's girl," despite the fact that she helped to support our family with income from her sewing business. She tends to deny her strengths rather than defining herself as a competent adult.

Only very recently have feminist researchers—primarily in psychology, sociology, and literature—begun to examine the mother-daughter relationship. Adrienne Rich, one of the first to make such a study, reminds us in *Of Woman Born* that although the mother-daughter story has been at the margins of cultural consciousness for centuries, it has rarely been told. Why hasn't this story been told? Whose interests are served by omitting the study of the mother-daughter relationship—and of mothering itself—from the curriculum? Why is it that, just at the moment girls reach puberty, whether in junior or senior high, they find themselves absent from the school curriculum? These questions are relevant, not only to incest survivors, but to all women and girls, for all girls are taught to be "nice" and "good," frequently at the expense of their intellectual and emotional development. Tragically, not only at home but also at school and in church, girls are taught to sacrifice their needs—and silence their voices—in order to avoid conflict. Such lessons, according to the authors of *Women's Ways of Knowing*, create a central dilemma for young women: "how to include both oneself and others" (9). This dilemma has been extremely difficult for me to resolve because I too was taught that a "good" woman, especially a mother, takes care of others even if it means she must sacrifice her own needs; however, as the authors of *Women's Ways of Knowing* conclude: "To seek connection with others by excluding oneself is a strategy destined to fail" (9). By the time I began graduate school in my late thirties, I knew that this strategy—of seeking connection while excluding myself—had failed for me.

Ironically, because I was determined to be a "good" mother—unlike my own mother—I too had been hooked by this sacrificial morality. I left a series of teaching positions, moving for the sake of advancing my husband's career, always with the hope that my turn would come if only I could be a good wife and mother. What I failed to understand is that, while structural inequities made such maternal sacrifices necessary, my dutiful deference would neither be acknowledged nor rewarded. As I learned during a painful divorce, if a woman gives up her professional goals in order to be a "good" mother and wife, the law does not reward this sacrifice. It is not surprising, then, that following my divorce, I wrote a feminist analysis of such structural inequities. While analyzing the costs of my mother's "feminine" speech, I was, in fact, trying to understand my own limited institutional, or public, authority. Ironically, I wrote this essay in order to complete the very graduate course,

"Introduction to Linguistics," that I had failed in 1969, ten years earlier. With the support of the women's movement, which had emerged in the intervening years, I found the courage to return to the same university—and to an introductory linguistics course—to reclaim my professional voice. Armed with linguist Robin Lakoff's analysis of "feminine" speech, I began to explore—tentatively, and not without guilt at what seemed a betrayal of my mother—my anxieties about authoring my life, and my texts. The essay I wrote for "Introduction to Linguistics" helped me earn an "A" in the course and, a few years later, after revising the piece to include personal disclosures, I submitted it to a feminist journal under the title, "I VIVIDLY REMEMBER, pretty well." This essay appears in the following chapter, along with my reflections—and an update.

CHAPTER 3

A Mother-Daughter Story

The heroine who wants to write,

or who wants in any way to be productive and creative...

must break from her mother,

so as not to be identified with maternal silence.

—Marianne Hirsch

Do mothers write their own experience as mothers?

What shapes and plots accommodate those experiences?

—Marianne Hirsch

A Daughter Analyzes Her Mother's "Feminine" Speech

My mother, the woman whose speech I will examine here, is a creative person. Although she lacks a formal education, she sews, quilts, gardens, and braids rugs. I admire her artistry, as well as her generosity and intelligence. But her habit of hiding that intelligence behind a kind of helpless "femininity"–such as her refusal to go anywhere alone or to be concerned with financial details– makes me wildly impatient at times. Perhaps that's because I haven't overcome certain "feminine" habits myself. Sometimes, for example, I'm politely deferential when I should speak up, or I'm confused when I should be angry. To liberate myself, I spend considerable time and energy recognizing my feelings, overcoming the habit of repressing or displacing them. Nevertheless, my fear of appearing too assertive, which Robin Lakoff names as the cause of "feminine" speech, often keeps me silent. This fear, Lakoff argues in *Language and Women's Place,* keeps women from being heard. Men, she says, learn that they will be "listened to and taken seriously," but if a woman "doesn't learn to speak women's language in a traditional society, she's dead."

Society has changed since 1975 when Lakoff's study was published, but I, for one, haven't reached the "postfeminist" era–or perhaps it would be more accurate to say that it hasn't reached me. For example, I didn't speak up when recently told [the year was probably 1982] that a man got a job for which I had also applied,

51

because he "sees himself as a manager, whereas you are perceived as more of a theoretician." As the curious shift to passive voice implies, I could only be defined by others, while the young man could "see himself." I didn't speak up, and this shifty parallelism still rankles. The emphasis in Lakoff's study, however, is not so much upon silence as upon those characteristics which make certain that even a speaking woman won't be heard. My mother's speech provides ample illustration of those features Lakoff identifies as "feminine"; her overuse of a variety of hedges, such as "maybe," "I think," or "I guess"; her use of questioning intonation where we might expect a declarative; her use of superpolite forms and empty adjectives; and her occupational lexicon, sewing terms such as "kick pleat" or "jumper." To this list I would add certain words that my mother characteristically avoids, having learned to regard them as "masculine": geographical terms such as "north, south, east, and west," and factual terms, especially numbers.

My analysis of the transcript of a trial in which she is the plaintiff reveals how costly, both financially and psychologically, "feminine" speech can be. Through it, although I agree with Lakoff's claim that "women's language" had to be learned for survival, my mother discredits herself, destroying her reliability as a witness in her own case and making it appear as if the truth must be located elsewhere—in the judge, for example, or the lawyers. She has been taught to locate truth outside herself, in experts and authorities; nevertheless, the jury system does not protect her from the need to present *her* truth credibly. What a double-bind! Lacking any other witnesses, my mother must take the stand to help her lawyer prove that the driver of a car which struck her, a pedestrian, was negligent. The defendant's lawyer will argue, of course, that my mother was somehow negligent. Since my mother's injuries were painful, involving hospitalization and loss of income, this is certainly a situation in which she wants to be listened to and taken seriously. As the judge points out in his instructions to the jury, the manner in which the truth is *presented,* such as "the accuracy of the witness's recollection" or "the degree of intelligence shown by the witness and the witness's ability to know and relate the facts," are crucial to determining "where the truth lies." The judge also cautions the jury to "consider, analyze and weigh only the testimony in exhibits presented in court." Besides the testimony of her doctor and photographs of her bruises, my mother has only her word.

Even with the help of a lawyer, the demands of public speaking are complex, particularly for a woman who has learned that her place is in the home. Only because she has been divorced and widowed, forced to become the sole support of my youngest brother, has my mother taken a job. She is walking home from the fabric store where she works as a clerk when she is struck by a car. The judge instructs the jury that, if they find her "entitled to recover damages," they are to

> award her an amount of money which will fairly and adequately compensate her for her injuries, giving consideration only to such of the following items shown by the evidence to have resulted from the negligence of Mrs. (the driver of the car). First, any pain, disability, disfigurement, embarrassment or emotional distress experienced by Mrs. O from injuries up to the time of the trial. There is no yardstick by which you can value pain and suffering exactly.

This yardstick will not be applied to the whole fabric of her life, nor will it measure the psychological stress of testifying. For my mother who, since childhood, has been afraid of public speaking, it is to be one of her most traumatic of life's trials. Having been raised on a North Dakota farm, she has learned not only the traditional domestic arts, but also the art of "keeping still."

Her attorney works to arouse the jury's sympathy while appearing to present only the facts. He begins, within the limits of admissible evidence, to provide "objective" biographical information:

Q. Now at the time of the accident, Mrs. O, how did you get to and from work?

A. Walked.

Q. Okay, now you've said in various proceedings in this case, you've estimated it to be two miles from your home to work, but since then we've checked. Do you recall—an estimate now what the distance is?

A. I guess it isn't quite two miles.

Q. Okay.

A. I don't know exactly.

Q. But you have checked and found it be somewhat under two?

A. Yes.

My mother, who customarily leaves such facts to men, has a marvelous memory for facts about sewing and gardening, but she is nervous. And she says "I guess," or "I don't know exactly," although her attorney has recently taken time to prepare her– "we've checked"–for this line of questioning. In establishing facts "closer to home," such as her daily responsibilities, her lawyer elicits a slightly greater degree of certainty:

Q. Your son J, at the time of the accident, what was he doing? Was he a student or what?

A. A student.

Q. He's now employed, I take it?

A. Yes.

Q. But at the time of the accident he required at least some attention and care?

A. He certainly did.

Q. All right. Did you then keep your own house, and take care of your house cleaning, your laundry?

A. Yes, I did.

Q. Your groceries. Things of that nature?

A. Barely, but I did. [While the lawyer strives to establish my mother's competence, she undermines him by answering "barely." Undoubtedly, she is emphasizing the fact that she had "barely" enough money, but in this context, it implies that she doesn't feel competent.]

Q. All right. How much were you earning at Minnesota Fabrics, at the time?

A. Approximately $2.55 an hour, I believe. [Ten years later, when she left her job, she was still making the minimum wage, although it had risen about a dollar an hour.]

Q. All right. And were you working pretty generally a forty-hour week? [Whenever she could: she had no other source of income.]

A. Never—yes. It never quite was that, but yes.

Q. All right. Now at the time of this accident where were you coming from? [My mother, who believes that geography is a male province, has never learned to give directions as he expects here.]

A. I usually drove—or walked up the slope to Humboldt, behind Humboldt School, and came around on the west-east, I believe.

At the time of the accident, my mother, whose father had recently given her a second-hand car, was just learning to drive. Having regarded her proper place as "in the home," she has been confined there, as much by her role as by poverty. As a result, like many women, she suffers from agoraphobia, and her confusion about directions reflects a deep-seated anxiety, not simply a lack of vocabulary. For this reason, she responds inappropriately to her lawyer's question. He corrects her:

Q. Well, okay. Try to pay attention to the questions. I'm just asking where you came from that night. [Although she is actually too attentive to this question, he now chides her, as if she were a child.]

A. Oh, I'm sorry. From Minnesota Fabrics.

Q. From work?

A. From work.

Q. You were going where?

A. Going home.

Q. Okay. Now in order to go from your work to your home was it necessary to cross 82nd Street?

A. Yes, it was.

Q. And did you have occasion to cross 82nd Street?

A. I don't understand.

Q. Did you—did you start to cross 82nd?

A. Yes. I crossed it.

Q. Now had you done this many times before?

A. Yes.

Q. And you were familiar with the area?

Being familiar with the area, having walked it daily for a number of years, is obviously not the same as having the linguistic ability to describe it accurately. And here's where the trouble begins. The lawyer's lexicon differs from her own, and their effort to maintain a cooperative exchange begins to unravel. He must behave as if she were capable of giving this description when, in fact, she is not. Yet he must not "lead the witness," or the defense attorney may object.

Q. Now does—the drawing on the board, does that fairly represent the general layout of the area—

A. (interjecting) Uh-huh.

Q. —in which you crossed that night?

A. Yes.

Q. Okay. And Humboldt would be one block to the east of Irving there (indicating). Is that correct?

A. I don't believe it's quite a block.

Q. Well, it's a short—a very short block?

A. Yes. Right.

A few lines later:

Q. Well, when you were in the hospital, did you feel pain in your hip?

A. No. Not—there wasn't—I think it was—It must have been when they moved me.

Again:

Q. On both sides?

A. Well, it's hard to pinpoint exactly where. I just don't know; it was excruciating, but I don't remember just—you know—

Although she has photos of her bruises, primarily on her hip and one leg, this exposure of intimate parts of her body–in pictures and language–embarrasses her. Furthermore, like most of us, she represses painful memories, especially those which are not allowed, or for which she cannot find the appropriate words. When the pain is emotional rather than physical, my mother usually says, "I just want to forget about it and get on with life." At these times, I can't decide whether this habit of forgetting comes from denial, a defense mechanism with limited usefulness, or from bravery. Either way, this habit now helps destroy her testimony's appearance of reliability. The accident is ghostly to my mother, who shies away from anything as precise as the names of body parts or numbers. Questioned about the length of her stay in the hospital, she answers, "I think it was twelve days," and about the number of days she spent in her hospital bed, "I suppose four days. I'm not really sure."

To a question about recent pain in her hip, she responds, "Well, I feel working on my feet–you know–eight hours a day at Minnesota Fabrics, that when I suddenly began to limp, I felt that that was–I felt myself that that was maybe from–from the accident." Maybe. But I would limp too, if I had to stand that long; I would limp because I couldn't stand it. If there is a causal relationship between the accident and her limp, she manages to make it opaque:

Q. And when did you start feeling pain in your hip area?

A. It wasn't right away.

Q. When was it?

A. I could say–I'm not sure. Maybe two months. [Pages later, she is still characteristically vague.]

Q. What problems did you have?

A. Well, just getting around. I don't know just what. [Here I want to distance myself.]

Q. Do you remember that?

A. I have no idea.

Q. If I showed you the bill would you—would that refresh your memory (indicating)?

A. Yes.

Q. How much did the replacement glasses cost?

A. I don't remember.

Q. Well, didn't you just look at the bill?

A. Oh. I thought that was just for the examination. [If he is exasperated, her lawyer doesn't show it.]

Q. Okay. Take a look at the top and make sure that that's the right bill.

A. House of Vision. Yes.

Q. Okay. Now was that—now do you know whether that was for the glasses or the examination?

A. I think it was for the examination. [She isn't certain what she reads.]

Q. And that was from doctor who?

A. I've forgotten.

Q. Can you read it?

A. I think it was Lindberg, but I'm not sure.

Ordinarily my mother reads very well, seeing is no problem for her. I feel irritated; I want to call her Mrs. O here since she doesn't appear as intelligent as she is. Why is she so nervous and confused?

It would help if I could joke now, but as Lakoff reminds us, many women have left that to men. I am such a woman; I rarely tell jokes.

But I have mostly overcome my mother's fear of open spaces, and I can read maps. It makes me angry when the defense attorney exploits my mother's incompetence, asking her to draw a map and describe it for the jury. Yet I also understand why, when her attorney objects, the judge does not sustain it.

Defense Attorney: I understand that you're not a professional map maker and I will do my best to ask you specific questions about the layout of the road and we'll put them in one by one. Okay?

A. I'd rather not.

Her Attorney: Well, go ahead, if you can. Try, as long as counsel's going to tell you how to do it. [Is he being ironic?]

This confusion continues for over ten pages of the transcript, despite my mother's protest that "at that time I was taking driving lessons and–and I just wasn't trained in maps and that sort of thing." The accident was, in fact, a great set-back for her slowly growing confidence in navigating–either on foot or by car–open, and very threatening, spaces.

Two pages later in the transcript (and many years later) she says, "I don't–I've never been good–if I could locate–I just can't– I'm trying to picture where Southtown is, and then I could get–" This litany of confusion and distress continues, reaching a climax of helplessness when the defense attorney challenges her memory of the moment of impact. Her phrase, "I vividly remember," appears to be only an empty adjective when followed by her fearful uncertainty.

Q. Would it be reasonable to–to say that your memory was fresher two years ago than it is today? [It has taken a long time to bring this case to trial.]

A. No. I vividly remember, pretty well—well, parts of it, I would say, of the accident, I vividly remember.

Q. All right. And other parts of it you might remember better two years ago than today?

A. I don't have any way of knowing that.

Her habit of hedging provides ammunition for the defense attorney. Ground has now been prepared for him to challenge her testimony in other areas, on matters which suggest that she operates impulsively and irresponsibly. Previous testimony indicates that she refused to accept a ride home, although it was late in the day and, possibly, dangerous to walk, particularly across a freeway/ramp intersection. "They knew I walked," she answers. The people who offered rides "knew I was doing it for my health's sake, because I–I was keeping my weight where it was supposed to be, by exercise." Her weight, about which she has now told a very "feminine" white lie, becomes an issue. Although she testifies that, at the time of the accident, she weighed a mere 130 pounds and was walking to keep trim, medical records reveal that she weighed considerably more.

The defense attorney continues to cut holes in the fabric of her character and credibility. He suggests that she was running, not walking; that she wrongly attributes her pain to the accident; that she was not seriously injured; and that her dark dress establishes her negligence. Her apparel becomes a costly issue:

Q. You indicated you were wearing a–a dark jumper?

A. Yes.

Q. And the blouse was some light color?

A. The blouse was a light-colored blouse.

Q. The jumper, I take it, was—was like a jacket, something like I'm wearing, so that the blouse would only—

A. More like a vest.

Q. Well, okay. the blouse would only show in front?

A. And the long sleeves.

This exchange becomes so convoluted that my mother seems to be saying, finally, that the jumper had sleeves. The judge who, like many men, lacks the vocabulary of a seamstress (some cultures have tailors, but they are rare in the United States), seeks clarification:

The Court: did you say that the jumper had sleeves?

The Witness: That's what I remember. Yes.

The Court: Oh, okay.

Her Attorney: I believe that now she misunderstands it. (to the witness) What do you remember as to the—

The Witness: (Interjecting) that I had a light-colored-a light-colored, long-sleeved blouse on.

The Court: What about the jumper? did the jumper have sleeves?

The Witness: No. A jumper is called a jumper. That—doesn't have sleeves.

Defense Attorney: Oh. Okay.

The Witness: That's why it's called a jumper.

I want to stop here, giving my mother a final, assertive moment when *she* defines for "the Court"—whose name stands in for this public place—a term from her sphere of expertise. For, of course, the last word in this court room was not hers. After deliberating for less than an hour on that Memorial Day Friday (a day my mother prefers to forget), the jury awarded her a sum which she no longer recalls. The transcript shows that the judge, annoyed with the jury which in its haste has failed to follow instructions–to determine the degree of negligence on both sides–concludes by declaring a mistrial.

A Mother as Narrator:
Reading, Writing, and Teaching the Maternal

When I turned in the preceding analysis of "feminine" speech to complete the final assignment in "Introduction to Linguistics," I made no personal disclosures. Instead, I disguised my mother's identity by naming her "Mrs. O." I pretended, in other words, not to know her. However, because I knew that personal disclosures would be acceptable to editors of the feminist journal, *Hurricane Alice,* I revised the essay, which was published as it appears above, using the title "'I VIVIDLY REMEMBER, pretty well': A Witness Against Her Self." Partly because I was a graduate student at the time the essay appeared, but also because I was ashamed, I did not disclose the consequences of my mother's "learned helplessness": the fact that her lack of authority–both at home and in public– enabled my father to sexually abuse my sisters for many years. As I reflect on this essay, which I first published so long ago (1983), I recognize–not without some guilt–that I was distancing myself from my mother by analyzing her lack of authority. Ironically, to establish my professional authority, I analyzed my mother's lack of an authoritative voice. Only in retrospect do I recognize that I was following an established pattern. As Marianne Hirsch says, "The heroine who wants to write, or who wants in any way to be productive and creative...must break from her mother, so as not to be identified with maternal silence" (45). In my first published work, I make such a break from my mother, distancing myself from maternal silence by analyzing how her "feminine" speech discredited her testimony in a court of law. I try to salve my conscience by praising my mother's domestic creativity—which, in fact, I do admire—and by acknowledging that I sometimes use "feminine" speech myself.

Furthermore, I explain that, having been taught "feminine" speech and behavior, my mother is not completely to blame for the fact that her testimony is discredited; nevertheless, I am, to a degree, engaging in mother-blaming. Even today, I am not certain: how much should a mother, who has so little institutional authority, be held responsible for protecting her children? I was asking this question as a daughter, despite the fact that I too was a mother at the time I wrote this analysis of my mother's helplessness. I did not want to acknowledge, even to myself, how similar I was to my mother at the time this essay was published: like my mother, I had recently been through a divorce and, as a result, my income had plummeted (from over $90,000 a year to less than $10,000) while my future employment was uncertain. Furthermore, like my mother, my divorce had left me without a car, making it necessary for me to walk to school and work. Also, like my mother, I had a son at home at the time of my divorce. Yet I was also different from my mother in significant ways: I was better educated: my mother had not gone to college, but I had completed an M.A., and I was supported by the women's movement which had already made an impact upon many institutions. Unfortunately, however, divorce law had changed very little: for example, my settlement (1982) did not recognize that I had given up years of income as a secondary teacher, as well as years of professional development, in order to be a "good" mother and wife—that is, in order to make geographic moves that advanced my husband's career. In divorce papers, my husband actually claimed that he had been the primary parent, and I had no opportunity to defend myself against this falsehood. Like my mother, I did not have narrative control. My divorce taught me that those (men) with money, those with the ability to hire the most verbally manipulative and intimidating lawyers, will invariably get what they want.

When I wrote the foregoing analysis of my mother's "feminine" speech, I was well aware that, even though a patriarchal society severely limits maternal power, it holds mothers, far more than fathers, responsible for the suffering of their children. I also knew that my sisters held my mother at least equally, if not more responsible for their suffering—despite the fact that it was my father who had sexually abused them. I sympathized with my sisters: why had my mother failed to intervene for them? At the same time, my mother was trying to help me through graduate school. She had just received a sizable inheritance, and she had sold her house in order to live with me and share expenses. I was ambivalent: I held my mother responsible for failing to help my sisters while, at the same time, I recognized that my mother lacked authority both in the family and in public. As illustrated in my analysis of courtroom discourse, my mother did not control her speech acts; rather, according to convention, her lawyer controlled her narrative with his questions. She was given no opportunity to simply tell her story without interference. When, I wondered, do mothers ever have the power to tell their stories? When do we hear the voices of mothers? Even daughters, I recognized, try to distance themselves from what Hirsch names "maternal silence," the silence that comes from not being heard by others. I remember my mother's voice, calling out at night to my father, "Where are you? Why don't you come to bed?" My father would just call back, "I'm just reading. Go to sleep." At home I was always listening for my father, afraid to fall asleep.

The fact is, my mother did not stop the abuse because, she claims, she didn't know it was taking place. My sisters have challenged this claim. Perhaps, even if my mother did know about the abuse, she assumed she could not stop her husband: after all, in a legal sense, his daughters were his property. This great imbalance in power between mothers and fathers, I came to understand—from my experiences as both a daughter and a mother—was the source of the problem: daughters could not expect protection from mothers as long as fathers were regarded as "heads" of families, and as long as fathers were also in charge of public institutions—the schools, the courts, and the churches. At the time of my marriage, despite my fear of men, I did not fully understand how this great imbalance of power would affect me. I was certain that, if I had an income of my own, I would maintain my equality. And when my son was born, I embraced motherhood, perhaps one of the more seductive institutions ever imagined. I wanted to be the best possible mother for my son—all that my parents had not been for me. Most of all I vowed *never* to abandon my son, always to love and protect him. In my willingness to sacrifice my own needs—my professional goals, in particular—to this ideal, I was trapped into playing the part of the sacrificial mother. Ironically, I had made a vow of maternal perfection in order to avoid repeating what had happened to me as a child. At the time, I had no feminist model for this demanding role.

How, then, could I fulfill the fantasy of the perfect mother? In fact, it is this very fantasy, as Nancy Chodorow and Susan Contratto have written, that inhibits individual and cultural changes in the family romance. Why is this so? They argue that the fantasy of maternal perfection induces the guilt that makes mothers the scapegoats for an unchanging, and deadly, culture. When mothers and daughters bear the guilt that fathers, with their sense of entitlement, deny, they are protecting abusive men. But how does one escape this trap, the trap of institutionalized motherhood? I began my escape when, in 1976, I decided to commit an act of destruction that would remove me forever from the contest of perfect motherhood: I chose to have an abortion. Although my doctor had promised me, following an ovarectomy, that I could not become pregnant, I became pregnant with a child that my husband (now my former husband) did not want. I felt betrayed by the medical profession and abandoned by my husband. I could not afford to raise the child on my own, and I had given up my job—in fact, three jobs—to keep our family together. I felt forced, in a violent culture, to choose *either* my child *or* myself when it should have been possible for me to choose *both* my child *and* myself. In order to feel some sense of agency, I used a violent vocabulary to describe the abortion. Yes, I was selfish; yes, I was killing a potential life. Yes, I was choosing myself, not the fetus; myself, not maternal suffering; myself, not some abstract principle.

Experience had taught me, after years of deferring my own dreams of a professional life, that I would have to give up one or the other: my dreams or my child. While still trapped inside this either/or morality, I had spent hours—during a five-year period in the 1970s—trying to figure how to love my husband and son without giving up my own dreams for graduate study. As I struggled with this dilemma, I kept studying the Kronos myth, which was also the interpretive model for my master's thesis. If I solved this riddle, in which a mother encourages and helps a son to slay his father, I might solve the riddle of my own life. The Greek myth goes like this: Kronos, who fears his children will try to steal away his power, as he had from his own father, orders his wife (and sister) Rhea to turn over her newborn infants to him. For years Rhea obeys. After swallowing each new infant, Kronos feels his power is secure. But Rhea finally grows tired of this sacrificial ritual and decides to trick her husband: when her next child, a son, is born, she wraps a stone in swaddling cloth and feeds it to her husband. He falls for the trick. Rhea manages to hide her son Zeus until he is full grown, at which time she persuades him to slay his father. As we know, Zeus succeeded in killing his father, an act of patricide that made him the most powerful patriarchal god.

Most of us are better acquainted with the story of Oedipus, another son who slays his father and becomes king. However, because the Kronos myth places more emphasis on the father's hostility to the son, I found it a more accurate depiction of patriarchal society. In the Kronos story, son Zeus slays his father–not because of an unconscious desire to possess his mother, which is how Freud explains Oedipus–but to defend himself against a hostile father. Gradually, I began to imagine my family–a father, mother, and son–as counterparts to Kronos, Rhea, and Zeus. Therefore, although I had been trained to read as a man–that is, to identify with the male protagonist–I found it increasing difficulty to ignore the plight of Rhea. As I began to identify with Rhea–as I began to read as a mother–I found it impossible to imagine myself as Kronos, a man capable of killing his own children, or even as Zeus, a son capable of killing his father. Kronos was particularly reprehensible: a man so indifferent to his children that his wife, simply by substituting a stone for a child, could fool him. Interpreting the Kronos story in terms of its gender implications, I asked, Who could I be but Rhea–ever faithful, ever submissive, a mother willing to feed her children to a monster? The story appalled me. Hadn't my mother sacrificed her daughters and sons to placate my father? Hadn't I therefore vowed not to sacrifice my child to the fathers?

The Vietnam War was escalating when I became pregnant in 1963 and, as my child grew in my womb, I vowed that, if the child were male, I would not allow him to go to war. Fiercely protective, I vowed to go in his place. I fantasized a time when all the mothers would find a way to collectively resist the call to war. I speculated that mothers, having been trained as peacemakers, as caretakers, would resist violence. Most mothers want to preserve lives, as Sara Ruddick argues in "Preservative Love and Military Destruction," not destroy them. Yet it was clear that Rhea had not sacrificed herself to save her children. Instead, she had sent a son to war against his father. I was forced to acknowledge that, historically, mothers have *not* succeeded in stopping war; in fact, they have often been active supporters of male violence. Likewise, according to the myth of Kronos, Rhea perpetuates male violence—whether she obeys or disobeys her husband: if she obeys Kronos, handing over her newborns to feed him, she perpetuates violence against her children; if she disobeys Kronos, aiding her son in his rebellion against his father, she perpetuates violence. Either way, it seemed to me, Rhea was the loser. Either way, she functioned in a sub-servient role: as a submissive wife, or as a helper to a heroic, rebel-lious, son. Her power could only be exercised covertly: she could trick, hide, or persuade, but she could not openly show her power, her anger. As I struggled to resolve Rhea's problem, I imagined myself in open rebellion against Kronos. Rather than aiding her son's rebellion, I thought, Rhea should take up arms against her destructive husband.

What could Rhea do? I kept asking this question, as my life stalled. My writing was blocked; I was emotionally paralyzed, unable to take action, unable to write a new script for my life. I wanted a script that did not force me to choose between caring for my son and caring for myself. I wanted, I see in retrospect, to remain a wife, protected by her husband, as I had not been pro-tected by my father. As it turned out, my decision to have an abor-tion was a painful dress rehearsal for the choice to save myself, even though it meant sacrificing my son to the trauma of divorce. During the 1970s, I had suffered from depression, not only because I had given up jobs, but also from feelings of helplessness engendered, in part, by the horrifying revelations of my two younger sisters: that they too had been sexually abused. I had deferred completion of my degree because I was afraid to face the truth of the Kronos myth: that I could not avoid sacrificing my son to the violence of a divorce.[16] I wondered: What is the point of finishing my thesis? I'm not going anywhere. The voice of shame chastised: "You failed linguistics. You don't deserve graduate school." The familiar father-voice intoned, "No wonder your husband won't move–despite the fact that you have moved for him, not once but three times–so that you can complete a doctorate. Do what is expected of a wife and mother." The voice of cold financial logic finished me off: as everyone knows, there are no academic jobs open in the field of English.

Fortunately, despite these oppressive internalized voices, the women's movement gave me courage to try again: I had the right to fulfill my professional goals even if it meant that I would have to give up living with my son. Giving up the daily parenting of my son was, by far, the most painful decision I have ever made. I missed him, missed kissing his cheek each morning to wake him for school, missed seeing his bright smile after school, missed his intelligence and humor. I knew, of course, that I would not have society's support for my desire to be both a parent and a professional, despite the fact that men assumed it was their "natural" right to have both families and careers. I recognized the truth of what the church–in collusion with economic, medical, legal, psychiatric, and educational institutions–had taught me: that I had no power to define maternal practice. That is why, beginning in the 1970s, I began to dream of writing a new script, a script in which mothers have the authority to define maternal practice. In this way, I might transform what has been defined as a passive and instinctive role into an active and intelligent role; eventually, I would use the idea of "narrating mothers" to transform the trauma of mothering into a new kind of authoring.

As Martha Wolfenstein says, describing trauma survivors: "Speaking about the disaster, in contrast to being haunted by memories that come against one's will, provides the possibility of turning passivity into activity. In retelling an experience, we voluntarily reevoke it. Narration is thus like play in that one can assume control over the repetition of an event which in its occurrence ran counter to one's wishes" (quoted in Janoff-Bulman 109). I wanted to imagine myself as a maternal narrator in order to assume some control over what had been my most joyful and most traumatic experience: maternal care of my son, and, as a result of my divorce, the premature loss of daily contact with him. Based on my experience, I recognized the value of Adrienne Rich's distinction between motherhood as experience and motherhood as institution. The actual experience of mothering may be joyful, as it was for me, but mothers do not control the institutional definitions of mothering. According to traditional definitions, a woman must sacrifice her life in the public realm, giving up the very authority she needs in order to be a strong, protective mother. Where, I began to wonder, can I find stories narrated by mothers? As Hirsch asks, "Do mothers write their own experience *as mothers*? What shapes and plots accommodate those experiences?" My desire to answer these questions is the reason that, after I found a tenure-line job, I set out to investigate the maternal perspective in literature.

How, I wanted to know, can we learn to read, teach, and write from this muted and marginalized point of view? I could not recall a single discussion of the maternal perspective in a classroom, nor could I remember reading a single narrative in the maternal voice. For that reason, seven years after writing the foregoing essay, in which a daughter puts her mother's speech on trial, I coauthored a collection of essays called *Narrating Mothers.* Along with my coeditor, Maureen Reddy, I point out in the introduction to this volume that the maternal perspective has rarely been employed in narratives, even those authored by women. Most women-authored narratives are told from the daughter's point of view. Furthermore, as I argue in my own essay in this collection, many readers ignore the maternal perspective even when a writer employs it. In "Civil Rights According to Mothers: Teaching Alice Walker's *Meridian*," I explain that male students fail to recognize the maternal point of view in Walker's novel, while most female students, especially those who are mothers, find this perspective central to the novel. Despite the fact that the central figure in this novel is black, while I am white, I could readily sympathize with her, primarily because she is forced to give up her child in order to claim a life, and a voice, for herself. Like Meridian, I was struggling to author my own life.

Thus, my analysis of *Meridian* opens with a focus on maternal oppression and violence: "One mother kills her child. Another longs to die on Mother's Day. These maternal tragedies in Alice Walker's *Meridian* illustrate what Adrienne Rich describes as 'the violence of the institution of motherhood'" (*Of Woman Born* 267; quoted in *Narrating Mothers* 239). The mother's willingness to sacrifice herself, as in the case of the mother who longs to die on Mother's Day, is more typical; however, given the oppressive conditions under which women mother—racism, poverty, rape, sanctions against birth control, lack of institutional and emotional support—it is remarkable that so few mothers sacrifice their child. One might expect that the frustrations of mothering, even under the best of circumstances, would lead to maternal violence toward children; however, as Sara Ruddick points out in "Preservative Love and Military Destruction," mothers usually "remain peaceful in situations in which they are powerful, namely in battles with their own and other children" (242). As both Herman and Jacobs emphasize, in 90 percent of the cases it is fathers or stepfathers, not mothers, who are the perpetrators of the cases of childhood sexual abuse. The reason for this great difference is that most women are raised to be empathic—to imagine the needs of children—while men are not.

Yet, as I have learned from teaching Alice Walker's novel, students often think of mothering as an "instinctive" activity which does not require much thought. In fact, as Ruddick explains in *Maternal Thinking*, motherhood is a complex activity, a discipline characterized by a concern for the preservation of children and for fostering their growth and social acceptability. Ruddick argues, further, that women should have the authority to define this activity. Ruddick has been criticized for her supposedly essentialist views, but she actually argues that even though, traditionally, women are more often mothers, both genders are capable of learning maternal thought. Ruddick is, of course, not the only feminist engaged in a critique of patriarchal views of mothering. As Jacobs notes, feminists have criticized psychoanalytic theories which view the mother as "merging" with her child (as if losing herself in the child's world view); instead, Chodorow and others argue, mothering is a complex social activity based on the relationship between parent and child. I certainly did not "merge" with my child; rather, out of my love for him, I became as attentive a listener as possible. However, according to my son, there was one period of his life when I was inattentive to him: during the years that I had no job outside the home. Having given up a series of teaching positions, I become a depressed and lonely stay-at-home mother. As a result, I became—quite against my best intentions—an inattentive mother. What painful irony!

As I was to learn from Jessica Benjamin's *The Bonds of Love*—too late to alter my own mother-script—the best mothers are those who assert their own needs and boundaries, rather than sacrificing themselves for the sake of others. Unfortunately, during the 1970s when I was struggling with the question of how to be a wife and mother without sacrificing my own needs, few feminist studies of mothering were available. Even today, despite the fact that for many women, mothering is "an epistemological revolution" (Belenky et al. 34), we are just beginning to understand why such a dramatic change occurs in women's ways of knowing when they become mothers. One of the reasons, as the authors of *Women's Ways of Knowing* point out, is that many women recognize that the survival strategies that worked in childhood are not always adequate for the task of mothering. When it becomes necessary to care for another person, one's world view alters dramatically. A tragic view of the world, for example, seems to be incompatible with maternal thinking. As I argue in, "Tragic Revelations," a paper presented at the Midwest MLA in 1993, strong mothers–mothers capable of protecting their daughters–are generally absent from "classic" tragedy. In classic tragedies, a daughter's relationship to the father is central, while her relationship to the mother is marginalized or absent. When a mother plays a major part in tragedy, as does Clytemnestra in "The Oresteia," she is soundly defeated by the patriarchs, sometimes with the collusion of her father-identified daughter.

The tragic vision may be incompatible with mothering because maternal thinkers, whether male or female, are concerned with preserving the next generation. For example, in Jane Smiley's *A Thousand Acres*, the narrator's decision to become a surrogate mother to her dying sister's children transforms the novel from the tragedy on which it is based–Shakespeare's *King Lear*–into a story of preservative love. As Smiley says in an interview with her colleagues (and mine), Susan Carlson and Faye Whitaker, "I think that in tragedy and a lot of Western literature the way everybody dies in the end can be viewed as a cop-out. If they were real men, they'd go back and clean up the mess that they left rather than just keeling over at the last chord" (17–18). If men were maternal thinkers that is exactly what they would do: go back and clean up the mess rather than keeling over. Those who love their children– that is, those who want to preserve and nurture them–don't have the luxury of keeling over. However, as readers we are more accustomed to Oedipal narratives which center on a male who, although an adult, is still struggling to resolve familial conflicts; therefore, we are taught–or is it only women who are taught?–to empathize with, even to "mother" adult males. In this way, the traditional canon has colluded with other patriarchal institutions in silencing maternal thinkers (of either gender) while, at the same time, holding mothers responsible for many of the ills of society.

However, even as I generalize about mothers, I am aware of the dangers of taking the experiences of middle-class white mothers as the norm. As my coeditor and I emphasize in *Narrating Mothers,* given economic and racial differences among mothers, it is important to use the plural when theorizing the maternal. No single mother, or group of mothers, can speak for all, not only due to economic differences, but also as the result of differences in race, ethnicity, sexual orientation, or generation. As I also learned, daughters cannot speak for mothers, nor can mothers speak for daughters—despite the fact that one might be a daughter-mother. As I know from both personal experience and research, even within a single family the differences in perspectives among women—between mothers and daughters, or among sisters—can be painful, leading to ruptures that cannot be healed. My father's sexual abuse of my sisters has, for instance, resulted in deep divisions: of my six siblings, three brothers and three sisters, I have frequent contact with only one sister. The loss of family—first through sexual abuse and later divorce—has been traumatic for me. Only by assuming narrative agency, only as an author, can I imagine myself as having limited control over these painful life events. However, before I could finally become an author, I had to complete my doctoral degree and find a tenure-line job. I managed to fulfill these goals, as I illustrate in the following chapter, by imagining Joyce Carol Oates as my friend.

CHAPTER 4

Sisterhood Is Powerful

You, sister, reading this:

I have no earthly way of knowing if you are already

involved in women's liberation, and if so, how deeply.

–Robin Morgan

The impulse to balance…tensions of unity and diversity,

commonality and difference, surely explains why

feminism particularly in the 1980s produced an entire

genre of anthologies based on personal…

narratives organized to show difference within a particular,

shared aspect of identity.

–Susan Lanser

My Friend, Joyce Carol Oates

Perhaps I should correct my title—which, after all, I borrowed from Elaine Showalter—and instead use the title, "By Reading Joyce Carol Oates I have Learned to Be My Own Best Friend." For, unlike Elaine Showalter who works with Joyce Carol Oates at Princeton, I am [in 1986] an older, academic woman constantly on the verge of unemployment. Ironically, it is my love for Oates's fiction—and my commitment to writing a book about her development as a writer—that helps to keep me in this precarious state. Nevertheless, Joyce Carol Oates is my friend: by speaking for me (when my own voice was not yet strong), her fiction has taught me to speak for myself; by courageously developing and changing (through the past twenty-five years), her fiction has taught me to insist on growth and change; and by continuing to insist on the value of a woman's perspective— despite often hostile criticism— her fiction has also taught me to persist, despite the sometimes harsh attacks on my own work. Recently, for example, I was introduced to an English class as "the woman who would talk about Oatmeal Mush," the male instructor's derogatory name for Joyce Carol Oates.

This introduction—which was rather a surprise to me, though perhaps it should not have been—took place on February 9, 1987, at a private liberal arts college in Georgia. I noticed that all the women in this English department had M.A.s (and taught composition only) while all the men had Ph.D.s. Clearly, the men liked it that way. I was there for a job interview, invited at the insistence of a newly hired woman dean who had met me at MLA. It became rapidly apparent that I had been invited to the campus so that the department could *appear* to support the new dean. What would she have done, l wonder, had she heard a young man, a temporary instructor in the department, introduce me to his students as "the woman who would talk about Oatmeal Mush?" Rather than answer him, rather than defend Oates or myself, l turned to the students and said: "Oates writes so much, but not so much mush. Let's talk about this story." We then began an animated discussion of Oates's well-known, frequently anthologized short story, "Where are you going, where have you been?" I shall return to this violent story, in which a rape-murder is anticipated after the story's ambiguous conclusion, later in the chapter.

First, however, I would like to place this famous short story within the context of Oates's development as a writer. Many readers may not know that Oates's "daughters"–her fictional female characters–have become increasingly powerful since the 1960s when "Where are you going?" was published. This growth in female power is apparent on a number of levels: (1) her women characters survive violent assaults; (2) they survive economically; (3) they compete in the professions, yet they recognize the dangers of becoming exclusively male-identified, and (4) in the 1970s and 1980s, some of her female characters develop a feminist consciousness. Oates's more articulate women, after a period of trying to think of themselves as "ungendered," recognize their mothers in/as themselves.

Although the details of Oates's life are not strictly parallel to those of any of her heroines, the trajectory I will outline has autobiographical implications which, I believe, are helpful in understanding the development of Oates's feminist consciousness. "All art," Oates has said, "is autobiographical," if not in particular details, then in the kinds of problems articulated–and sometimes "solved"–in a given work. I will focus in this chapter on an act of violence that Oates reworks obsessively in her fiction (both in novels and short stories). Specifically, for Oates, this violence is rape, and for me, rape *within* the family: incest. In an autobiographical essay in 1982 called, "Stories That Define Me," Oates has stated that she was the victim of "not quite clinical molestation." I will illustrate how this "playground" violence enters Oates's fiction, in novels published in 1966 and 1986, but first I would like to give my own autobiographical response to "Stories That Define Me." In this essay Oates describes how she became a writer–a process that each time yields a different (revised) Joyce Carol Oates–out of a desire, not simply to escape a world of violence, but to transform it. "I write," she says, "with the enormous hope of altering the world–and why write without that hope?" Now this is a bald, powerful statement, nothing timid about it, and it empowers me.

What does not empower readers like me–a reader who has witnessed her father's sexual abuse of a sister, abuse that continued for many years–are writings such as Jane Gallop's "The Father's Seduction," in which Gallop cites Luce Irigaray to critique Freud but, finally, to defend psychoanalysis from attacks by survivors of childhood sexual abuse. Gallop writes, "The recent emphasis on real incest threatens to deny important psychoanalytic insights in the same gesture that it perhaps correctly accuses Freud of a blind spot." Gallop goes on with her defense of psychoanalysis, arguing, "Irigaray's more complex accusations–'not simply true ... nor completely false'–about father Freud's defensiveness are finally more useful to a feminist understanding of the binds of the father-daughter relationship." How has Gallop determined that Irigaray's "more complex accusations" are more "useful" to feminists than are accusations by victims of actual incest? Certainly accusations of both actual and psychological rape are equally complex! Finally, Gallop insists that mental seduction is more damaging than actual rape: "Briefly, the veiled seduction, the rule of patriarchal law over the daughter, denying her worth and trapping her in an insatiable desire to please the father, is finally more powerfully and broadly damaging than actualized seduction" *(Daughters and Fathers* 107). Why the necessity to put into competition psychological and actual forms of paternal rape? (I wish, Jane, you could have observed my mother, a victim of that more "veiled" seduction, a woman so trapped in her "insatiable desire to please the father" and the father-husband, that she did nothing to rescue my sister from abuse, and, in fact, denied the abuse until all three of my sisters became victims.)

I do not think it surprising, as Gallop apparently does, that paternal rape (by fathers, or uncles, or older cousins) is so widespread. In this culture, men readily assume that, because they "own" women and children, they have the right to use them as they see fit. Slave owners made this same argument. How useful, I wonder, is psychoanalysis to slaves? Not until my father's funeral in 1976, when I wrote, "I am my father's daughter" in the funeral register, could I begin to write. And not until this moment have I written so openly about my origins in shame, in family shame. Even now I feel that my testimony on this topic will be discredited, that it will "taint" my authority (which must remain lofty and theoretical to be "important"). 1 also wonder: will my story merely arouse male readers (assuming men will read such writing as this)? As Christine Froula says in *Daughters and Fathers,* Judith Lewis Herman "notes that incest victims frequently report that men find their histories arousing, as though they too envy the place of bad father" (135). Will a story that I write to liberate myself become the stimulus for a man's pornographic fantasies? Another (childhood) fear ignited by this writing: Will I be rejected, will I be abandoned? (Victims of incest often remain silent for this very reason, and certainly they/we have been abandoned.) Victims also fear that they may destroy their families: I have certainly said nothing for years because of this fear; nevertheless, my family of origin has been almost destroyed because of this violence. Victims also learn to protect their fathers, whom they recognize as financially more powerful and emotionally more independent than mothers. While my father still lived, l could not speak openly. Now, however, l gain courage because of publications like *Daughters and Fathers*, and I continue writing.

Few such feminist publications were available when I first began to read Joyce Carol Oates in 1972. At that time, her fiction helped me to feel that, one day, I too might speak out against violence and injustice. It certainly helped me to complete my master's degree and then insist upon my right to graduate school in 1978. By 1983, as I wrote my dissertation, l kept dumping this explosive autobiographical material into a fifth chapter, a chapter that I never wrote. It was my strategy for delaying a writer's block until a time when I could better afford it. Sure enough, my fear emerged again in the summer of 1988, as I wrote an essay on teenage runaways—many of them victims of sexual abuse. With perfectionism bordering on self-censorship—which Madelon Sprengnether describes as symptomatic of abuse victims—I wrote and rewrote my essay until my body was so contorted by pain that I required physical therapy. As l stood to read my essay at a conference the next fall, l nearly fainted. At the end of the session, I was able to continue, but not in my own voice: I read a poem by Joyce Carol Oates. Her voice saved me, once again.

Even Oates's title, "Stories That Define Me," liberates me, for it insists that one life may consist, not of a single story—the story perhaps of childhood victimization—but rather of "stories," and not stories imposed by others, by those who assume language belongs to them, but *stories* created by me, in the company of other women. How splendid to read Oates in the company of other women (past and present) who imagine new worlds into existence.

And in "Stories That Define Me," Oates reminds us that our reading, not only our actual lived experience, shapes our writing, or sometimes (mis)shapes a woman's writings. Oates writes:

> Hadn't I absorbed the unmistakable drift of certain prejudices, certain metaphysical/anatomical polarities? Even the otherwise egalitarian Thoreau, whose *Walden* I read at the age of 15 or 16 and have prized forever, even Thoreau, who understood that slavery is obscene because all men are equal, tells us matter-of-factly in "Reading" that there is a "memorable interval" between spoken and written languages. The first is transitory, a dialect merely, almost brutish, "and we learn it unconsciously, like the brutes, of our mothers." The second is the mature language, the written language—"our father tongue, a reserved expression."

Oates continues, "One wonders if brutes achieve a written language, are they no longer brutes? Or is their writing merely defined (by others) as brutish?" A blank space follows and, in the next paragraph Oates shares the fact of having been molested repeatedly as a child and, later in her life, repeatedly attacked for writing that is violent. "Why is your writing so violent?" "Why is your writing so brutish?"

So frequently has Oates been attacked, under the guise of this "innocent" question, that she finally replied, in a *New York Times Book Review* essay appropriately called, "Why Is Your Writing So Violent?" (1981). The question, Oates rightly states, is always "ignorant," always "sexist." The violence in her fiction does not come from her fantasies, it is obviously everywhere, and women are its frequent victims. Is there a connection between such acts of violence and Thoreau's widely shared (perhaps unconscious) view that the language belonging to men is civilized whereas the "mother tongue" remains brutish? Yes. I believe so. The "father tongue" which Oates constantly challenges and revises seems to me an elaborate (mythical) denial system, an "official" language that allows men to define women, not as rightful users of language, but as outside it, as "brutes" or "sleeping beauties." From the beginning of her writing career, as, for example, in *A Garden of Earthly Delights* (1966), Oates has challenged such stereotypes. Her heroine in *A Garden* is at once brutish—that is, uneducated and illiterate, born into a family of migrant workers—and angelic, a beautiful goldenhaired child, a favorite of her father's because she embodies his dying soul. Oates grew up not far removed, historically or geographically, from poverty (six miles south of Lockport, New York, in Niagara County), and her depiction of migrant workers contains certain fictionalized autobiographical elements.

The most important, for my purposes, are her depictions of Clara's mother—(whose outlines remain blurry)—and her depictions of sexual abuse. In *Marya, A Life* (1986), written twenty years later, Oates returns to these images, but with significant differences: Marya's mother, unlike Clara's, comes into clear focus at the end of the novel, and Marya, unlike Clara, not only survives, she prevails: she becomes, in fact, an academic and a writer. On a structural level, as well, the differences in the two novels are significant. In *Marya*, the first five chapters center upon Marya's encounters with different men—her father's corpse, her cousin, her eighth-grade teacher, Schwilk, Father Shearing, Emmet Schroeder—but this "personal" novel shifts focus. In chapter 6, Marya's friendships with women, with Imogene Skillman in particular, become central. What Marya discovers is that competition sometimes destroys friendship or love. Marya also discovers that, like many a heroine of romance, she has been seeking her mother in men, such as Maxmillian Fein, her father-professor-lover. In the final chapter, Marya searches directly for her lost mother. By contrast, in *A Garden of Earthly Delights,* Clara never recognizes her need for a mother; she defines herself solely in terms of her relationships to men.

Oates divides the novel into three parts, each bearing the name of a significant man in Clara's life: Carleton, her father (Part I), Lowry, the lover who abandons her (Part II), and Swan, the son who nearly kills her (Part III). Swan finally shoots his surrogate-father, Clara's husband, aptly named "Revere," and then turns the gun on himself. Clara survives the slaughter, but only physically. In her midforties she enters a nursing home where, sustained by Revere's money, she watches television, endlessly. Oates writes, "She seemed to like best programs that showed men fighting, swinging from ropes, shooting guns, and driving fast cars, killing the enemy again and again until the dying gasps of evil men were only a certain familiar rhythm away from the opening blasts of the commercials, which changed only gradually over the years" (384). Clara, then, never escapes the world of violence; it has penetrated her imagination, victimizing her. Furthermore, her author, Joyce Carol Oates, has not yet discovered structures that will enable her to transform a heroine defined exclusively by her relationships to men: to father, lover, and son.

As in the novels of George Eliot, Oates's earlier heroines did not become her equals. The problem is that in order to claim language, Oates, like Eliot, had to first imagine herself as male or, at best, genderless. As Oates had explained, she recognized very early that it was better to be Lewis Carroll, the writer, than to be Alice, his character. It is better to be a writer than to be written, better to be an author than to be authored. Some critics, such as Myra Jehlen in "Archimedes and the Paradox of Feminist Criticism," have suggested that the novel imposes restraints that force a woman to write as a man. I would agree that, during the 1960s when Oates was learning the craft—that is, before she had begun to revise the novel's conventions—this gender issue caused her difficulty. In *A Garden,* for example, despite Clara's centrality in the novel, Oates keeps her heroine at a "safe" distance. What I mean is that Clara's experiences, her poverty and sexual vulnerability, sometimes parallel Oates's own experiences so closely that she can not yet bring her past (or Clara's) into closer focus. In *A Garden,* although Oates protests against the view of "a fall" into sexuality, she splits the act of rape–incestuous rape–into the experience of two characters, Clara and Rosalie, one a survivor, the other a victim. Clara escapes her father's incestuous fantasies, though her father seeks her everywhere before his death as if Clara might redeem him; Clara's friend Rosalie does not escape incestuous rape.

The two little girls had played together in an abandoned car lot, a setting that recurs in *Marya,* but only Clara has the power–the seductive appearance, intelligence, and good fortune–to escape poverty by charming a man who is "fatherly" toward her and who marries her. Rosalie, however, bears her *biological* father's child. When the people in a nearby town find out, they beat to death Rosalie's father, Bert, a migrant worker. The scene is violent and, to me, terrifying. It is a scene that many a victim of incest imagines might happen if she tells. She pictures the townspeople

> dragging Bert out of his shanty. One man jumped down, another was behind Bert, and with a shove they got him out. He lost his balance and fell in the mud. Then some of the men in the town rushed over and began kicking him. Clara saw a spurt of red. She saw his face lifted by someone's boot, his head snapped back, and then he was lost in a rush of legs. The only shouting came from that group. Everyone else waited. People around Clara were inching back. "You let him alone, I'll kill you!" Clara screamed.... Then she saw Rosalie's mother in the doorway. She was screaming at the men who were beating her husband.... Clara could not make out anything except two words–"His property, his property." (79)

87

Rosalie's mother, like the mother of many victims of family sexual abuse, believes in father right, in father law. Before this law women, children, and the poor of all races are helpless "property."

Patriarchal law itself engenders violence and chaos, as this mob scene suggests. In this scene, Oates may be depicting the chaos of her own emotions: her anger and pity, her grief and perhaps shame. As people around Clara "inch away"–as victims of incest expect others to inch away–Clara pleads for the life of the father, the sexual abuser, and in this moment the author's self-division seems evident to me: if she takes on the power of the father (his law, his language) will she become a destroyer? If she rejects this power, will she perish? In this novel Oates does not resolve the dilemma; the problem remains like a frozen memory, left behind in the abandoned car lot. The two girls in *A Garden of Earthly Delights*, separated forever by Rosalie's fate (her victimization by her father), never return to their childhood playground, a vacant lot where "junked automobiles all around them looked as if they had crawled...and died." As they played in abandoned cars, they had smiled, these two girls, not knowing why, and Clara had seen "windows everywhere...cracked as if jerking back from something in astonishment; the cracks were like spider webs, like frozen ripples in water" (65). Sexual abuse destroys their friendship.

Moving forward twenty years, from 1966 to 1986, Oates creates another abandoned car lot, another "playground," in *Marya, A Life.* This time Oates brings the scene of sexual abuse into closer focus. Rather than "jerking back from something in astonishment," an astonishment that freezes memory and creative movement, Oates now identifies that vague "something" as the repeated scenes of molestation by a cousin. Marya, who later becomes an academic and a writer, has been abandoned by both parents, left in the care of an aunt and uncle, when the sexual abuse occurs. Chapter 2 of the novel opens, without introduction, with these words:

He instructed her to hold still. Not to move. Not to move. And not to look at him either. Or say a word.

Marya froze at once. "Went into stone," as she called it. And stared at the grimy partly broken windshield of the old car. And said nothing.

It was only Lee, her cousin Lee, who liked her. Who liked her most of the time. Who meant her no harm....

He was twelve years old, Marya was eight. He didn't mean to hurt her and he never really hurt her unless by accident....

In the smelly old Buick at the back of the lot, Marya knew how to go into stone; how to shut her mind off, to see nothing without closing her eyes. She was afraid only that her neck might snap: she knew how chickens' necks were rung, how a garter snake might be whipped against the side of a barn and its secret bones broken. Lee was strong—it was a joke around the house how strong he was. [Here the scene shifts but Oates courageously returns to a fictionalized version of a painful memory.]

"Be quiet," Lee would say, grunting. "Or I'll wring your skinny little neck."

She never closed her eyes because—how did she know this?—the gesture might anger him, might make him rough.

She stared at, must have memorized, the windshield of the old wreck. It was cracked in cobweblike patterns that overlapped with one another, doubly, trebly, dense and intricate and fascinating as a puzzle in a picture book. A maze; such things were called, a labyrinth. *"Can you get to the center without raising your pencil point and without crossing any line?"*

[Marya tries, as my sisters have told me they had tried, to lose their pain by intense concentration, as if leaving their bodies behind.]

Sometimes Marya could do it at the first try, sometimes she couldn't. If she got angry, she cheated: but then getting to the center didn't count.

[Marya wonders how many people have died in these cars. She sees bloodstains. She waits for Lee to finish, as my sisters must have waited.] When it was over Lee wouldn't wait to catch his breath but drew back from her at once, flush-faced, panting, his wet lips slack. He never looked at her–they never looked at each other at such times. He rarely spoke except to mutter, "Don't you tell anybody, you."

Hold still. Don't move. Don't tell. (15–18)

These are familiar injunctions, *"Don't move. Don't tell."* Victims of incest, and other kinds of rape, are either killed or cautioned against speaking out. And society often conspires with the abuser, shaming the victim, forcing her to bear the responsibility for the rapist's violence. To give an example of blaming the victim: a number of students in my freshman English class at St. Olaf College [in 1986], on reading Oates's story "Where are you going, where have you been?" blamed the victim of rape. She should have obeyed her mother, wrote the students, she should have stayed home like her "good" sister June. When I returned these papers for revision, I showed them photographs of three young women–ages thirteen, fifteen, and seventeen–all of them victims of rape and murder, all of them pictured in a (1966) *Life* magazine article called, "The Pied Piper of Tucson." These, I said, are photographs of the victims, the "raw material" of Oates's story. Do they deserve violent deaths for disobeying their parents? (I ask this question with open anger.)

What did you mean, I asked Joyce Carol Oates in an interview in 1973, when you wrote in *The Edge of Impossibility* that "violence is always an affirmation"? To answer this question, she used the rapist as an example. "The rapist," she said, "seeks to unite himself with something beyond himself, but his desire for this union has been twisted." Perverted. Love twisted into violence, into a wish to obliterate the other, to swallow up the other's threatening identity. Clara, staring into the violence of a television program, gets lost, but Marya, Marya is found. After she receives a letter and a photograph from her mother Vera Murchison, Marya stares into the blurry photograph, "waiting for the face to shift into perfect focus" (310). Although the picture is still slightly blurred, Marya sees more clearly (and looks more closely) than did Clara, who saw only a series of "formless" women with "formless" bodies who took her biological mother's place. It is knowledge–that we are "of woman born"–everywhere violently repressed. What Oates affirms in *Marya*, and in many other novels, is the possibility of dreaming into existence a culture which doesn't require us to define ourselves at the expense of another, a culture which allows each of us a center, a voice, a face, a story.

As I complete this chapter in the winter of 1989, I am a tenure-line assistant professor at Iowa State University. *The Journal of Popular Culture* will publish my essay on "Where are you going, where have you been?" in its winter issue. Self-doubt (a legacy of my nightmarish childhood?) surfaced as I proofed the galleys for this essay, called "An Unfilmable Conclusion: Joyce Carol Oates at the Movies" (the short story had been made into a 1986 movie called "Smooth Talk"). Would readers find my essay about rape and murder too positive? Perhaps I tried so hard to emphasize the means by which Oates transforms an act of violence into a story of survival–a woman writer's survival–that I distorted my thesis: that violence against women will not stop until our society undergoes a spiritual transformation. I wonder: Did my personal background once again misshape my writing? Or is it the conventions of academic discourse that inhibit my search for an authentic shape for my truth? I don't know.

In the meantime, despite self-doubt, I continue to write, thinking of Joyce Carol Oates as my friend. I imagine her as part of my story—she could be an older sister, for example—and Oates has imagined me as part of her story. Because I wrote to her about her fiction, about sexual abuse in particular, she generously imagined me a character in her novel *Bellefleur*. I am Yolande, an older sister who rescues her young sister Germaine (born a hermaphrodite) from sexual abuse. Just as Oates makes Elaine Showalter a character in *A Bloodsmoor Romance* (Miss Elaine Cottler who ran for president of the United States), she creates a space for me in her fiction. And in that space, I imagine myself into being. I see myself as having many lives to live, many stories to tell.

Sisterhood and Conflict

While it is unlikely that Elaine Showalter will ever read, "My Friend, Joyce Carol Oates," she has acknowledged my membership in the feminist community by including my essay, "'An Unfilmable Conclusion': Joyce Carol Oates at the Movies," in the collection she edited for Rutgers Press, *Where Are You Going, Where Have You Been?* It would appear, then, that my attempt to join the sisterhood—a desire evident in my echoing of Showalter's title—has succeeded. Without such recognition by "sisters," I would not have a voice; therefore, unlike more self-confident younger feminists, I do not find it necessary to "slay the mother" to achieve a voice of my own. It is my strong need for affiliation with the feminist community, and the fact that I am part of the same generation as Oates and Showalter, which prompts me to imagine these famous women as helpful, slightly older sisters or friends. Indeed, as I mentioned in chapter 1, my need for sisterhood is so strong—undoubtedly because my father attempted to destroy any trust between my sisters and me—that I find controversy among feminists deeply disturbing. Even as I recognize that debate is both healthy and necessary, I become anxious when feminists disagree.

Part of my anxiety arises, I understand, from my personal past: our family had no effective methods for resolving conflicts. When conflict occurs in my family, we withdraw into silence, sometimes a silence that lasts for years. Therefore, when I learned that Joyce Carol Oates's fiction was not warmly received by most feminist scholars, I became anxious. As a graduate student, I worried that, because I had chosen to write about Oates's fiction, I would be excluded from the feminist community. I also knew that without some support from the feminist community, I would not be able to write a book about Oates's novels. For that reason, I was very happy to learn, while still in graduate school, that Showalter was an admirer of Oates's fiction. And fortunately, after presenting a paper on Oates's novel *Bellefleur* at the Modern Language Association in 1985, I found additional feminist support for my work on Oates, this time from Sandra Gilbert. It is largely due to such feminist support that my book—*Lavish Self-Divisions: The Novels of Joyce Carol Oates*—was finally published in 1996. Without the work of feminist scholars such as Eileen Teper Bender, Joanne Creighton, and Ellen Friedman—all of whom preceded me—I certainly would not have persevered in my work on Oates.

Unfortunately, it was also in 1985, just at the time feminist critic Cara Chell announced that Oates was writing feminist fiction, that Oates's novel *Solstice* was attacked by well-known feminist writer Joanna Russ in *The Women's Review of Books*. Russ criticized the novel for its supposed appeal to "prurient appetites" (Bender 158), describing *Solstice* as a "Sadistic lesbian novel." Oates replied to Russ in a letter to the *Women's Review of Books*, explaining, "I have never written a sadistic lesbian novel," but defending her right to do so. Ironically, this controversy over *Solstice* mirrored the very competition—a power struggle between two women—depicted in the novel itself. Furthermore, *Solstice* portrays the very problem that Joanna Russ (or "Joanna," the first-person authorial voice of *The Female Man*) warns us is a major problem in establishing either a woman's identity, or a women's community:

> There is the vanity training, the obedience training, the self-effacement training, the rivalry training, the stupid-ity training, the placation training. How am I to put this together with my human life, my intellectual life, my solitude, my transcendence, my brains, and my fearful, fearful ambition? (151)

How can these contradictory aspects of the self be united, reconciled? According to Annis Pratt, Russ answers this question in the imagery and plot of *The Female Man*, and in her authorial comment: "To resolve contrarieties...unite them in your own per-son" (111). Oates holds a remarkably similar view of contraries as evident from her preface to a collection of critical essays called *Contraries* (1981): Blake's "Without contraries is no progression." Furthermore, despite Russ's attack on *Solstice*, this novel examines how a woman is to redefine herself, including her "fearful, fearful ambition," while maintaining friendships with other woman. The novel answers this difficult question by creating a balance of power between the "feminine" Monica, who becomes the novel's narrator, and the "masculine" sculptor Sheila, both of whom may be viewed as aspects of Oates's authorial consciousness. By uniting these gender contraries, *Solstice* suggests that Sheila (who repre-sents the novelist's image-making power) and Monica (who repre-sents the novelist's narrative voice) are aspects of the creative process. Authorship becomes, in short, a process in which the writer divides herself up lavishly into all her characters, but also a process during which characters actually "talk back" to their author as they claim their own voices.

As I argue in *Lavish Self-Divisions*: an author is not a single voice, nor a single story. I stand behind this claim; however, it does not resolve the conflict between Oates and Russ, or within the larger feminist community. It does not, for example, explain why, as Jane Gallop notes, Susan Koppleman attacked Oates so harshly in *Images of Women* (1972). Since Gallop expected the first collection of feminist criticism to "trash" male writers, she was surprised to find Koppelman's "unusually vehement" attack on *them*: "[A]t no time does Miss Oates separate herself from her characters and say, 'This sexism, like their racism, their ignorance...their poverty, is part of their victimization'" (quoted in Gallop's *Around 1981* 94).[17] Koppelman charges that Oates "does not separate herself from her characters," that she lacks sufficient critical and moral distance from her bigoted, impoverished characters. Since subsequent critics, such as Linda Wagner Martin, have repeated this charge, though usually in milder tones, I felt threatened: How would I, a critic without an established reputation, defend Oates from such unjust charges? Fortunately, at the time I was writing my book on Oates, feminists began to examine the issue of conflict within feminism. With the appearance of *Conflicts in Feminism* in 1990, I learned that even well-established feminists, such as Jane Gallop, Marianne Hirsch, and Nancy Miller, found it painful when young feminists such as Toril Moi built their arguments by *"trash-ing"* other feminist work (350, my italics).

How, I wonder, is it possible to debate ideas without destroying the very feminist community necessary to my academic survival, particularly my survival as an author? Fortunately, during the 1980s, Oates began to examine the "dark side" of relationships among women in her fiction—relations between mothers and daughters, especially, but also between sisters and friends. As Showalter says of *Marya, a Life*, "Oates never idealizes the process by which Marya comes to the decision that at midlife she must reclaim a matrilineal past. The community of women is not idyllic, but torn by rage, competition, primal jealousies, ambiguous desire, and emotional violence, just like the world in which women seem subordinate to and victimized by men" (*Ms.* 50). In this and other novels of the 1980s, Oates shows how matrophobia often gives birth to sororophobia. As Helena Michie emphasizes, "Sororophobia...has much in common with, owes it very existence to, is even we might say a daughter of 'matrophobia'" (9). Nevertheless, says Michie, sisterhood "remains a distressingly utopian term" (8), as if the bond were devoid of competition and envy. "Why," Michie asks, "should the concept of sisterliness not include, among other elements, competition and envy?" (9).

Probably because of my need for affiliation, I do not usually regard other feminists who study Oates's works primarily as competitors although I do admit to some disappointment when other Oates scholars do not cite my work. Because Oates has frequently been attacked by both misogynist and feminist critics, I was pleased when, during the 1980s, a growing number of feminist scholars began to define Oates as a feminist writer: Ellen Friedman in 1980; Elaine Showalter in 1983; Cara Chell in 1985; Eileen Teper Bender in 1987; Marilyn Wesley, Jo Anne Creighton and Lorna Sage in 1992. During the same decade, I was baffled when Bonnie Zimmerman omitted any discussion of Oates's postmodern novels from her essay, "Feminist Fiction and the Postmodern Challenge" (*Post-Modern Fiction* 177–80) and surprised when Gayle Greene, declaring that Oates is "not feminist" (25), omitted her from *Changing the Story: Women Writers and the Tradition.* By contrast, my study of Oates demonstrates that, during the past three decades–decades which parallel the emergence of the second wave of the women's movement–Oates has developed into a powerful feminist writer. While it is true, as Henry Louis Gates, Jr., points out, that Oates refuses "to add to our supply of positive role models" (28), it is equally true, as Showalter says, that "no one can argue with the writer's need to grow, to experiment, to take all of human experience for her province" ("Women Who Write" 31).

Although I am now more professionally secure, I often wonder: How is it possible to disagree in public—especially in this era of backlash—and maintain a strong feminist community? To some extent, my experience as a feminist collaborator—as a coeditor of one anthology and contributor to nine anthologies published during the 1980s and early 1990s[18]—provides an answer to this question. Particularly through my collaboration with Maureen Reddy, my coeditor for *Narrating Mothers*, I learned that despite our differences, we could—if we were open about our conflicts—maintain our strong friendship. Although Maureen is younger than I, she taught me a great deal. I began to revise my own writing process as I noticed, for example, that Maureen wasted no energy on self-doubt, that she was unafraid of criticism, and that she did not rely as much as I did on feminist authorities. Symptoms of my dependency were evident in my tendency toward digressive arguments with other feminist critics, as well as in my excessive use of quotes. My self-confidence grew stronger through this experience of feminist collaboration, particularly as I learned (as I had never learned from my family) that it is possible to resolve conflicts and maintain relationships. Undoubtedly because of my personal history—I had not been taught any skills for coping with conflict, and I was afflicted with habitual self-doubt—my development as a writer had been impeded.

At the same time, I have learned from researchers such as Carol Gilligan, Lynn Mikel Brown, Jill McLean Taylor and others that, for many middle-class white girls, self-doubt begins in the middle school years, while conflict is pushed underground. While it is comforting to recognize that I am not alone in my anxieties about conflict—young girls are still being taught to avoid conflict—it is disturbing to discover that feminists have had little educational system that continues to expect girls to practice "niceness" at the expense of developing assertive voices. As Gilligan argues, "For girls to remain responsive to themselves, they must resist the conventions of feminine goodness; to remain responsive to others, they must resist the values placed on self-sufficiency and independence in North American culture" ("Teaching Shakespeare's Sister" 10). It is wonderful to find these words, words that affirm my personal struggle against "feminine goodness," as well as my efforts to reimagine authorship not as a solo, but as a collaborative performance. No one is completely self-sufficient. As I happily acknowledge in *Authoring a Life*, without the support of the feminist community, I could not have claimed a voice, nor would I have found a way to author my life. Therefore, I remain committed to the development of feminist curricula and pedagogies, not only in college literature classrooms, but also in middle schools and high schools.

That is why, in the chapter which follows, I advocate the teaching of a young adult novel that depicts father-daughter incest. Although I recognize that well-intended teachers and parents will oppose bringing this topic into middle school literature classrooms, I believe that the pedagogical risk is worth taking. Why? My answer is that if my sisters had read a novel about father-daughter incest designed for young readers, they might have escaped years of traumatic suffering, particularly if they had been guided by a feminist teacher. Therefore, I dedicate the following chapter to my sisters while, at the same time, I acknowledge that this novel also speaks for me, a girl once silenced by shame, a girl who was once a "schoolaholic," like the novel's protagonist. First published with the title, "Father-Daughter Incest in Hadley Irwin's *Abby, My Love:* Repairing the Effects of Childhood Sexual Abuse During the Adolescent Years," this chapter contains no personal commentary; however, it is, as should become quickly apparent, autobiographical. For this reason, I am especially grateful to Jane

Tompkins for her support of this chapter prior to its publication in *Children's Literature Association Quarterly* in 1992. In a letter (dated 1991), which Tompkins copied to me, she wrote,

> Unlike an awful lot of professional literary criticism these days, this essay does not aim to show off the writer's expertise, her ability to conceptualize in a complicated way, or her theoretical acumen. The aim of the essay is to address a real life problem in a way that will be helpful to its readers. Daly provides a powerful, detailed, subtle, and well-informed analysis of highly charged material–the novel deals with a teenager's recovery from a long-continued sexual abuse.

The fact that Tompkins, a feminist I admire, has found my effort to "address a real life problem" of value to readers gives me some assurance that sisterhood is still powerful!

CHAPTER 5

Politics and Pedagogy: An Incest Narrative in a Middle School Classroom

The survivors did not only need to survive
so that they could tell their story; they also needed
to tell their story in order to survive.

–Dori Laub

Authorship not only expresses itself through narration,
it also develops through narrative.

–Mark B. Tappan and Lyn Mikel Brown

ABBY, MY LOVE, OPENS with a high school commencement address, a valedictory speech by Abigail Morris, or "Abby," as she is known to her family and friends. Authors Lee Hadley and Annabelle Irwin, whose pen name is Hadley Irwin, have carefully positioned their female protagonist at the threshold of leaving home, just at the moment of her entry into adult life. The question central to the novel, "What are the effects of childhood sexual abuse upon a daughter's development?" is dramatized by this opening, for often an incest victim experiences a crisis at times of transition, finding herself unable to manage increased responsibilities. By beginning with Abby's commencement address, the authors also reassure young readers that Abby will not only survive adolescence, she will actually triumph. Such a triumph is plausible for a young woman who survives father-daughter incest by becoming, in her words, a "schoolaholic," a teenager addicted to school, participating in every possible extracurricular activity in order to avoid going home. This strategy of avoidance, a realistic one for some victims of family sexual abuse, does provide a limited though temporary means of self-protection, but it does not help Abby to heal.[19]

In order for the healing to begin, as this novel skillfully conveys, she must reach out for help, share her painful secret, and work with a therapist trained to help incest victims confront and

103

then let go of terrifying memories and debilitating behaviors. Not all victims are as fortunate as Abby; not all find someone to listen and help.[20] That is why, I believe, it is important for all of us to learn how to recognize the symptoms of sexual abuse and how to respond in humane and effective ways to signals of distress. Over the centuries, at least since Biblical times, society has denied the reality of childhood sexual abuse, often blaming the so-called Seductive Daughter, as in the Old Testament story of Lot.[21] But since the 1970s, with the advent of the women's movement in the United States, our society has begun to acknowledge the reality of childhood sexual abuse and often, but not yet always, to effectively intervene. *Abby, My Love,* published in 1985, reflects this hopeful change, showing young readers that help is available, even as it informs them of the devastating effects of father-daughter incest.

Father-daughter incest, which may not result in intercourse but which always involves secrecy, is a form of sexual exploitation estimated as affecting one out of every one hundred daughters in the United States. To put the statistics in somewhat different terms, one million American girls have been involved in incestuous relations with their fathers; 16,500 cases occur each year.[22] One of the most recent, well-publicized revelations of childhood sexual abuse is the story of Marilyn Van Derbur, Miss America in 1957, who disclosed in *People* magazine (1991) that from the age of five to eighteen, when she was finally able to leave home, she was sexually violated by her millionaire father. Many of Van Derbur's symptoms—such as a lack of trust in adult males, a desire to achieve perfection in her work, and careful control of her feelings—are similar to those of Abby Morris; the difference is that Abby does not have to wait until she is well into adulthood before she can tell her secret, as Van Derbur did, to a trusted male friend. That is why, as I explained in the preceding chapter, I advocate teaching father-daughter incest narratives as early as middle school.

Providing Abby with a neighborhood friend, a young man named Chip to whom she finally tells her terrible secret, is but one example of Hadley Irwin's considerable insight into the needs of their adolescent protagonist, as well as the needs of their young readers. Furthermore, because Chip is the narrator, his telling of Abby's story allows readers to experience his struggle to understand and to sympathize with Abby's sometimes puzzling behavior, but from the point of view of someone close to their own age. Abby learns to trust Chip, an exceptional young man who, when Abby tells him her secret, wisely consults his mother about how to help Abby. Chip's mother, a warm and self-sufficient widow of the Vietnam War, comforts both young people and also finds the right kind of help for Abby. By contrast, Abby's mother at first tries to hide the fact that the abuse has occurred, a response characteristic of some mothers of incest victims who actually deny that abuse has taken place. This consideration of the incest victim's lack of support leads me to an important question: In what kind of families does incest occur? I shall consider this question very briefly here, developing it further in my discussion of the effects of childhood sexual abuse upon Abby.

Research demonstrates that father-daughter incest occurs in families at all income levels. Abby's family, for example, is clearly middle class; her father is a dentist, her mother a homemaker. Yet, according to one sociological explanation—called "the conflict theory"[23]—Abby's family exhibits a key trait of incestuous families: an unequal distribution of power. Abby's mother lacks a college education and has no economic independence from her husband, a situation that makes it difficult for her to offer genuine protection to her daughter. In other words, lacking financial resources, how would she herself survive if she confronted her husband with the abuse? Yet the conflict theory, with its emphasis upon the unequal distribution of power between mother and father, is incomplete. "The power relations in the family do not suffice to explain why fathers frequently take advantage of their superior position to make sexual use of their children while mothers do not" (55), as Herman argues in *Father-Daughter Incest*. "It is the sexual division of labor, with its resultant profound differences in male and female socialization," Herman explains, "which determines in mothers a greater capacity for self-restraint, and in fathers a greater propensity for sexually exploitative behavior" (55). In other words, because admission to adulthood requires the male's repression of all maternal capacities, fathers frequently lack the ability to nurture. The Morris family is traditional in both its sexual division of labor and in its imbalance of power. For example, it is Mr. Morris who decides that Abby will stay home alone with him on Saturdays while his wife and youngest daughter go shopping, a plan that does not elicit a word of protest from his acquiescent wife, despite Abby's obvious discomfort.

Although Mrs. Morris does not yet know about the abuse and would have no obvious reason to protest her husband's plan, she does not pick up the distress signals her daughter tries to send her. It takes young Chip, now a senior and one year older than Abby, to pick up her distress signals, listen to Abby's secret, and offer to help her. Nevertheless, Hadley Irwin takes care not to engage in mother-blaming; instead, the novel provides descriptions of the Morris family that enable us to see the vulnerability of both Abby and her mother.[24] Evidence that the authors have carefully researched the topic of father-daughter incest is apparent, not only in their effective depiction of its damaging effects upon Abby, but also in their prefatory thanks to both Anna Stone, a Social Services Supervisor, and to Jeanne Beardsley, a Clinical Social Worker. Most important, however, is the fact that Hadley Irwin use their knowledge to offer realistic reassurances to young readers: yes, terrible things happen to children; some parents actually hurt their daughters rather than protecting them, but some adults, such as Chip's mother and her soon-to-be husband, Jake, can be trusted to help. Furthermore, though incest is deeply injurious to Abby–in ways that I shall detail here–she does find effective therapy and she does prevail, as we know from the outset.

As Abby asserts in her valedictory speech, "We are not alone. We are not powerless.... We control our own lives," and furthermore, although the abuse occurred within the privacy of her family, Abby has learned that "Nothing that happens to us affects only us. Nothing we do affects only ourselves. We belong to the world, and the world belongs to us" (4). This is important news for the isolated victims of childhood sexual abuse, news that Chip, as narrator of the novel, conveys to readers with his usual flair for comic relief. Relating the details of Abby's commencement address, Chip reports that "Old Redundant," the principal, introduces the valedictorian with his customary "illiteracies": "A high honor, irregardless of the other awards she has won" (9). This infusion of humor is an important ingredient in the novel, not only for readers, who need temporary relief from so emotionally oppressive a topic, but also for the development of a trusting relationship between Chip and Abby who first meet when Abby, still in grade school, moves into the neighborhood. The novel itself depicts Abby's years in high school, with major emphasis upon her development from age fifteen to seventeen, by which age sexual desire has usually emerged. Chip's good humor helps to ease Abby's deep anxieties even as it provides some release for his more ordinary adolescent nervousness about girls.

The young pair distance themselves from the tensions of a potentially romantic relationship by adopting personas, taking the parts of Mildred and Millard Fillmore, a role-playing strategy familiar to Chip from having acted in plays, and appealing to Abby because of her highly developed verbal ability, as well as her need to escape her own distressing identity. Before detailing how these adult personas facilitate the development of a trusting relationship between Chip and Abby, I should mention that the

CBS movie based on *Abby, My Love*–an "After School Special" that aired in April 1991–does not develop this linguistically playful dimension of the novel.[25] No doubt because the producers wanted a movie that would run for less than an hour, they omitted this psychologically complex facet of *Abby, My Love,* but they do portray an episode in which Abby and Chip visit an antique shop where they try on hats that inspire them to play different characters. This donning of personas is, for Abby, not just play, but also a defense mechanism that allows her temporary relief, a flight from her identity, even an escape from her body, which she has come to hate.[26]

The novel provides us with many clues as to how frequently Abby tried to avoid being alone with her father, a clear indication that she felt herself a prisoner in her own home. As a consequence, she tells Chip that she hates her name, that she has dreamt of escaping from her bed, and that the watch she wears, a gift from her father, seems more like a "handcuff." Thus, the persona Abby adopts–a name invented for Mrs. Millard Fillmore whose birthday Chip suggests they celebrate–is not just for sport, as it is for Chip. For Abby, this alternative self protects her from the possibility that, because of her attraction to Chip, her feelings will erupt, a dangerous possibility for her because she feels such shame and because she fears that, should she lose her careful self-control, she may reveal her secret and lose Chip. The degree of Abby's anxiety surfaces on their first date while Abby, the "schoolaholic" who has volunteered for the duty, is cleaning up the gym after a school dance. Having turned off the lights in preparation for leaving, she says to Chip–as if playing a childhood game of hide-and-seek– "You'll never find me," but she immediately becomes frightened with the game. Chip wonders why, when he had barely touched her, "she made this awful low muffled sound as if she were going to be sick or something" (62). As readers, we may be as baffled as Chip, but also as attracted to her as he is.

Abby's puzzling response to Chip's touch, along with her complicated explanation about why she can't go to a Friday night movie–she says she has to clean house on Friday nights so that she can go shopping with her mother and her sister on Saturdays–inspire Chip to invent a celebration as an occasion for a second date. Hence, he creates the imaginary birthday of the presidential wife, Mrs. Millard Fillmore–Abby to play the part–without knowing why such play-acting appeals to Abby. Chip, telling us Abby's story after the fact, is now able to understand Abby's desire to be someone else, and also understand her sometimes peculiar behavior. Of the need to clean the house on a Friday night, for example, Chip first thinks, "It was an organized house, all right, but it sounded more like an institution to me" (64), though he later comprehends her desire to avoid Mr. Morris. Chip also understands, in retrospect, why Abby doesn't laugh when he describes his old Volkswagon as "New, Used, Abused." The fact is that Abby, who has named the car "The Phoenix," has come to identify with it, thinking of the car not only as a source of freedom but also as an metaphor for her own body which, as readers learn along with Chip, is indeed "New, Used, Abused."

Once again, the movie producers lost an opportunity to convey important information when they eliminated "The Phoenix," replacing it with a newer, more ordinary car. For, as a metaphor of Abby's body, The Phoenix also tells us, by indirection, what must happen to Abby in therapy, that she must "die" if she is to be "born again" as a healthy young woman. The self that must die–the split subject depicted as Abby/Mrs. Millard Fillmore–must be transformed into a healthy, integrated young woman. Significantly, it is as Mildred Fillmore that Abby begins to tell her secret to Chip, as if it might be a fiction, a dream. Abby begins,

Mildred must have been four or five....She used to have these nightmares. Sometimes, you know, it's hard to decide whether you're asleep or awake when you're little. Anyway, there'd be this man in her room. Sometimes just standing in the doorway or at the foot of her bed. Sometimes bending over her. Sometimes sitting on the bed and touching her. (author's ellipses, 104)

Chip responds, understandably, with confused sympathy. "That's an awful dream for a kid to have," he says. But Abby goes on to disentangle reality from fantasy: "Mildred tried so hard to stay asleep when she felt the hands," she says, and Chip responds, "Maybe it was just someone seeing if she were all right" (104).

Such a comment, a denial of what Abby has just said, might have discouraged some victims, many of whom sense when listeners do not want to know the terrible details of incest. But Abby, who initially hides behind her "Mildred" persona, persists, clarifying her story to her trusted friend. "Chip!" she insists, "His hands were inside my pajamas between my legs! Then it got worse!" (104). Finally, confronted with this ugly detail, he asks Abby, "He hasn't actually.... I wanted to say 'raped you,' but I couldn't get the words out," when she interrupts, "He has" (104). Abby goes on to explain that she is afraid her younger sister will be her father's next victim and also that she is afraid to stay alone with her father when her mother and sister leave three days early on their family vacation. Moreover, she is, as often happens in such cases, afraid that Chip will hate her. Fortunately, Chip does not regard Abby as "used goods," nor does he exploit her lack of self-esteem, as a less compassionate young man might have. Instead, because he has been raised by a mother he respects, Chip is amazed at Abby's fear that he will "hate" her or blame her. "I hate all right!" he says, but "Not *you*! It's that... that.... Not even the words I'd learned in the locker room fit what I felt" (author's ellipses, 105). Understandably angry with Abby's father, Chip will have to manage his anger effectively if he is not to frighten Abby, a large demand for someone so young.

110

Chip's next question is one that most of us, in his place, would ask, "Have you told your mother?" (105). To this Abby responds, "I've tried. But she couldn't hear me. It's all mixed up. We're a family. He's my father, and he's her husband" (105–106). The point is, of course, that her mother is too "mixed up" in the family to see Abby's reality clearly, to see that Abby is being treated as a "little wife" rather than as a daughter. Still, Chip wonders why Abby hasn't told anyone else before this, given the fact that the abuse began years earlier. Abby explains, "Because there isn't anyone else. Who would believe me?" (106). However implausible, her fear is actually realistic, given the history of incest victims whose credibility has frequently been denied and who have actually been blamed for seducing their adult fathers.[27] This tragic history of the silencing of children, especially daughters, in a father-dominated culture, makes Abby's silence understandable. Even today, when credibility is at issue in cases of sexual abuse, many adults choose to believe the more powerful father, not the daughter.

For that reason, Chip is plausible as the person likely to believe Abby and to take her side. Also, as Abby knows, Chip has a good relationship with his mother, the person he is likely to consult in order to seek help. Nevertheless, it is not surprising when Chip, despite his sympathy for Abby, engages in a common form of denial, thinking that "things like this just didn't happen. Oh, maybe in really poor families or with alcoholics or drug pushers, but not with families who lived just down the street" (107), a reaction at once plausible and instructive to readers, who might have thought exactly the same thing. Chip also wonders, as most readers will, "If it was true, how could Mrs. Morris not know it, and if she knew it, how could she let it happen?" (107). Indeed, if Chip was puzzled by Abby's behavior, wondering, for example, why she hated her name, why she hated her watch but wore it anyway, why she disappeared inside herself sometimes and why she kept space between them, then why wouldn't Mrs. Morris have noticed too? Most of all, Chip reflects upon how Abby "talked about being two people at the same time and why being Mildred was so important" (107). He now thinks back, too, to Abby's reaction to his description of The Phoenix as "New, Used, Abused": "It was the story of her life," he now understands. Nevertheless, once Chip tells his mother Abby's secret, the story of, as he says, "the ugliest word in the language, 'Incest,'" hope becomes possible (108).

Like a phoenix, the almost "schizophrenic" Abby/Mildred will be born again as Abigail Morris, a young woman capable of claiming her name, her body, and her self. Abigail's year-long therapy occurs off stage, a wise decision by the authors, considering the age of their readers. During the period of Abby's therapy, Chip does receive one postcard from her, telling him that "Mildred Fillmore was married twice," concluding with the puzzle, "You'll never guess his first wife's name" (130). This clue sends Chip straight to the library where he discovers that Fillmore's second wife's name was, of all things, Abigail. Comforted by this clue to Abby's quest for identity, Chip decides to deal with Abby's long absence—an absence also likely to be inexplicable to young readers—with the understanding that "Mildred really was in Secaucus, discovering her name was Abigail" (133). What Hadley Irwin conveys by way of this play with names is that therapy helps Abby to heal the psychic split within. She reclaims the mute child, the child who could not cry out in the night, but lay in obedient silence as her own father violated her body, murdering her soul, and depriving her of a childhood.

In fact, Abby has had no childhood, a truth poignantly implied when she first proposes to Chip that they skip school for a secret holiday. She says, "May third is Mrs. Millard Fillmore's birthday. We are going to celebrate, no matter what. You and the Phoenix and me" (88), explaining that, "We are going to be sick that day. Very, very sick. For just one day we are going to be juvenile and delinquent. We are going to be irresponsible...we're going to be kids" (88). Chip does not yet understand why Abby imagines them as "anything else" than kids, nor does he understand that Abby is sharing this secret to test whether she can trust Chip with a far more serious secret. That Abby can allow herself just one day to be a kid is a tragic consequence of childhood sexual abuse. Indeed, only through therapy will Abby acquire knowledge of rights she should already have learned as a child: that she has a right to say "no" to an exploitive adult, even a parent; that she need not carry the burden of her father's shame; that she was an innocent child, not guilty of seducing her father or, in any way, causing his behavior; and that she need not assume responsibility for holding together a family that has failed her.

Only in retrospect, and after great pain, does Abby learn that, though she has lost her innocence, she is not to blame. This insight is one of the most important for rape victims to accept, both emotionally and intellectually; otherwise, they cannot learn to cherish themselves, despite the tragic failure of their fathers to do so. Of course, when she first tells Chip what her father has done, Abby does not know that she is guiltless, which is why she asks Chip not to "hate" her. Typically, Abby assumes responsibility for what her father has done, behavior consistent with Mr. Morris's selfish expectations, such as the expectation that Abby will behave as an adult in their sexual liaison. Even at age twelve, as Chip had noticed earlier, Abby had sounded more adult than her father. Initially an admirer of such maturity and intelligence, Chip tells us, for example, that

> listening to Abby talk was like listening to the engine of a finely tuned sports car, a Porsche or a Lamborghini. Most of the time she spoke in whole sentences, maybe even paragraphs, not at all like the other kids my age. It was kind of eerie, really. There she was, only twelve

years old, but she sounded so much older, like she was an adult and I was the kid. She wasn't condescending or anything. She was just different. (7)

Fortunately, Chip is secure enough to admire a girl like Abby, rather than being intimidated. At the same time, however, he describes her formal speech as somehow "eerie," as if he senses another level of meaning in Abby's polished style. What he senses, of course, is a highly intellectualized adult persona, the public self that contains the mute child inside, the child who has been forced to perform as an adult sexual partner to her father without concern for her own feelings of abandonment and violation. This reversal of child and adult roles is even more obvious on one occasion when Chip, encountering Abby and her father alone at the playground, observes how Abby tells her father they had better go: "It's getting late and Mom might be worried," she says, in a manner that makes Chip think, "Just for a moment she sounded as if she were the mother and he was the little kid" (36). Indeed, Chip has a point. Abby is certainly assuming adult responsibility, inappropriate in a twelve year old. This kind of over-responsible behavior, as well as the confusion in roles—as Abby performs as a wife, physically and psychologically—is characteristic of many incest victims.

In such cases it is often assumed that it is the mother's failure as a wife that creates the daughter's role confusion. In fact, incest does occur more frequently in those families where mothers are ill and/or overburdened with the care of many children, but to blame the mothers in such families is to ignore the fact that these immature fathers expect their sexual demands to be met regardless of circumstances.[28] In short, mother-blaming distracts attention from the childish behavior of the incestuous father who, though he may hide his dependencies behind authoritarian dominance, damages his children with his narcissistic demands. Mr. Morris, for example, obviously uses his daughter as if she were an extension of his own ego, as if she has no needs or feelings that diverge from his. As Jessica Benjamin argues in *The Bonds of Love*, dominance masks those dependency needs that our society's gender stereotypes prevent some men from admitting into their consciousness. Once repressed, such needs may be perverted into an authoritarian character structure, a sadistic personality that cannot acknowledge the autonomy of an "other," whether that other is a wife or a child. Mr. Morris, for example, has not only denied Abby a separate identity as a child, he continues to deny her the right to construct an autonomous identity as an adolescent.

Without such autonomous selfhood, Abby cannot survive, not only as a sexual being, but in all aspects of her being. Indeed, as Jessica Benjamin reminds us, it is a paradox that, as we grow up and strive to acquire independence, someone must recognize that independence.[29] In other words, even to acquire freedom, we need the help of other people. But Abby does not have the help of parents healthy enough to recognize her efforts to develop the independence to survive when she leaves home. As we know, healthy parents encourage adolescents to strive toward autonomy while maintaining a balance between granting too little or too much freedom, as Chip's mother does. By contrast, unhealthy parents such as Mr. and Mrs. Morris are too self-involved, too immature themselves, to nurture Abby's desire for spiritual and psychological growth. Tragically, not only has Abby missed the development that normally occurs in childhood, she is now threatened with the loss of important developments that take place during adolescent years as well. Her fragile and premature adult persona, because it is not integrated with the mute child within, cannot be maintained, particularly at times of transition—such as high school graduation—which place additional stress upon a young person.

At such transition points, the mute child—"New, Used, Abused"—makes its demands known, if not in the form of a breakdown, then in the inevitable perpetuation of the abuse, either in

115

self-destructive behavior such as drug abuse, promiscuity, or self-mutilation, or, in some cases, the abuse of others, especially children. As Alice Miller emphasizes in *Thou Shalt Not Be Aware: Society's Betrayal of the Child*, the only sure antidote to cycles of violence against children—violence that does not remain contained within families, but erupts in society at large—is to tell the truth, to break the silence. In *Abby, My Love*, the silence is finally broken and, just as important, the truth is acknowledged rather than denied. Yet denial remains a possibility, as Alice Miller reminds us, for some adults tend to identify with the more-powerful parents, rather than with the victimized children. Even in Chip's initial response to Abby's revelation, we can see the very human tendency to deny the occurrence of so horrible a crime.

For example, Chip has the habit of using humor when uncomfortable, and when Abby tells him that she dreams of flying, of leaving her bed at night, he quips, "You've read too much Peter Pan," at which Abby jerks away angrily, leaving him to wonder what he has done wrong. "I stood like a stupe and watched her go," he tells us, "I had no idea what I had done" (47). Of course, only after Abby shares her secret and after Chip observes Mr. Morris's jealousy when his daughter dates, does it become apparent to him why Abby would wish to fly away from her body, escaping her bed and her home. At first Chip thinks that Abby and her father look "like a kind of Norman Rockwell cover on one of those old *Saturday Evening Posts*—a portrait of a father and daughter" (35)—and the CBS movie opens with just such a scene: Mr. Morris is seated at his daughter's play table, having tea with the rest of her "children," her dolls and stuffed toys. How ideal, most of us will think as we watch the pair turn toward the house and enter it, Mr. Morris's arm resting gently on his daughter's shoulder. This scene, repeated later in the movie when Abby has entered puberty, becomes ominous once we have learned, along with Chip, the nightmare going on inside the Morris household.

Although Hadley Irwin's decision to employ Chip as narrator initially denies Abby a narrative voice, this technique serves the important purpose of enabling readers to discover the truth from a sympathetic but sometimes confused perspective. Like Chip, we see the father-daughter relationship as "ideal" until we are finally forced to give up this interpretation. Not only do we see Abby's desperate efforts to escape being alone with her father, we also hear his sometimes inappropriate remarks to Chip, remarks such as, "Glad you stopped in. Most of the time it's like a harem around here" (55). A harem? No wonder Abby fears her father may harm her younger sister, a fear that research shows is warranted since incestuous fathers do not stop with one victim.[30] Through Chip's eyes, we also observe the family together, sensing the strained relationships. Visiting the Morris household with his mother, a travel agent arranging the family vacation, Chip reports that

> by themselves Pete and Abby and Mrs. Morris were real, but when I saw them together they were all out of focus–like a blurred photograph. Pete, who was always in action, hardly moved. Abby, who always bubbled with crazy ideas, retreated into that world of her own, and Mrs. Morris didn't just chatter, she babbled as if she were trying to fill up the empty spaces in the room. (73)

The strain in this family is palpable, especially in Abby who "was sitting still as if frozen" (74) as her father arranged for his wife and Pete to leave for Chicago three days earlier than he and Abby would leave. Mr. Morris offers the plausible excuse that he must remain at work while Abby finishes out the semester. As in other instances when Abby seems somehow there but not there, Chip wonders about her puzzling behavior.

It may well be, in fact, that some readers will wonder how Chip manages to be so patient with Abby, but the authors make his patience plausible in a number of ways. First, as a teenager, Chip has just begun to date, and he thinks it possible that all women behave strangely. Second, Abby and Chip create such a delightful play fantasy with the roles of Mildred and Millford that readers will see the pleasure in their relationship. Finally, since the revelation of Abby's secret comes in the tenth chapter of a thirteen-chapter novel, the pacing is just right, building the mystery, but allowing for a plausibly swift resolution of the crisis. As previously stated, not all victims have the good fortune to be heard and helped, as Abby is, but Hadley Irwin demonstrates how such an outcome is possible. In the novel's last three chapters especially, readers will learn how the disclosure of Abby's secret leads to the process of healing during her junior year in high school in time to give the valedictory speech. Beyond the close of the novel, the authors hint, there is also the possibility of a romance between Abby and Chip. While such a conclusion is important in terms of the reassurance it offers young readers, it also provides information important to adults who may teach this novel, perhaps along with the CBS movie, in their middle school English or reading classes.

The authors wisely avoid making a monster of Mr. Morris, which would frighten those young readers who may also be incest victims, and they also do not engage in mother-blaming. Hadley Irwin understand that ambivalence toward one's parents is one of the most difficult and most damaging consequences of incest. For when love and hate are so intermingled, either against the perpetrator or toward the parent who failed to protect the victim, the possibilities that the survivor will develop trusting relationships as an adult are severely limited, particularly without therapeutic help. The authors wisely show young readers that some adults can be trusted. For example, the fact that Chip can trust his mother, who is strong where Mrs. Morris is weak, balances the novel's portrayal of mothers. Chip's mother responds in the best possible way to the revelation of Abby's secret, hugging Abby and reassuring Chip that he has done the right thing to tell her. The fact that Chip also trusts his father-to-be-, Jake, a mature man who, in contrast to the selfish Mr. Morris, is considerate of Abby and Chip's feelings, balances the portrayal of fathers. A judge who understands the legal and social dimensions of the problem, Jake tells Abby and Chip, "It's all right. She needs help. It's something she can't do herself. *It's a secret that must never be kept*" (115). Then he adds, "Once the secret is shared, the healing can begin," one of the most important lines in the novel (116).

The authors are also realistic in their portrayal of the victim's early response to such reassurances from adults. Some weeks after the revelation, she admits to Chip that since telling her mother about the sexual abuse, "Nothing's changed" (123). Finally, Abby tells Chip that she has begun to consider more self-destructive measures, such as, "Making myself sick. Getting fat. Running away..." (author's ellipses 123), even suicide. At this point, Chip drives her directly to Human Services, leaving her at the child protection agency. Her final words to him indicate her ambivalence about reporting her father's crime: "'Is it possible,' she began in a small, shaky voice, 'to love someone and hate him at the same time?'" (123). Following Abby's report of the abuse the CBS movie shows Chip's mother informing Mrs. Morris of the sexual abuse—which Mrs. Morris initially denies—and also shows Mr. Morris being taken away by police in handcuffs. Such a scene might well frighten some incest victims; therefore, I prefer Hadley Irwin's portrayal of Abby's ambivalence about disclosure. Indeed, such ambivalence is warranted for, in some instances, not only does punishment of the perpetrator remove the family's only source of income, it also angers the mother, who blames the daughter for their precarious economic situation. As if to anticipate such fears on the part of their young readers, Hadley Irwin takes care to portray how confidentiality can protect a family, and how economic consequences can be managed, at least by a middle-class family like the Morris's.

Meanwhile, we wait with Chip–who finally dates a little, but without much enthusiasm–for Abby to return to the story. Abby's return, though hinting of romance, leads only to one sweet kiss after the annual Collinsville High Snow Ball. Both Abby and Chip arrive at the dance without dates, and so when Chip asks Abby to dance, she turns him down. This doesn't discourage Chip, who knows that Abby doesn't like to dance and therefore says, "The Phoenix waits without," an old joke between them, to which Abby replies, "Without what?" Chip replies on cue, "Without gas or oil... or us!" (137). It is during this reunion that the Phoenix finally dies. "I think we have a dead bird,"(136) says Chip. Abby also apologizes for making Chip wait so long for her death and rebirth, sensing his anger. Chip acknowledges his anger: "I was angry with Abby, who'd kept me bouncing up and down for almost a year like some foolish ball on a trained seal's nose" (137), but one sure sign of Abby's mental health is her ability to accept his anger without fear or defensiveness. Characteristically, victims of incest do not know how to express emotions of any kind, having been forced into silence about their own needs and desires. But anger creates special difficulties for survivors who, because their anger has such deep roots and goes unexpressed for so long, seems to the victim to threaten annihilation of everything in its path, like a long dormant volcano. Often, for this reason, incest survivors act out their anger in self-destructive ways, such as self-mutilation, drug abuse, or promiscuity. Abby had instead chosen an overly intellectualized adult persona, a mask to control the long-frozen feelings that her affection for Chip threaten to thaw. Yet we see that therapy has helped Abby recognize, as she tells Chip, "that there's nothing wrong with being angry. Not with yourself, I mean, but with someone else" (137).

The mute, angry child within Abby might have sabotaged her chances of becoming valedictorian of her graduating class;

instead, Abby has integrated the public persona, the overly intellectualized adult who, as Chip noted very early, spoke in "whole
sentences, even paragraphs" (7), with the private child who has
been abused. This newly integrated young woman, the Abigail
Morris who speaks at commencement, is capable of telling her
own story, capable of controlling her own narrative. Chip has
obviously acted as Abby's editorial assistant for the valedictory
speech, and as he listens, he thinks, "I had told Abby to delete
that!" (142). Nevertheless, his comment has a happy tone, for Chip
recognizes, as readers do, that Abby has learned to make her own
choices, set her own boundaries, and write her own scripts, making her own deletions and additions. Happily, Abby even manages
to conclude with a surprise for Chip, who thought he had memorized every line of her speech, closing with a quote from "one of
our little-known and unheralded presidents: Millard Fillmore"
(142), which is, in fact, one of Chip's quips, "If you can't chew it,
spit it out" (142). Of course, Abby has "spit it out," as this serious
joke reminds us.

Had she not done so, her story would have been told through
"hysterical" symptoms, that is, through the language of her body, a
body frozen with fear, a body unable to "let go" of anger and pain
of the past and therefore unable to enter the future as a healthy
adult. What Freud's first patient, Anna O., named "the talking
cure"–the process of sharing one's story in order to construct a self
capable of self-authoring–has helped Abby, enabling her to untan-
gle her ambivalence toward her father, ambivalence that would
have interfered, not only with her sexuality, but with many significant facets of her personality. Abby now believes in her own
authority, as is evident from the speech she writes and which she
so ably presents at graduation, as well as in her insistence upon the
right to name in her own way what she has experienced. We learn,
for example, that when her father described his actions as "bad
parenting," as "out of control," or as "loving too much," she has

rejected all such definitions. As she tells Chip, "He was wrong! He did something terribly terribly wrong!" (138). At the same time, she rejects Chip's descriptions of Mr. Morris as "sick" or as "an animal," neither label a help to her. "I can't hate him," she says, "I hate everything he did, but I can't hate *him*" (138), a distinction between the evil act and the one who commits that act which finally frees her from disabling ambivalence.

In the novel, it is Chip who experiences the anger that some readers may feel, both toward Mr. Morris and, because she is so weak, toward Mrs. Morris as well. Teachers need to know, since anger will also surface during classroom discussions, that such anger may discourage incest victims from revealing their secrets to a trusted teacher. For example, if students express anger toward Mr. Morris by demanding harsh punishment, the victim may react with fear, for she both loves and hates the perpetrator.[31] However, if a teacher wisely asks angry respondents to consider how the incest victim may feel if her father is "put in jail for the rest of his life," or even "killed," as some may suggest, classroom discussions may encourage some young women to overcome their shame and tell their painful secrets. In these cases, of course, teachers are required by law to inform authorities, and most will also want to respond to the young victim in humane and helpful ways. Teachers also need to examine their own emotional responses. For example, one teacher might unconsciously identify with the adult and against the child, therefore tending to minimize the damaging consequences of sexual abuse, while another teacher might actually over-identify with the victim and attempt to "help" by angrily attacking the parents, thereby frightening a victim into silence. As Miller explains in *Thou Shalt Not Be Aware*, denial may take a variety of forms.

Therefore, teachers should be forewarned that some parents, particularly in the current political climate, will object to the teaching of any novel which is critical of adults. Some parents may insist that what goes on in families is private and "none of the school's business." For example, in a 1985 *Phyllis Schlafly Report,* under the sensational headline, "Parents Speak Up Against Classroom Abuse," Schlafly quotes letters from angry parents, all of whom object to classroom discussions of such topics as suicide, death, drugs, shoplifting, teen pregnancy, and abortion. "Who are the Typhoid Marys who carry such poison into the classroom?"(1) asks Schlafly, an inflammatory question implying that simply to discuss such problems causes children to act them out. "We recently lost a son to suicide from what he learned at school," says one letter writer; another charges, "My child was required in class to see the movie, 'The Lottery'... about a mother being stoned to death in front of her own child." The assumption by Schlafly and these angry parents is that antisocial behavior is being promoted in public classrooms through discussions and journals that encourage youngsters to disclose personal problems. Schlafly objects strongly to journal writing because children might reveal family secrets. What she implies in her argument is that children should not know about these problems, as if not knowing, or "agnosis," as James Moffett terms it, is the solution. However, as illustrated in chapter 6, the desire to "protect" innocent children from knowledge may, in fact, be an attempt to protect frightened or abusive parents, often at the expense of their children.

CHAPTER 6

My Father/My Censor:
English Education, Politics, and Status

Religious values collaborate with the ideology

of individualism and with sexism

to censor the full capability

of what people can say and write.

–David Bleich

Literacy is the power to make oneself

heard and felt, to signify.

–-Charles Schuster

WHEN JANE TOMPKINS ANNOUNCES her intention to deliberately transgress the public-private hierarchy, a hierarchy she defines as "a founding condition of female oppression" ("Me and My Shadow" 123), I immediately want to join the revolution. I want to believe, as do Tompkins and others, that "the reason I feel embarrassed at my own attempts to speak personally is that I have been conditioned to feel that way. That's all there is to it" (123). I want to echo Jane's defiant, "To hell with it!" (123) and speak assertively, shamelessly, loudly. But for me, although conditioning is certainly a major part of what inhibits me from speaking, there's more to it. At this very moment [in 1992], as I struggle to resist the voice inside (a paternal voice) which tells me to censor personal disclosures that have a profound bearing upon my work in English education, I must confront the powerful emotional inhibitions, the fear and shame, that enforce the conditioning for secrecy. I know that Tompkins is right when she says that "an epistemology which excludes emotions from the process of attaining knowledge radically undercuts women's epistemic authority" (123). As I can testify, my epistemic authority has been enhanced by acknowledging that my analysis of father-daughter incest in *Abby, My Love* was not simply an academic exercise, but an attempt to integrate my private and public selves.

Especially when she fears self-revelation, the writing process can be excruciatingly painful for a survivor of incest. For example, in the summer of 1988 while composing an essay on teenage runaways in Joyce Carol Oates's fiction, I twisted my body into such painful contortions that I had to see a doctor. In the fall of 1988, when I tried to present this paper at the Midwest Modern Language Association, I nearly fainted–to the understandable irritation of the session chair. What I wanted to say then, but couldn't yet say in public, was that I know from personal experience, as well as formal research, that many runaway girls are incest victims. In 1990, after finally making connections between the sexual victimization of adolescent runaway girls and their lack of narrative authority, I submitted a revised (but still confused) version of this same paper on teenage runaways to the editors of a collection called *Anxious Power*. As I wrote this essay, "Anxious Power in the Early Fiction of Joyce Carol Oates," I was obviously anxious about my own epistemic authority, not only that of Oates and her female characters. Fortunately, because of the patience of the editors of *Anxious Power*, I revised the essay to their satisfaction–though not to mine. In the process, I recognized the effects of my emotional autobiography upon my lack of confidence as a writer. Finally, as I write this chapter, I am beginning to map the emotional terrain of my reading and writing, discovering previously hidden connections among my personal, professional, and political selves. This journey into my own "heart of darkness" is frightening, but wonderfully liberating. As I reassemble my various selves into a stronger and more coherent writing persona, I feel as if I am writing–to use Emily Dickinson's wonderful phrase–with my soul at "white heat."

Until now, for example, I never understood that my concern with social and professional status can be attributed to the fact that I am the child of an immigrant: my father came from Norway when he was six years old. Indeed, it worries me to admit my concern with status because, as everyone knows, such self-disclosure can be risky in a status-conscious academic world, a world in which what others know about you can be used against you. In short, it isn't just conditioning—but one's realization about the actualities of power—that makes self-disclosure risky. To be vulnerable is to risk the loss of authority. Any classroom teacher knows, intuitively: *If I look anxious, students won't respect me; I must look confident, no matter how afraid I feel.* Because part of me does not want to give up my status, does not want to risk my authority, I would rather not tell you how my work in English education has roots deep in my nightmarish childhood. But, following the example of Tompkins and others, I'm going to say "to hell with it." After all, I am a newly tenured associate professor of English at Iowa State University, the "second best" university in the state, and I now claim some professional status. And this status, though not apparent in my salary, will soon to be reflected in spatial terms: I have been promised a private office in Ross Hall. For the first time in eighteen years of teaching—seven years at three different high schools, four years as a graduate student teaching associate, and seven years as an assistant professor (five of them at Iowa State)—I will have a room of my own in an English department. I'm enough of a skeptic, however, not to believe in this room until I actually inhabit it.[32]

Furthermore, my status as a professor of English education—not English—remains troubling to me for reasons both professional and personal. It is easy to explain the professional dimension of the problem: any association with secondary English teaching is considered, if considered at all, as a second- or third-class academic assignment. I think everybody knows this; therefore, I hardly need to add that my problem is neither an individual nor a local one. "A chronic lack of status vis-a-vis other disciplines" is a problem for anyone associated with departments of education, according to John Goodlad who directs the Center for Educational

Renewal at the University of Washington ("Goodlad Tests His Vision" 1). Goodlad argues that education acquired "its stepchild position" because, historically, "teaching was a female occupation in a society that 'didn't value the female intellect" (1). Little wonder, then, that women who teach in our public high schools, as Jo Anne Pagano once did, report being "troubled by questions of power and authority" (44). She says, "I suspect that a female intellectual of working-class background is among those most likely to be troubled by such questions. We know how radically one can be changed by one's education" (44). I share Pagano's preoccupation with questions of power and authority, not only because I am a female with a working-class background, as she is, but because, as I have explained, I experienced the violence of "father rule" as a child. I shall return to this personal issue, but I shall begin with the problem of status in the professional realm.

The College of Education at Iowa State certainly suffers from a chronic lack of status; however, I doubt that Goodlad's solution—to give teacher education programs "a position in academe comparable to law schools"(1)–will be implemented here. In fact, a recent survey of department chairs in the College of Liberal Arts and Sciences, shows that, of the 46 percent who responded at all, few regard teacher education as part of their department's mission. Some respondents, according to Assistant Dean J. D. Beatty, suggested that a land grant research university should not be in the business of teacher education. I don't know whether my colleagues in the English department share this view; however, teacher education certainly has a problem with visibility in my department, despite the fact that between one-fourth and one-third of our English majors seek certification in secondary teaching. The invisibility of teacher education became obvious during our recent external review: specialists in creative writing, linguistics, literature, and rhetoric were invited to evaluate the department's performance while English education was ignored. As a consequence, and despite my successful effort to meet with the evaluating team, English education was mentioned in only one sentence of the report. One consequence of this chronic lack of status is that, as both Catharine Stimpson and Henry Louis Gates, have pointed out in *The MLA Newsletter* and in *PMLA*, respectively, changes in literary studies–changes in the canon, in particular–are not reaching the high schools. The empty rhetoric of our "Education President" (George Bush) may not have been the only impediment to effecting such change; the attitudes of some of my colleagues have also impeded educational reform.

But my quick course in English education's lack of status among English professors began long before I acquired a tenure-line position. As I was about to begin my job search, a kindly gentleman scholar counseled me to omit or at least "play down" my experience as a secondary teacher. "It may be important to you," he said, "but hiring committees won't be favorably impressed." However, because jobs were scarce and because I did see some jobs advertised as combination literature and English education positions, I chose to mention–on one unobtrusive line of my vita–my experience teaching high school English. Because I had a supporting program in English education, along with a strong commitment to the teaching of English in our public schools, I hoped to work in both areas. While teaching at a liberal arts college, where I held a one-year-only position, I received a second lesson in English education's lack of status. Invited to participate in the Teacher Education Committee, I heard, to my astonishment, angry resistance from a first-year, tenure-line faculty member who had been placed on the committee, obviously against her wishes. Yes, she acknowledged, she had been a high school teacher, but she had become a college teacher in order to "escape all that." What she meant to escape, I understood immediately, was all that work, all that low status, all that sexism. I sympathized with this woman's anger and with her resistance to serving in the "pink ghetto" of English education; at the same time, I found it painful to experience what felt like rejection from an academic woman who wanted to bury her past—a past which I also wished to escape—rather than integrate it into the present.

As I have said, this professional problem of mine—the low status of English education in a university English department—has roots that reach deeply into the early years of my personal history. It isn't easy to dig up these personal roots, exposing them to readers who may prefer not to know the state of my soul. Yet I want to write about this tangle of professional and personal roots, partly in the hope that it will help me to resolve my ongoing internal debate about status. A public admission of the self-doubt disease may not necessarily lead to a cure, but I believe that this kind of writing may be therapeutic, not only for me but for some readers. For many years, long before I dared think of myself as a writer, I thought of myself as a reader and, in retrospect, I recognize that reading has also been a form of therapy for me. Indeed, my commitment to reading and writing—to English education—probably started in grade school. I enjoyed reading, and I was recognized as a good reader. I remember, for example, that when my sixth-grade teacher posted the number of books each of us had read, I was often at the head of the class. Even then, I liked the status. But in retrospect, I see that I also liked the safety of reading, the escape it provided from the painful realities of my childhood. Reading was a space where I could try to understand myself and my chaotic family, an imaginary place where I had the power to survive bad things, perhaps even imagine changing them. As a child, I certainly didn't have the power to change the terrible things that were happening to my sister.

Many years later, as I began to write about literature, I did not recognize how reading and writing about literature had enabled me to make sense of my personal past. In fact, through analyzing fictional characters, I distanced myself from the autobiographical while, at the same time, I found a "cover" for self-analysis. Even now, when personal criticism has become more acceptable, I struggle to overcome my resistance to self-disclosure. If I propose writing an autobiographical essay, my immediate impulse is to withdraw the proposal, to write something else. For incest survivors, the writing process is characterized by excessive self-criticism, almost to the point of self-erasure, as Madelon Sprengnether has noted. The inner debate is always: to tell or not to tell, to write or to erase. For example, as I write this chapter, I say to myself, it's easier for Jane Tompkins or Nancy Miller to write personally than it is for me; after all, they don't have such a shameful secret to confess. That's the voice of the child-victim inside, the voice that cries, "poor me." I have to resist that voice, even as I embrace her. All right, let's admit that it may be more difficult for survivors of sexual abuse to put into practice the slogan, "The Personal Is Political," but that's no excuse for not trying. For many years, I associated this feminist slogan exclusively with my discontent as an intellectually frustrated, unpaid middle-class housewife; the slogan did not authorize me to speak of the pain and outrage of father-daughter incest. Indeed, if I wrote about incest, I doubted I would ever be admitted into the academy, let alone become a tenured professor. Nevertheless, I was encouraged to write academic essays in the personal voice in graduate school, primarily by feminist scholars at the University of Minnesota–Shirley Nelson Garner, Toni McNaron, and Madelon Sprengnether.

Consequently, as I wrote my dissertation, I gradually acquired the courage to focus more explicitly on the problem of fathers and daughters. However, this closeness to the autobiographical forced me to invent an imaginary chapter where I could dump "digressive" and deeply disturbing personal material. This survival strategy was fairly effective at the time. If I had stopped for therapy then, I would not have completed my Ph.D., and without the degree I would not have had any chance for employment. I had no other source of financial support because of my divorce; hence, I couldn't afford the luxury of self-disclosure at the time. At present, having a reliable source of income and having finally published an autobiographical essay called "My Friend, Joyce Carol Oates," I can come out of the closet without so great a risk to my well being. Perhaps even more important, I have begun to experience the exhilaration of genuine creativity, the almost visceral discovery of connections, of mental maps, among once fragmented pieces of knowledge.

At the same time, I would prefer to write in the personal voice without having to use the word *incest*–a word that still bothers many people. For example, not long ago when, at a dinner party, I told a woman–who had asked about my current research–that I was writing about incest narratives, she turned away in embarrassment. Since the word *incest* no longer embarrasses me, and since the topic is so much in the news, I had not expected it to embarrass her. Yet the reluctance to talk about incest remains powerful even in the 1990s. I have noticed, for example, that some reviews of Jane Smiley's Pulitzer Prize winning novel *A Thousand Acres* avoided comment on its tragic plot, father-daughter incest, even when these same reviews emphasized Smiley's allusions to Shakespeare's *King Lear*. People who buy the novel expecting another vision of Iowa as a "Field of Dreams" will certainly be surprised. Attempts to censor Smiley's novel have already appeared in newspaper reports–for example, in 1994, the headline, "Levy Fails though School Bans Jane Smiley's Book," appeared in a Lynden, Washington, paper. "Conservative Christian activitists complained about the explicit language and portrayal of incest and adultery in a struggling Iowa farm family" (quoted in *The Iowa State Daily* 1).

But I am not innocent of such polite silences myself. Hadn't I, for example, comforted myself for years with the knowledge that my father had, in fact, not actually sexually abused me, only my three sisters? This refusal to think of the stories of my sisters as part of my own story had made it easier for me to continue my denial. But this self-censorship was, I believe, a form of betrayal since it left my sisters to bear the shame. Indeed, one tragic consequence of society's taboo of speaking about incest is that it leaves children to bear the guilt for crimes committed by fathers (and in rare instances, mothers) against them. By finally recognizing myself as a victim too–in the sense that my reality was denied–I began to claim strength as a survivor. Yet I had to defend this position recently when a feminist psychoanalytic critic argued that women who criticize Freud for suppressing the truth of the actuality of father-daughter incest are, in her words, "speaking from the place of the victim." I countered that I claim authority by writing from the place of a survivor, not a victim, a survivor critical of Freud's belief that "hysterics lie"–that is, that daughters fantasize their abuse by the father. She disagreed, arguing that feminists can't "have it both ways," can't both criticize Freud and, at the same time, use his theories. But why not? Why do we have to accept the whole Freudian package? My hunch is that this woman fears identifying with "victims," preferring to identify with the more powerful father figure.

The views of this woman worry me. For if everyone shared her beliefs, I would lose the sympathetic audience I must imagine in order to write at all. I know, for example, that without a close friend who for many years acted as a sympathetic reader of my many anguished letters, I would never have dared to go on to graduate school. When I told this friend my story, my secret, she did not reject me; her belief in my story gave me hope. While in graduate school, I often began academic papers by writing letters to her, imagining a trusted reader in order to start writing for less sympathetic professors. It is apparent to me, based on my own difficulties in imagining a sympathetic reader, that my father's betrayal has for many years handicapped my ability to write and speak with confidence. In fact, when unable to write, I have kept my habit of introspection alive solely through the act of reading, through imaginative association of literary characters with my family and myself. I remember the great relief I felt when I read *Crime and Punishment* during the summer after tenth grade: if Dostoevsky's killer could find forgiveness and even love, maybe my father could too. Although I didn't understand it at the time, it is also likely that my own imaginative identification with the hero's violent acts gave me a safe outlet for my own unarticulated rage. I could imagine myself acting as violently as Raskolinkov without becoming a tragic figure myself. I could also identify with Raskolnikov's victims without, at the same time, becoming a victim myself.

In other words, the habit of reading allowed me to look within and thereby resist censoring the "truth" of my personal experience. My formal education did, however, place constraints upon such self-investigation because, as Judith Fetterley points out in *The Resisting Reader*, women of my generation were trained to read as men. It did not occur to me that my academic training had forced me to deny my discomfort about the portrayal of women in classical literature. Why, I wondered without daring to ask, did the story of Lot place the responsibility for incest on his daughters? And why, despite the king's own capacity for violence, did Shakespeare encourage us to sympathize more with King Lear than with his daughters? Literature is one way that our culture has conditioned women not only to sympathize with destructive men, but to find them attractive. This conditioning of my sympathies made it possible for me to hold my mother accountable for my father's crimes without taking into consideration her oppression—the oppression of all mothers—in a male-dominated culture. I did not begin to ask such questions about the politics of gender or to read with an awareness of gender politics, until I entered graduate school. Still,

I value all those early years of reading as a "man" because at least I learned the habit of introspection, the habit of looking for and analyzing my own shadow. Jean Kennard has given a name—"polar reading"—to this kind of imaginative experience.

This habit of seeking self-knowledge through reading saved me, I am certain, from the practice of denial or repression. By contrast, it was my father's habit of denial that enabled him to abuse my sisters for many years. The same habit also made him ripe for membership in the John Birch Society, a political organization which he joined in the late 1950s and which sanctioned his psychological need to project his own "shadow" onto the Communists. Now, as an English educator, I oppose censorship: I stand with people like James Moffett, with members of the National Council of Teachers of English who support "The Right to Read," and with feminists who urge women to "break the silence." I stand against censors like Phyllis Schlafly, the John Birch Society, and my father. In my research on censorship, a topic I address in English methods classes, I have discovered a powerful relationship between my father and me, between "me and my shadow." He tried not to see his shadow, while I have seen my shadow, and his. My father, who should have gone to college, instead became a director of the John Birch Society, a patriot who resisted "Communism" in his public speeches. I achieved my father's dream of graduating from college, but I resist the rule of the father by writing as a feminist. When, in the register at my father's funeral in 1976, I wrote, "I am my father's daughter," it was the first time I declared myself in public, claiming both my father's authority and his secret—and its shadow—as my own.

It took me many more years to reject what Ursula Le Guin calls the "father tongue" (quoted in Tompkins 127) in order to begin mapping the powerful personal/political connections between English education, the John Birch Society, my father, and me. The revelation of this nexus of relationships enables me to feel

more at home in the world of knowledge, and it helps me to recognize that the status of English education is not simply my individual problem but an issue for all of us who care about good
public schools. When critics complain, as David Simpson does,
that "the move to autobiography is almost never accompanied by
any real analysis of what an individual's position in a culture or
society is" (Heller A8), I answer that by writing in the personal, I
finally understand my own academic politics: I understand that
my father's right-wing politics—a politics which asserts the authority of father rule—frightened me into silence about my experience
as his daughter for many years. This fear also dictated my decision
to pursue a low-status "female" occupation, delaying my entry into
higher education, and plaguing me with self-doubt during my job
search. During these same years, the feminist movement helped to
shape me into the kind of academic I am today: a resistance
fighter. Although my resistance to the political right began in my
father's house, in silent rebellion against his definition of his
daughters as his property, this resistance could not have developed
without the women's movement, specifically its collective claim to
public power. My mother could not claim such power; her life was
exclusively "personal" and domestic. Raised to believe in the rule
of the father, she was silently angry for years about the little
respect she earned by cleaning my father's house and caring for
his children—cooking and sewing and gardening for all of us, her
husband and seven children.

She went to bed exhausted, apparently too tired to hear my
father visiting my sisters in their bedrooms. One night, however, I
remember hearing my mother call my father's name even as my
sister, lying next to me, struggled against his sexual advances. My
mother's voice did not have the power to stop my father; he called
back that he was reading, and she made no further protest. Why, I
wonder to this day, wasn't reading enough for my father? Why
couldn't he have devoured his books instead of his daughters? The

answer, or at least part of the answer, is that my father's reading of right-wing literature allowed him to rationalize "father rule" and to project his own shadow onto the "Communists." By defining Communism as "the enemy within"—a phrase often used by John Birchers—my father could avoid looking at the enemy within himself. It must have been a great relief to him to read Robert Welch's words, "For *our* enemy is the Communists, and we do not intend to lose sight of that fact for a minute. We are fighting the Communists—nobody else" (Forward to the Fourth Edition ii). For years my father's "enemy within," his own shadow, escaped detection as he searched for betrayers of our "republic" everywhere. Along with other John Birchers, he was instructed by *The Blue Book of the John Birch Society* to look in the Supreme Court and "Impeach Earl Warren," to "Investigate Communist Influences at Vassar," and to document grievances of "Women Against Labor Union Hoodlumism" (Welch 91). While my father projected his own shadow onto the Communists, my sisters saw it looming beside their beds at unpredictable times in the night. When one of my sisters told me that, in an attempt to keep him out of her bed, she wrapped herself tightly in her sheets, I pictured a death shroud. A child cultivates the habit of self-reliance very early in her life if she believes that no one will respond to her cries for help.

As a child, I couldn't find a place—a safe place—in my own home. In 1991, as a consequence of my marginal status in an English department, I often felt homeless, as I did as a child. I did not belong in an Education Department, nor did I wish to go there, but I couldn't seem to find a place in my own department. This sense of homelessness was heightened by the fact that I visited student teachers in area secondary schools during one full semester of each year. The fact that I had once been a high school teacher myself added to this sense of isolation: whereas I had once been treated as a colleague by secondary English teachers, I was now regarded with suspicion, as someone who saw herself on a higher plane, as someone from "higher" education. Having felt isolated and marginal all my life—another characteristic of survivors—I was uncomfortable working at the hierarchical borders between these educational institutions. I wanted to transform these borders, creating more egalitarian and personal relationships with my colleagues in secondary English classrooms, but institutions offer little support for this kind of labor. Whether the work is inter-disciplinary or inter-institutional, such border crossings seems to confound the system. Fortunately, my position was redefined in 1994—I would no longer teach undergraduate methods courses nor supervise student teachers—thereby resolving one of the great frustrations of my professional life.[33]

However benign its intentions, for years my department had insisted on defining me in way that fit its narrowly specialized concepts of scholarship and teaching. Expected to limit myself to fulfill "programmatic need" in English education, I experienced a recurrence of my old shrinking man nightmare, a nightmare that woke me repeatedly during the month's prior to my graduation from college. In this nightmare, I struggle to keep the man beside me from shrinking. When a crowd jeers at me, I run to the library for protection, but the man running beside me, my twin, shrinks until he is small enough to be carried in my hands. It is a dream, I believe, about the necessity of shrinking as I try to fit people's expectations of me, a dream about trying to escape a feminine role that makes me a second-class citizen by forcing me to project all my "masculine" traits onto a man. It hasn't helped that I am a small woman, described over the years as "petite" and "cute," words that also meant "trivial." But I fight against trivialization, refusing to shrink. For example, at a Theory/Pedagogy Conference at Indiana University of Pennsylvania in the spring of 1991, I opened my talk about "Teaching Alice Walker's *Meridian*," by calling attention to the fact that "theory" was clearly the privileged term at the conference, but I wanted to reverse the hierarchy, beginning my talk with emphasis upon pedagogy, upon actual classroom experience. Calling attention to my subtitle, "Civil Rights According to Mothers," I explained that after teaching Walker's novel in three different college classrooms, I discovered that the theme of motherhood was invisible to young male readers, whereas it was a central theme for most women. Based upon student responses to Walker's novel, which I cited in my paper, I argued against a phallocentric and racist canon and against exclusively "masculine" reading practices, and for inclusion of women's writing as well as attention to a perspective often silenced in our culture: the maternal. "How did you dare to say that?" a woman asked me afterward.

"What is your location?" I asked immediately. She was still in graduate school, she said. My location as a tenure-line professor in a department where feminists are numerically strong, I explained, means that I can risk making arguments for the inclusion of writing by African American women. In time, she could do the same. This is the kind of exchange that keeps the "shrinking man" nightmare at bay, the kind of moment that suggests how my work might make a difference. At such times, I reminded myself that my work in English education—between English and Education Departments, between universities and high schools, between literature and rhetoric—was a location as rich in possibilities as it was in contradictions. The experience of mentoring future secondary English teachers, for example, had been most satisfying, and I remain enthusiastic about teaching a graduate course called "Teaching Literature and the Literature Curriculum." This course is a potential site of cultural transformation, a place to enact my commitment to improving education, and to encourage activism in students who plan to become teachers themselves. In this course, I make assignments that require graduate students to examine the institutions, curricula, and canons where they hope to teach, whether at the high school, community college, or university. Students read works such as Paul Lauter's *Canons and Contexts,* as well as selected essays from Elizabeth Flynn and Patrocinio Schweickart's *Gender and Reading.* They examine how identity themes of gender and race, along with class, shape their reading responses, and they study white male identity themes in traditional canonical works, such as *The Scarlet Letter,* in contrast to themes in *Uncle Tom's Cabin* by Harriet Beecher Stowe and *Our Nig* by Harriet E. Wilson.[34]

The syllabus states the objectives of English 521 as follows: The purpose of this course is to examine the relationship between a literature curriculum, its goals and/or canons, in a variety of teaching contexts. The question of what literary works should be included in our "canon" remains highly controversial, as does the question of what a "canon" should do. Is a canon simply a means of transmitting a "white" cultural heritage, for example, or is it a body of works that enables us to critique and redefine our culture? "Whose Canon Is It Anyway?" African American critics are asking, as are feminists, both of whom want representation in what has historically been a "white male" canon. In English 521, students explore the debate over our literary canon, particularly in terms of its implications for curricula and classroom practice in a variety of different contexts: in secondary schools, in community colleges, and in higher education. We ask, for example: Do canons drive the curricula in these various contexts? Should we even have a canon? And, if so, should it reflect cultural diversity? Do classroom teachers have great freedom to teach whatever texts they wish? What part do anthologies play in curriculum decisions? What part does the community play? When does censorship become a problem? Do we, in fact, need to have a shared cultural heritage, and should teachers of literature understand the transmission of this heritage—or a critique of the canon—as their primary goal in teaching? How do these considerations affect students at different grade levels?

I take pleasure in teaching this course because it allows me to affirm the value of cultural diversity and to demonstrate connections between politics and the teaching of English. Gerald Graff may think that the battle to transform the canon has been won, but this is certainly not the case in Iowa's secondary English classrooms, especially those located in buildings where, throughout the 1980s, pictures of Ronald Reagan were often placed conspicuously in the lobby outside the principal's office. Censorship, though it goes by the name of "excellence," is also evident in Secretary William Bennett's ideal reading list, first published in 1988, a list of American "classics" for grades nine through twelve that recommends writing by only one white woman, Emily Dickinson, and only one black man, Ralph Ellison. Thus, the question that Henry Louis Gates, Jr. asked in 1989, "Whose Canon Is It, Anyway?" remains controversial for many secondary English teachers in the 1990s. As one student teacher told me, books by African Americans, ordered in the late sixties and early seventies, now often gather dust in storage rooms while English teachers go "back to the basics" of traditional grammar. In effect, spending hours on prescriptive grammar teaches submissiveness to higher authority and, at the same time, functions as an effective form of censorship. Teaching English 521 allows me to talk about how censorship efforts increased in the 1980s as secondary English teachers tried to diversify the canon, and about how to join with other faculty and their professional organizations in order to develop strategies for collective resistance.

In English 521, I have also presented a lecture on censorship that identifies what James Moffett calls "agnosis"–the desire not to know–as the chief characteristic of the censoring mind. According to the editors of *The Right to Literacy*, "what James Moffett calls 'agnosis': not wanting to know, the fear of knowing," may be the greatest threat to literacy, greater even than the threat of government, schools, or poverty (5). In *Storm in the Mountains* Moffett analyzes community censorship that erupted into violence in Kanawha County West Virginia in 1974 when the state attempted to adopt Moffett's coedited series of language arts textbooks, *Interactions,* which had been published by Houghton Mifflin. Moffett explains, "The Kanawha County case prefigured an increasing American trend toward a sort of de facto theocracy, an evangelical governance of the nation that, under the guise of defending freedom against Communism, feels justified in moving toward a police state at home while intervening militarily in countries abroad" (191). The drama had all the ingredients Margaret Atwood uses to such good effect in *The Handmaid's Tale.* The key players in the case were Alice Moore, the wife of a fundamentalist preacher in a mining community called St. Albans in Appalachia; the John Birch Society, along with Mel and Norma Gabler of Texas; the Magic Valley Mothers Club; the Christian-American Parents; Concerned Citizens and the Reverend Marvin Horan who led a boycott of the school and who was later imprisoned for setting off a bomb in an elementary school. Two shootings took place after mine workers joined the protest. As one high school student said, "They're shooting people because they don't want people to see violence in books" (quoted in Moffett 19).

In her objections to *Interaction,* Mrs. Moore, the wife of the fundamentalist minister, followed guidelines spelled out by the Gablers:

> Textbooks must not intrude into the privacy of students' homes by asking personal questions about interfeelings [sic] or behavior of themselves or parents...must recognize the sanctity of the home and emphasize its importance as the basic unit of American society... must not contain offensive language...must teach the true history and heritage of the United States...shall teach that traditional rules of grammar are a worthwhile

subject for academic pursuit and are essential for effective communication...shall encourage loyalty to the
United States...and emphasize the responsibilities of
citizenship and the obligation to redress grievances
though legal processes...must not encourage sedition
or revolution against our government or teach or imply
that an alien form of government is superior. (Quoted
in Moffett 23)

These guidelines must have comforted my father. If textbooks
could not "intrude upon the privacy of the student's homes," then
his nocturnal crimes would remain hidden from the scrutiny of
public authorities. The same argument for student privacy is evident in an article called "Parents Speak Up Against Classroom
Abuse" when Phyllis Schlafly identifies journal writing as invasion
of privacy of the home. At the end of a long list of parental com-
plaints against the discussion of suicide, drugs, abortion, and teen
pregnancy, Schlafly asks, "Who are these Typhoid Marys who
carry such poison into the classroom?" (1), creating antagonism
toward teachers who center their classrooms around student needs
and interests. The implication is that teachers who promote knowledge of such activities stimulate students to try them. "Agnosis,"
not-knowing, is what Schlafly counsels.

In 1976, two years after the eruption of violence in Kanawha
County and four before the election of Ronald Reagan, my father
died at the age of fifty-six. His own shadow, which for many years
he misidentified as the "Communists," finally killed him. Since he
had worked feverishly to elect Barry Goldwater, I think he would
have been happy to know that Ronald Reagan was elected in
1980, but I'm not absolutely certain. Before his death, he may
have begun to look within at last: in the hospital, as he lay dying
and talking aloud in his dreams, he said, "There's more than one
version of the Heidi story." Perhaps, had he told his version of the

Heidi story–about how his love for his daughters became a way of hiding his shadow–he might finally have recognized the enemy within. Perhaps he would also have recognized Ronald Reagan as the official embodiment of our society's collective denial of its tragic divisions of class, gender, and race. Denial, or agnosis, Moffett explains, is "a self-limitation of the natural human faculties of understanding" arising out of a "resistance to descending into the self to understand others through understanding the self," a resistance to introspection that leads to the "need to keep attention focused on things outside" (182–84). This description certainly fits my father, but in some ways it fits me too, though I hope not as much now as in the past. Moffett wisely acknowledges that "Everyone resists *some* knowledge. Some things we don't *want* to know" (184). Because Moffett acknowledges his human limitations, he gives me the courage to do likewise.

As I read *Storm in the Mountains,* I often wrote comments in the margins as I recognized the psycho-social connections between my father's habit of "agnosis," his sexual violence, and his right-wing politics. For example, when Moffett refers to Erich Fromm's *Escape from Freedom,* I recalled that Fromm had given me insight into my father's behavior and that I had loaned my father a copy, hoping he would see Fromm's point that just as Nazism answered a longing of the German lower middle classes "to escape from the self-responsibility of freedom into authoritarian submission" (Moffett 194), the John Birch Society answered his need to escape from his overwhelming responsibilities as the head of a large family. But when I asked my father to discuss *Escape from Freedom* with me, he told me he had "lost" the book. What a loss. My father had always seemed more of a boy than a man, terribly insecure behind his authoritarian views. I kept thinking of my father as I read other psychological studies, all written after World War II, that Moffett had consulted in order to understand the authoritarian, censoring mind. At one point, citing a psychological survey by Goldstein and Blackman, Moffett establishes a link between the authoritarian personality and the desire for status: "the authoritarian individual is proper and concerned with status and success, a problem stemming from his parents' insecurities with status" (194). As the eldest child of a Norwegian immigrant family, my father inherited insecurities about status from his mother. In a letter from my grandmother, written shortly before her death, this anxiety is evident: *"After one winter in school the Teatcher said J. was ihead of his class," she wrote, "If it was somting he did not understand he came right up to her and asked she said."*

Wanting to preserve only her proud memory of my father's status in the classroom, she denied what he had done to his daughters. In her one cruelty toward me, she refused to listen to me read an autobiographical essay I had published about my Norwegian ancestry. In this essay, called "Of Bread and Shadows, Beginnings," I did not reveal my father's crime, but my grandmother refused to hear the ending, where I wrote, "My father's story—which is also mine—is not a circle that closes neatly. It still casts a shadow." I couldn't bear the idea of a closed circle, the image of generations repeating the lives of their parents. I preferred to think instead of a spiral: in a spiral movement, I return to the shadow to confront and move beyond it. Yet it seems that I have inherited, along with many Americans, this preoccupation with status. What an irony: immigrants come to the United States to escape oppressive hierarchies only to erect them once again. We can move away from home, but apparently we cannot leave behind the effects of child-rearing practices that create censoring minds, minds like those of my father's. As Moffett explains, those adults who score high in dogmatism and who have a tendency toward censorship have often been raised in homes where expressions of ambivalence toward parents were not tolerated. I am not certain that my paternal grandmother was "dogmatic," but she was a self-sacrificing Christian mother whose stifled anger was displaced onto "outsiders." I was once shocked to hear my kindly grandmother make an antisemitic remark, but there's a logic in her displaced hatred: since she could not express ambivalent feelings within her home, she had to find a public outlet for them.

Citing the work of Rokeach, Moffett explains that this censorship of ambivalence in childhood leads, as in the case of my father, "to a narrowing of possibilities for identification with persons outside the family [and] to the development of closed belief systems" (196). Certainly my father was handicapped in his ability to identify with people outside his family; his incestuous acts are symptomatic of this crippled consciousness. According to Rokeach, those children who develop a closed system of belief compensate "by a self-aggrandizing and self-righteous identification with a cause," (quoted in Moffett 197), a statement that gives me insight into my father's fanatical devotion to the John Birch Society, one of the organizations which helped to fuel the violence in Kanawha County, West Virginia. But why, finally, is this analysis of my father relevant to my work in the academy? The answer is plain, though not simple: my understanding of my father teaches me that intelligence severed from emotions cripples human beings. Forced to deny their handicaps, these emotional cripples perpetuate victimization through their unexamined child-rearing practices, practices in the private domain which shape emotions that, in turn, are placed outside the bounds of scrutiny in university classrooms.

This understanding of my father/my censor brings me to a resolution: no matter how great the risk, and it is considerable, I can no longer teach as if my students and I are all talking heads. I make every effort to bring together in my classroom and in my writing what has previously been sundered into private/public aspects of my personality. As Tompkins says, "An epistemology which excludes emotions from the process of attaining knowledge radically undercut[s] women's epistemic authority" (123), and, as I know from personal experience, such an epistemology creates households like the one I grew up inside, households in which mothers and daughters stifle their fury, households in which fathers act out their repressed—and therefore distorted—emotions.

To underscore my point about the need to transgress the conventions of academic writing and the unwritten rules of the classroom which sever public and private, as well as minds and emotions, I shall return to Moffett's study of censorship, particularly to his analysis of a censor's comments about the "The Lottery" by Shirley Jackson and "The Stone Boy" by Gina Berriault. I want to demonstrate that Moffett himself does not see the gender politics being played out in these stories, nor in the censors' comments about them, despite their relevance to the problem of censorship. Moffett says that censors claim to object to the teaching of "The Lottery" because it is "an absurd story about a town which offers a human sacrifice by way of a lottery" (174). Moffett's response is gender blind. He says, "I would speculate that book censors...find this story appalling because it points to the possible price of groupiness—the sacrifice of the individual—and suggests that close community—the very lifeblood of our objectors—thrives on traditions that retain rude exactions as well as support and security" (174). He fails to note that it is a woman, specifically a mother, who is the human sacrifice in this story. This fact does not escape the notice of a censoring parent quoted in Phyllis Schlafly's newsletter who says, "My child was required in class to see the movie called 'The Lottery.' This is a bloody and upsetting film about a mother being stoned to death in front of her own child" (1). Father-dominated societies have long been predicated upon maternal sacrifice, but those who repress the (m)other cannot bring this shadowy knowledge to consciousness.

Another example of Moffett's gender blindness occurs in his analysis of a censor's remarks on "The Stone Boy," a story that Moffett calls "a parable of not wanting to know" (183). Moffett notes that from the objector's phrase, "'The story is abnormal,' one

149

might get the completely false impression that the story deals with incestuous feelings" (181). When the boy, whose emotions are "petrified" after accidentally killing his brother, goes to his mother's bedroom during the night, the repetition of the word *terror*, Moffett says, "would make it pretty hard for even the most prurient reader to sexualize the passage" (181). Moffett notes the objector's use of inappropriate sexual innuendoes, but he does not identify the gender of the censor. Moffett may have been unable to determine this censor's gender, but he does not appear to be troubled by this lack of knowledge. In accord with conventions of academic writing, Moffett consistently refers to censors in gender-neutral terms. Although astute in recognizing the hidden racism behind the written rationales provided by censors, Moffett fails to highlight the gender politics being enacted in his own discourse. Nor does he see a relationship between a censor's objections to portraying maternal sacrifice in "The Lottery," and a censor's inappropriate sexualizing of the boy's feelings toward his mother in "The Stone Boy." Yet these acts of censorship are related: because our society represses the (m)other—an act of self-censorship more severe in men than in women—the repressed feelings toward the mother become vulnerable to distortion. It is the male's greater need to deny ordinary human dependency that leads to this repression and hatred of the maternal. Once repressed, healthy love for the mother becomes distorted by sexual (incestuous) desires. At bottom, I believe, this denial that we are "of woman born" leads to the desire for domination.

As Jessica Benjamin says in *The Bonds of Love*, "Domination begins with the attempt to deny dependency" (52). Fear of dependency is understandably more severely repressed in most males than in most females, but it must be confronted by all of us if we are to become a healthier society, a society capable of integrating its dark continent—the maternal body, and the knowledge of mortality—rather than projecting it upon an outside "enemy." Moffett notes "the almost obsessive apprehension about being classed with or reduced to beasts" (153) in the objections of censors, but he links this apprehension only to racism, making no mention of its link to sexism. "Reversion to animality runs as a motif throughout typical fundamentalist thinking and connects inherently with racism, since a racist's hierarchy of lower to higher strains of human beings usually anchors lower end in the animal world," says Moffett (155). He recognizes that "racism is a displacement onto others of bestiality suspected in oneself," and he sees displacement as the strategy of "people of low self-esteem" who are threatened by kinship with animals (156). Our kinship with animals is most apparent at moments of birth and death, but the desire to deny this reality permeates Western thought—religious, philosophical, and scientific. In another chapter, however, Moffett does acknowledge that "the moral and commercial right" oppose the Equal Rights Amendment, probably because they perceive equality for women "as a menace both to survival of the family and to male sexual identity in particular" (215).

The "pro-family" movement emerged out of this coalition which made "frenetic efforts to shore up the father image" (Moffett 216). Along with other right wingers, my father believed that "fighting enemies outside is strength; finding weaknesses inside is itself weakness" (Moffett 221). Supported by the profamily movement's efforts to shore up patriarchal authority, my father would undoubtedly have tried to prevent the teaching of father-daughter incest narratives which expose abusive fathers. In one of our last conversations, at a time I had separated from my husband and was planning a divorce, my father tried to counsel me back into my bad marriage. "Don't play father to me," I said, finally voicing my opposition to his hypocrisy. He looked stricken, and his eyes begged me to rescue him. I refused. Because he had failed to look within—because of his affliction with "agnosis"—he forced my sisters to bear the burden of his crimes. His model of authoring gave him the only voice in our family, just as the traditional literature canon has spoken only in the father's voice. Hence, rather than valorizing a literary canon which promotes a violent masculinity at the expense of women, children, and the poor of all races, we should promote narratives that, as Tompkins argues, perform the important "cultural work" (*Sensational Designs*) of inspiring readers to transform an unjust society.

The question is, What kind of cultural work can be accomplished through the teaching of father-daughter incest narratives? Chapter 5 gives a partial answer to this question by focusing on the middle school classroom; chapter 7 takes up the question of which narratives to teach—and how to teach them—in the college literature classroom. In this dialogue with a student, who is also a survivor of childhood sexual abuse, I also illustrate a major thesis of *Authoring a Life:* that authoring is always a collobrative act. Not only through speaking, but also by listening attentively, an English teacher may nurture a speaker's capacity for self-authoring. I propose a model of authorship in which the older generation—of which I am now a part—shifts its attention away from self-authoring (a task which, one hopes, requires less attention as we mature) in order to focus on the task of other-authoring: nurturing and mentoring the young. In contrast to the psychoanalytic model of authorship, a model in which the son violently wrests authority from the father while the daughter remains the father's property, subject to his transgressive desire, this model emphasizes the gradual transfer of authority to the young. This work of mothering or mentoring, as the authors of *Women's Ways of Knowing* emphasize, has the power to transform our ways of knowing, as well as our ways of teaching. Such cultural work should be at the heart of the literature curriculum from grade school through graduate school.

CHAPTER 7

The Scarlet Letter I: Incest Narratives in the College Literature Classroom
(with Laura Armstrong Randolph)

Personal consciousness, individual oppressions,

lived experience—in short, identity politics—

operate in the classroom both to authorize

and to de-authorize speech.

—Diana Fuss

Once teachers begin to view their students

also as possessors of authority,

the process of knowledge contruction changes.

—Frances A. Maher and Mary Kay T. Tetreault

SECRECY IS A DEFINING FEATURE of father-daughter incest, according to Judith Lewis Herman, and this secrecy has, until recently, been maintained by our canon and in our classrooms. Because the traditional canon replicates the dynamics of the patriarchal family, it has forced daughters, whether as writers or readers, to bear the burden of this secret. Such enforced silence is as harmful as the incestuus act itself, for it shatters a woman's perception of reality, placing her under a "cognitive cloud" that makes her unsure if she knows what she knows (Belenky et al. 60). She wonders, "If no one talks about it, did it really take place?" This cognitive confusion interferes with a woman's ability to think and learn, to read and write. Only when a daughter tells her story—a critical step in the recovery process, according to Herman's *Trauma and Recovery*—is she able to reconstruct a meaningful life. Yet, as Christine Froula points out, in some ways, the situation of literary daughters mirrors the relationship of daughters in the incestuous family, as described by Judith Herman and Lisa Hirschman. For example, Froula explains, because the daughter is "prohibited by her father from speaking about the abuse, [she] is unable to sort out her contradictory feelings of love for her father and terror of him, of desire to end the abuse and fear that if she speaks she will destroy the family structure that is her only security" (112). With the advent of the women's movement in the late 1960s, a great change took place:

daughters began telling their traumatic stories at speakouts, as well as in memoirs, autobiographies, poetry, and fiction.

Those who wish to teach father-daughter incest narratives, now have a great range of options: early examples include Maya Angelou's autobiography, *I Know Why the Caged Bird Sings* (1969), and novels such as Joyce Carol Oates's *them* (1969) and Toni Morrison's *The Bluest Eye* (1970).[35] It was in the early 1970s that feminists began to challenge the Freudian theory that hysteric patients had only fantasized paternal sexual abuse. In 1971, at a conference on rape sponsored by the New York Radical Feminists, Florence Rush presented one of the first theoretical papers to argue that incested children, usually girls, were not to blame, and that sexual abuse, most often committed by fathers, should be understood as part of a "pervasive pattern with antecedents of social acceptance that reach far back into history" (Brownmiller, Intro. to Rush ix). In the 1980s, numerous studies—Rush (1980), Herman (1981), Miller (1984)—criticized Freud's theories and confirmed the pervasive pattern of father-daughter incest. According to Herman, the estimates of women who survive some form of sexual abuse in childhood and/or adolescence ranges from one in three to one in five (*Father-Daughter Incest* 12). As these researchers recognize, father-daughter incest itself is not taboo. What is, or was, taboo was for daughters to talk about it.

Given the severity of the crime, literature teachers might assume that few students in their classrooms have been affected, but as the authors of *Women's Ways of Knowing* discovered, one in five women in any college classroom is likely to be a survivor of childhood sexual abuse (Belenky et al. 59). Those who teach the daughter's incest narrative might also assume that their classrooms are supportive of survivors; however, because professors rarely encourage students to share personal experiences, and because survivors rarely self-disclose in the classroom, we know very little about how students are affected by these narratives. In order to break this silence, I have invited an undergraduate English major, Laura Armstrong Randolph, a survivor of paternal sexual abuse, as I am, to analyze our responses to reading, discussing, and writing about these narratives. Our purpose here is not to engage in personal therapy but to participate in a larger feminist project: the work of cultural change. For as Froula suggests, when daughters break their silence, their stories "uncover the structure of hysteria as a culturally induced repression of paternal sexual abuse" (note 2, 132). In our view, the college literature classroom is a place in which the "talking cure" may be used, not for individual therapy, but to resist the "culturally induced repression of paternal sexual abuse." Using feminist theory, as well as relevant personal experiences, we explore how such a talking cure might work in college literature classrooms.

Given the power of the daughter's story to challenge patriarchal authority, it is surprising that these narratives have met with such positive reception during the past two decades. Somewhat less surprising is the fact that we have now entered a period of backlash—in the 1990s, the credibility of the survivor's story has frequently been challenged or trivialized—and our analysis has been influenced by this growing hostility.[36] In particular, because we haven't space to address the problem of "false memory,"[37] an issue likely to arise if we include a discussion of autobiographies, we have chosen to analyze only novels. Before beginning our discussion of pedagogy, which focuses primarily on a paper on father-daughter incest written by Ms. Randolph, we must first explain how we came to work on this topic together. In the fall of 1995, after reading Smiley's *A Thousand Acres*, a novel which had been assigned in my undergraduate senior seminar, "Women Novelists and the Tradition," Laura informed me, both in a written response and during a visit to my office, that she was upset by the novel's depiction of incest. Because she is a survivor of childhood sexual abuse, she explained, this topic was of great importance to her. At that point, I informed Laura that

I too was a survivor, and we decided to study this topic in a tutorial. During the following semester, we would read feminist theory on the topic, as well as eight or nine contemporary novels depicting father-daughter incest.

At the same time, during spring semester 1996, Laura was enrolled in my seminar, "The American Canon Debate." As she began to reflect on the relationship between the canon and the daughter's incest story, she decided to make this the topic of her seminar paper. Below is the paper that Laura wrote—with our follow-up conversation embedded, in italics, in the text. To save space, we have omitted Laura's title page and merged our bibliographies. Our dialogue explores the following questions: Which contemporary novels most effectively portray the daughter's perspective? Which theories of father-daughter incest offer the most powerful explanations of these narratives? and, finally, How do institutional mechanisms operate to silence disturbing "unauthorized" narratives of victims—both students and teachers? Here, then, is the paper Laura wrote.

With a Hook and an I:
An Analysis of Bastard Out of Carolina
and A Thousand Acres

The incest narrative has until the late twentieth century been highly disguised—as, for example, in Shakespearean romances or Mary Shelley's *Frankenstein*—and even hidden within the pages of traditional literature. Now that the paternally enforced silences are being broken, most often in novels by women, our literature is being flooded with incest narratives. However, many of these works are not accurately approaching the subject of incest and its detrimental effects. Incest, it seems, has simply become a "hot topic" on which writers, through the advent of television talk shows, are making a buck. As an incest victim/survivor, I take extreme offense at this obvious exploitation of a group that has already been subjected to one of the greatest forms of exploitation in human relations.

To explain this point, I compare two novels containing the incest narrative, Jane Smiley's *A Thousand Acres* and Dorothy Allison's *Bastard Out of Carolina.* Before analyzing these two novels, I first examine the institutional structures which enforce or suppress such works. The literary canon is, for example, a structure which continues to suppress the works of Others while including those that continue to function within the white, male-dominated world of the canon. Therefore, it is necessary to examine some of the current theoretical debates over the canon and introduce feminist theories of incest narratives.

The Canon Debate

The American canon debate has intensified in recent years. In this age of postmodernism, scholars have offered widely varying definitions of the canon, its functions, and its construction. The most accurate and encompassing definition of the American canon may be found in Paul Lauter's *Canons and Contexts* where he states that the canon is

> that set of authors and works generally included in basic American literature college courses and textbooks, and those ordinarily discussed in standard volumes of literary history, bibliography, or criticsm.... It encodes a set of social norms and values; and these, by virtue of its cultural standing, it helps endow with force and continuity.... The literary canon is, in short, a means by which culture validates social power. (23)

159

Lauter's assertion that the canon shapes American culture in profound and profuse ways cannot be denied. Lauter further states that "the works and authors generally considered central to a culture are those composed and promoted by persons from groups holding power within it" (49). The above definition of the canon is not confined to the words of the texts or the dusty books on one's shelf. It claims that the canon is an amazingly powerful vehicle through which, in part, we define our culture. This definition also allows for critical reviews of the works our culture claims as our literary history; furthermore, it allows for the critique of those norms and values that our culture through literature holds in such high esteem.

Another institutional structure that must be considered, especially in relationship to the canon debate, is the academy. Within the ivory towers of our nation's leading institutions of higher education are the professors who hold the power that controls what we read. It is within these walls that American culture is defined because it is within these walls that the mandates of what constitutes "good" literature are constituted. Robert Hemenway states that "no writer, no book, is likely to be accepted into the canon without the sanction of the university curriculum" (63). If that is the case (and I do believe it is) then the power of university English curricula is enormous. It illustrates that the shaping of the American mind actually does lie primarily in its universities. It also places the burden of canon formation upon these institutions. With that comes the "privileging" of texts that support the hegemonic views of the white, male world in all aspects of our culture. As Hemenway states: "The political and class assumptions in the metaphor of privilege all too often reflect the political and class assumptions of the academic study of literature" (64).

One example of such a political assumption is reflected in the fact that our heritage, the literary canon on which we base our cultural beliefs and values, is steeped in narratives of, by, and/or about the father. But what about our literary mothers? Where, if at all, do they fit in—both in terms of their daughter's literary and literal lives. Sandra M. Gilbert answers these questions in "Life's Empty Pack: Notes toward a Literary Daughteronomy." She explains that the "literary mother seems necessarily to speak both of and for the father, reminding her female child that she is not and cannot be his inheritor" (258). It is for this reason, then, that the daughter writer inherits a "figurative empty pack" (258).

Having inherited this "empty pack," some literary daughters are responding to this lack of maternal heritage in their own works. As Gilbert says, the majority of our literary mothers have written in the father tongue, rather than in an innovative mother tongue. At the same, as Gilbert says, there have also been, historically, revisionary daughter-writers. Allison is emerging through this revisionary process—a mother-daughter tradition—while, in contrast, Smiley has failed to break with the father. She continues, as I shall illustrate, to speak in the father tongue. Allison's incest narrative, by contrast, revisions the long hidden incest narrative of our phallocentric literary mothers and fathers.

In short, political and social views, however disguised, are intrinsic to literary texts. For that reason, the traditional English curriculum has a dramatic effect upon which incest narratives will be considered acceptable. It is highly unlikely, for example, that a narrative of such force as Allison's *Bastard Out of Carolina*, which depicts a working-class victim of paternal incest, will ever be included within the English curriculum. It is possible, however, that *Bastard Out of Carolina* might be taught in women's literature or women's studies courses. However, the taboo of speaking about incest in the college classroom still exists; therefore, even though the incest narrative may be part of the plot, it is rarely the primary focus of classroom discussion. For example, *The Bluest Eye* is frequently taught; however, attending to other aspects of the narrative, such as its critique of racism, allows the instructor to dismiss, ignore, or make short shrift of the scene in which Cholly sexually

violates his daughter, Pecola. By focusing on other conflicts, professors or students may avoid this uncomfortable topic.

*D: I agree with you. In my fall 1995 seminar, "Women Writers and the
Tradition," the course's focus on intertextuality probably gave us an excuse
to avoid an in-depth analysis of incest in* A Thousand Acres. *At the
same time, I consciously avoid exerting too much control over discussions
but, rather, encourage students to raise questions. Perhaps, when discussing
father-daughter incest, this strategy is not the best since it does not provide
public support for survivors who are afraid—or even ashamed—to speak
about incest in public.*

*R: I think that some of the women had strong opinions about the incest, but
they didn't—for a variety of reasons—speak up.*

*D: Perhaps they did need more support from me. I wish these women had
voiced their opinions more strongly. But as a feminist professor, I am also
concerned about alienating males or male-identified students: one accusa-
tion of "male bashing" can poison the classroom atmosphere.*

The Incest Narrative

Incest is by no means a new topic. In almost every past and present culture in the world, strict social norms have forbidden sexual
relations between parents and their children. Even the most
"sacred" Western world text, the Bible, contains specific reference
to the condemnation of incest. Lynda E. Boose discusses the
impact of this decree in her essay "The Father's House and the
Daughter in It: The Structures of Western Culture's Daughter-
Father Relationship." In the following passage, Boose examines
phrases in Leviticus that pertain to incest:

> When the codified taboo emerges in Leviticus 18, it
> places almost every conceivable family female—mother,

> sister, aunt, cousin, sister-in-law, niece, daughter-in-law,
> granddaughter, and so on—off limits. Conspicuously, the
> only one not included is the daughter. As Judith Lewis
> Herman comments, "The wording of the law makes it
> clear that...what is prohibited is the sexual use of those
> women who, in one manner or another, already belong
> to other relatives....The patriarchal God sees fit to pass
> over father-daughter incest in silence." Nonetheless, the
> unstated taboo is implicit. Though it "forbids [the father]
> to make sexual use of his daughter," no particular man's
> rights are offended, should the father choose to disre-
> gard this rule. (64)

This blatant silence on the issue of father-daughter incest has
played a major role in silencing incest narratives. Since one of the
very books that so many turn to for guidance fails to directly
acknowledge and condemn father-daughter incest, it is no wonder
that it has, for centuries, remained a "privatised" form of family
violence.

However, feminists have begun to challenge father-rule, and
to speak out about the ways in which institutions perpetuate this
violence. For example, in Christine Froula's examination of the
interconnectedness of literature and sexual abuse in "The
Daughter's Seduction: Sexual Violence and Literary History," she
claims that

> woman's cultural seduction is not merely analogous to
> the physical abuses that Freud's parents claimed to have
> suffered from but continuous with them....Herman
> shows that the abusive father does serious harm to the
> daughter's mind as well as to her body, damaging her
> sense of her own identity and depriving her voice of
> authority and strength. For the literary daughter—the

women reader/writer as daughter of her culture—the metaphysical violence against women inscribed in the literary tradition, although more subtle and no less difficult to acknowledge and understand, has serious consequences. Metaphysically, the woman reader of a literary tradition that inscribes violence against women is an abused daughter. Like physical abuse, literary violence against women works to privilege the cultural father's voice and story over those of women, the cultural daughters, and indeed to silence women's voices. (121)

This silencing has been occurring for hundreds of years within the Western world. It is only recently that women, in great numbers, have found their authority of their own voices and now refuse to accept their literal or literary father's voice and story.

D: As an English major in the 1960s, I was such an "abused daughter," forced to study a literary tradition that inscribed violence against women. Judith Fetterley maintains that this tradition continues. Do your professors continue to privilege the father's voice and story?

R: Overall, yes. However, there are feminist professors at Iowa State who are trying to end the silencing of women.

In my analysis of *A Thousand Acres* and *Bastard Out of Carolina*, I demonstrate that Smiley continues to speak in her father's voice while Allison is denouncing and reclaiming with full force the authority of her own voice.

A Thousand Acres

Jane Smiley's *A Thousand Acres* is a revision of Shakespeare's *King Lear.* Set in the middle of Iowa on a hog farm, a patriarchal family, similar to Lear's family (three daughters and their father), discover the truth about themselves and their life as a family. The novel is narrated by daughter Ginny who, at the beginning, has no memory of paternal incest. Her sister Rose, who does remember, is consumed by rage and hatred resulting from her father's abuse. The third sister, Caroline, is "evidently" not a victim of their father's violence. Also central to the novel is Jess Clark, who ultimately becomes the lover of both Ginny and Rose.

Smiley won both the 1992 Pulitzer Prize and the National Book Critics Circle Award for *A Thousand Acres*. Proclaimed as a great work of contemporary literature, it has been accepted into the college curriculum (at least at Iowa State), so it is being validated as canonical literature. However, while Smiley is successfully revisioning *King Lear*, the novel's incest narrative actually perpetuates the tradition of literary violence against women. As Gilbert explains, the literary mother or daughter often becomes, in turn, the voice of the "Law of the Father." This is exactly what Smiley has done. In terms of the incest narrative, she does not break out of the confines of her literary father's house, nor does she attempt to. In fact, she revels in it, as the following analysis will show.

D: It's hard for me to understand how, on the one hand, Smiley revisions Shakespeare's Lear *while, on the other hand, she fails to break out of the father's house—that is, fails to transform the incest narrative. However, I am receptive to your analysis, partly because Smiley herself acknowledges that she has found it easier to write from the paternal than the maternal perspective, despite the fact that she is the mother of three children. In "Can Mothers Think?" she says that writing as a mother is difficult primarily because there are few literary models.*

R. It's hard to imagine that Smiley, and others of her generation, found so few maternal literary models. In my generation—I was born in 1970, the year The Bluest Eye *was published—it has been relatively easy to find such models. However, because of the backlash, I can see that many students in the next generation, those entering college now, have not studied the mother-daughter canon.*

My first criticism of *A Thousand Acres* is the placement of Rose's declaration of their shared abuse. It follows the scene in which the father accuses Ginny of being a "bitch," "barren whore," "slut," and "dried-up whore bitch." It is only after these accusations that Rose relates to Ginny what she remembers about their childhood. At that time Ginny still insists that she does not remember. The incest narrative also does not begin—is not revealed—until after the reader has witnessed Ginny begin a sexual affair with Jess Clark, and to compound matters, Ginny's husband, Ty, is constructed as a halfway decent man which only makes Ginny's adultery seem even more vicious.

D: If we consider how much the male students liked Ty, I can see the problem: you are suggesting that Ginny looks bad, by comparison to her "good" husband Ty; therefore, by the time Ginny recalls the incest, readers have already judged her harshly.

R: Yes. I recall, for example, that some of the male students, along with some women, spent a good deal of time praising Ty, Ginny's husband. I want to make it clear, however, that I do not think Ty is a good man. Larry Cook is his ideal, the kind of man he wants to become.

Only after readers have been subjected to all of the above subplots are they allowed to hear the incest narrative. Smiley's insistence on placing the incest narrative after the father's story "privileges" his story, undercutting Ginny's and Rose's story of incest. In this way, through the manner in which she sequences the narrative, Smiley continues the tradition of literary violence against women and the privileging of the father's narrative.

D: Smiley does say, "I was determined to stick with the plot [of Lear] as far as I could all the way to the end" (Berne 37). Do you mean that the incest narrative is almost buried by the many plots set in motion early in the novel?

R: Yes, in part, that is what I mean. However, I want to emphasize the fact that Smiley allows the daughters to tell their stories only after the father tells his. It's still the story of a father, and what his daughters do to him—his insanity, his land, his property. The story is always about him; it's never about what he has done to them. I don't think Smiley has a strong enough grasp of actual incest to be able to effectively portray it in literature.

D: Smiley insists she is critiquing the father' story. She always objected, she says, to productions of King Lear which ended "Isn't Lear great" because she saw him as a narcissist (Carlson/Whitaker 7–8). Furthermore, rather than seeing Goneril and Regan as monsters, she asked, "Why are the sisters so angry?" and answered: "Well the only women I've ever met who were that angry have been abused; they haven't necessarily been sexually abused but they've been abused or mistreated or brutalized in some way" (Carlson/Smiley 9).

R: I think she's wonderfully imaginative in rewriting King Lear, but the profound horror of incest seems beyond her imagination.

D: Are you suggesting that, because Smiley does not give us a full and graphic depiction of the incest, she has not fully imagined its horror from the victim's perspective?

R: Because Ginny recalls only a brief moment of abuse—"I had looked at the top of his head, at his balding spot in the brown grizzled hair, while feeling him suck my breasts" (228)—then nothing. Although Rose and Ginny speak about the abuse, readers never overhear Ginny's inner voice, nor do we come to understand how she has internalized the abuse. Ginny's distance allows readers to distance themselves.

The second issue I have with Smiley's incest narrative is the way in which Rose almost denies that the rape ever took place. When Rose tells Ginny that their father sexually molested her, she states:

> But I was flattered, too. I thought that he'd picked me, me, to be his favorite, not you, not her. On the surface, I thought it was okay if he said it was, since he was the rule maker. He didn't rape me, Ginny. He seduced me. He said it was okay, that it was good to please him, that he needed it, that I was special. He said he loved me. (190)

Although most incest victims go through some of the above feelings, and most perpetrators use such arguments to convince their victims that it is natural and normal, I object to the statement, "He didn't rape me, Ginny. He seduced me," in which Rose denies the abuse.

D: Is it your view that the word seduction misrepresents a father who forces a child into a sexual relationship? In the novel, of course, it is Rose who uses the word seduction, not Smiley. But Smiley herself uses the term seduction in an interview when she says, speaking of Larry Cook, "He pursues a kind of seduction of Rose that he would be ashamed of if he could look at it with any perspective" (Carlson/Whitaker 10).

R: In my view, Smiley's word seduction is an excuse for the father's action, a way of condoning rape.

D: Alice Miller, who has written an excellent critique of Freud's theory of infantile sexuality, agrees with you. She says, "The word 'seduction' reinforces the wishful thinking of the adult, who assumes that the child shares his or her desires; these projections are absent in the word 'abuse'" (126). However, in fairness to Smiley, I want to point out that feminist critics such as Jane Gallop and Christine Froula have also used the word seduction to describe the father's linguistic appropriation of the daughter's voice.

R: There's a difference between the ways that Miller and Froula use the term. Froula is referring to a psycho-linguistic appropriation, whereas Miller objects to the term being applied to physically enacted sexual abuse. Feminists are so afraid, so silenced, on this topic of incest that we still refrain from using the term abuse or rape. But to return to my analysis.

What else is the sexual act committed upon a child, if not rape? Does lack of resistance constitute consent? Rose's denial of the raping of her body by her father is another continuation of the tradition of violence against women in literary works. Smiley is not deconstructing this myth; she is supporting and promulgating it throughout her novel.

D: So, as you interpret A Thousand Acres, *because Smiley fails to critique her character's view of incest, she, as the author, perpetuates misconceptions about incest?*

R: Yes, Smiley has, in my view, misled all of her readers and violated the trust of those readers who are actual incest survivors. I think we have to hold Smiley accountable for delivering Rose's lines, "He didn't rape me," without ever challenging words that actually deny the incestuous act.

D: So you think that Smiley's choice of a limited first-person narrator, a narrator who lacks a feminist consciousness, leads her to abandon the very readers for whom she says she is writing? I ask this question because Smiley says, "If we teach King Lear *to seniors in high school, then the rhetoric of the play asserts that women and daughters have very little leeway and men and fathers have very great leeway. Well, that's not something I want my daughters to believe" (Carlson/Whitaker 27).*

R: In that case, she should rewrite her novel. She should write in a maternal voice rather than a paternal voice.

A further contention I have with Smiley's incest narrative is with a conversation later in the novel between Ginny and Rose in which they discuss their father's abuse. The conversation follows the death of Rose's husband, Pete, as well as Rose's announcement that she too is having an affair with Jess Clark. It is Pete's death, and his anger at his father-in-law, that prompts the conversation. Rose says,

> "I want what was Daddy's. I want it. I feel like I've paid for it, don't you? You think a breast weighs a pound? That's my pound of flesh. You think a teenaged hooker costs fifty bucks a night? There's ten thousand bucks. I wanted him to feel remorse and know what he did and what he is, but when you see him around town and they talk about him, he's just senile. He's safe from ever knowing. People pat him on the head and sympathize with him and say what bitches we are, and he believes them and that's that, the end of history. I can't stand that." Her voice thrilled up the scale.
>
> I said, "I feel weird. I must be really tired," but I knew it wasn't fatigue. Then I said, "Okay. Here's a question. Did you know that Jess Clark slept with me?" (303)

My dispute with the above conversation is that it aligns the sisters' competitive pursuit of Jess Clark with their father's molestation, as if these relationships are parallel.

D: If I understand you correctly, you object to the fact that the sisters seem to be the active agents, pursuing a relationship with Jess just as, by implication, they actively pursued a sexual relationship with the father. This makes them the "seductive daughters," despite the fact that they were children, living in their father's house, subject to his laws.

R: That's exactly what I am saying.

D: In fact, Smiley does say in an interview, "I think Shakespeare's very right about how some kind of unresolved rivalry over the father might work itself out if the daughters were once again in a position where they were both interested in the same man" (Carlson/Whitaker 11). This kind of rivalry didn't develop between my sister and me—in fact, I still feel guilty that I escaped most of the sexual abuse because my sister absorbed my father's attentions—but then I don't believe that all victims have the same experience. My question is this: do you think that two sisters, both incest victims, might become confused enough to imagine themselves rivals for their father's sexual attentions.

R: Yes, I do believe this is possible. However, Smiley does not place the above conversation, the rivalry between Ginny and Rose, in a narrative sequence that would alert readers to the fact that this rivalry results from— is caused by—the incest. At this point, Smiley is so concerned with her relationship to Shakespeare that she provides no authorial insight into the effect of sexual abuse on the daughters.

Again, Smiley continues the traditional pattern, writing an incest narrative, as in the Biblical story of Lot, in which the daughters seduce the father. By sandwiching the discussion of the father's abuse between a discussion of the sisters' separate but shared affairs with Jess Clark, Smiley suggests that, just as the seductive daughters competed for the father, they now compete for Jess. Such a view suggests, implicitly at least, that the father was not the agent of the abuse.

D: Smiley does say, "If every writer has some kind of secret, totally grandiose ambition, mine would have been when I was writing this book that no one would ever be able to read King Lear *the same way again" (Carlson/Whitaker 27). Do you think that her desire to follow Shakespeare's plot leads her to recreate his view of sibling rivalry?*

R: Yes, and as a result her novel suffers. I believe that when dealing with a topic as volatile as incest, the author has a responsibility to portray this sibling rivalry, not from Shakespeare's point of view or according to his plot structure, but from the point of view of the daughter.

D: When I read this exchange between Rose and Ginny, I thought about Shakespeare's plot, not about understanding, more fully, why incested daughters might, years later, compete for the love of the same man.

R: The majority of readers will not have read King Lear; *they are taking Smiley's authorial word—through the voice of Ginny—as the "truth" about how incest functions even though, in my view, she doesn't fully understand how incest disrupts sibling relationships and distorts the victim's sexuality. I do see the distinction between Smiley and her character; nevertheless, I hold Smiley responsible for the vision of the work as a whole. A major problem is that Ginny is an incredibly weak character.*

D: Ginny narrates the story of her family's destruction almost without emotion. At first I thought of her detachment—her almost disembodied voice—as a flaw. But such flat affect may, quite possibly, be one result of sexual abuse. And it is clear that Ginny hasn't sought any therapy; even at the end of the novel, she seems depressed and isolated. Smiley explains her choice of narrator as follows: "I never considered making it Rose's story because I always perceived Rose as more angry than Ginny, and that was for purely narrative reasons—an angry voice can't write a novel because a novel can't sustain that kind of monotonous pitch. . . . Rose, being as single-minded as she is, would just be too shrill and too monotonous to sustain the narrative" (Carlson/Whitaker 26).

R: Why not have an angry narrator? I object to the notion that an angry voice is necessarily "shrill and monotonous." Perhaps the real problem is that Smiley couldn't sustain that kind of anger.

D: I'm not sure whether a narrator as angry as Rose would turn off readers, but Ginny—who was angry enough to attempt to kill Rose—has cer-

tainly not worked through her anger. Did you know that Dorothy Allison believes that it is dangerous for a writer to be too emotionally involved? She told E. J. Graff that, before writing Bastard, *she "wrote out her anger in* Trash *and could move beyond it—and use it" (46).*

R: I believe that Allison probably did write out her anger—the self-destructive anger—but she still uses that anger. For example, Allison's narrator claims her anger and directs it at the father. By contrast, Ginny's anger is misdirected toward her sister. Furthermore, we are asked to believe that Ginny finds it possible to imagine her father's crimes because she discovers her own capacity for evil. How can one equate brewing a batch of poison sausages—an attempt at murder which is, in fact, not realized—with the rape of a child? Ginny attacks an equal, her sister, whereas Larry Cook attacks his children, exploiting his authority as a parent.

My final criticism is Smiley's handling of the incest narrative at the end of *A Thousand Acres*. Ginny has left the farm, Rose has died, Ty has moved to Texas, and Rose's girls live with Ginny. Ginny's final statement, in which she contemplates the past, deals with her father and herself:

> And when I remember that world, I remember my dead young self, who left me something, too, which is a canning jar of poisoned sausages and the ability it confers, of remembering what you can't imagine. I can't say that I forgive my father, but I can now imagine what he probably chose never to remember—the goad of an unthinkable urge, pricking him, pressing him, wrapping him in an impenetrable fog of self that must have seemed, when he wandered around the house late at night after working and drinking, like the very darkness. This is the gleaming obsidian shard I safeguard above all others. (371)

My objection is that, in the end, Ginny still defines herself in relation to her father. She has not accepted the authority of her own voice; otherwise, the last words from her mouth would not have focused on her father, but on herself and her daughters. With this close, Smiley privileges the father's story. Another aspect of the ending that illustrates Smiley's failure to escape the father's tongue is her insistence that Ginny leave the farm alone. Here, Smiley is expressing the myth of individualism that American culture is based on; however, one cannot heal the wounds of incest alone. It is not possible. Frankly, it is not possible to do anything at all on one's own. There is ultimately an interconnectedness that we all need to survive. Smiley's denial of community support for the female illustrates just how trapped within the white, male, bourgeois world she is.

D: So even though Smiley herself views this ending as a revision of traditional tragic closure, primarily because Ginny moves beyond revenge (the desire that drives most tragic plots) in order to mother Rose's children, you feel that she hasn't succeeded?

R: Smiley may have moved beyond tragic closure; however, she doesn't shift into the maternal voice. In fact, Ginny , who isn't very persuasive as a mother, says, "I recognize that they [Rose's children] do not have a great deal of faith in my guardianship, though they like me, and we get along smoothly" (369).

D. It seems that students, like Rose's children, don't have much faith in Ginny either. Even though I pointed out that Ginny is the novel's narrator, student writers consistently overlooked Ginny's narrative role, even when it was relevant to their arguments .

R: By the end of the novel, I had truly forgotten Ginny's role as narrator.

D: Since you were not the only student to forget that Ginny, not Smiley, is the narrator, I am left to speculate as to why Ginny's narrative presence made so little impression. Were these students naive readers who conflated the author and her characters? It might also be that Ginny's "I" is simply not very powerful—perhaps because she has disassociated her mind and emotions.

R. In A Thousand Acres, *we have both ends of the spectrum: one daughter who is, presumably, too angry to speak, the other too emotionally disembodied to speak with authority. This may accurately reflect the effect of sexual abuse on victims; however, readers are not likely to understand—without a few clues from Smiley—why Ginny speaks almost as if she were a reporter, rather than a participant in tragic events.*

Bastard Out of Carolina

Dorothy Allison's *Bastard Out of Carolina* was a 1992 National Book Award Finalist; however, it has not received the same critical attention that *A Thousand Acres* received. The novel is also within the genre of autobiographical fiction which, in my opinion, adds to its authority. As E. J. Graff writes, "Allison grew up much as does *Bastard*'s Ruth Anne, nicknamed Bone. . . . She was abused by her stepfather whom her mother was unable to leave" (42). Smiley does not claim that *A Thousand Acres* is autobiographical fiction; that explains why, in my opinion, she is unable to portray the incest narrative. Although the imagination is a powerful tool, some acts may be beyond the imagination.

Allison is actively revising the incest narrative in *Bastard.* Rather than writing as a traditional literary mother, she is breaking the long traditional literary violence against women. The incest narrative in this novel is not masked by other elements of the plot; although other elements do exist, the primary focus is the incestuous abuse. Smiley, on the other hand, distracts readers from the incest narrative with numerous subplots, such as the affairs of Jess Clark, the issue of property inheritance, and the battle over family versus corporate farming. Thus, she buries the incest narrative within the struggles of the male, middle-class Iowa farmer.

Allison's novel, set in the southern United States, centers on a poor working-class extended family. This focus on the working-class poor breaks the boundaries of the white bourgeois novels that permeate the canon. Allison deftly defends the working-class poor by inverting the middle class's slang name for the poor— "trash." Metaphorically, she illustrates how in the river near her aunt's home, "Trash rises.... Out here where no one can mess with it, trash rises all the time" (180). Here, Allison directly confronts the cultural stereotype that all poor people are poor because they want to be, or they are stupid, or lazy. Instead, Allison challenges that belief by inverting the responsibility onto those who define the poor as "trash." In contrast, Smiley's character's are all middle-to upper-middle-class Iowa farmers. The values within Smiley's work are supposedly the values of all good Americans, with the exception of the incest narrative. It is unfortunate that Smiley did not make use of these so-called family values of Midwestern, middle-class family and juxtapose them against the tyranny and exploitation that exists within many of these families.

D: Here our interpretations differ. I see A Thousand Acres *as a critique of traditional, patriarchal middle-class family values, particularly the father's hunger to possess the land and to exploit it, as he exploits his daughters, without concern for the generation to follow. The novel's imagery of water, poisoned by fertilizers, lying just beneath the surface of the prairie—causing cancer and sterility—suggests an analogy between the abuse of the land and of women. What do you think of this interpretation?*

R: I can see this; however, I don't find it compelling because Smiley still maintains and privileges the father's voice.

Allison chose, as her narrator, a prepubescent girl whom she names Bone. It is through this clear-eyed child that we hear about the incest. In contrast, Smiley's narrator, Ginny, who initially has no memory of the abuse, tells the incest story only through the eyes of an adult caught in the mystical fantasy of the ideal family. The world which Allison constructs is primarily female oriented. However, it is female oriented within the male patriarchy, an element that Allison never lets the reader forget. The story begins with Bone's "illegitimate" birth, and her mother's fight with the male patriarchy to claim "legitimacy " for her child. The story then evolves as the reader is introduced to Bone's extended family, including her crucial aunts and uncles.

The aunts take an active role in Bone's development, and the uncles are by no means passive, but the crucial element, in my opinion, is how Allison also structures the community of women that surround Bone. This is a definite break from the traditional incest narrative, and a shifting from the father's story to the daughter's. The reader is, from the very beginning, given the narrative through the words of the daughter, Bone. The father's story is never told, and it is only through Bone's interpretation of events that we receive the narrative.

D: Why do you think it so important that Allison makes Bone's relationships with women, rather than the father, the center of her story? Do you have in mind some feminist theory?

R: No, it's not feminist theory; it's experience. Every male authority in my life—father, stepfather, uncle, priest, boyfriends—has sexually abused me. For that reason, I feel support and acceptance primarily in a community of women. I also think that only a strong community of women, along with feminist men, can end the cyclical pattern of sexual abuse. At the same time, my position has been strengthened and expanded by feminist critics. As a result, I don't feel as isolated.

D: I have come to a similar conclusion. However, my view comes primarily from reading feminist critics, from my analysis of the absence of mater-

*nal voices in literature (*Narrating Mothers, *1991), and from my study of father-daughter incest in the novels of Joyce Carol Oates. In* Lavish Self-Divisions *(1996), I argue that Oates's novels of the 1980s illustrate that the incested daughter must shift her alliance from her father to her mother if she is to recover. At the same time, I believe that before a daughter can make this shift, she must analyze her relationship with the father. Smiley's novel provides such an analysis.*

R. My problem is that Smiley's main character doesn't make this analysis; if Ginny had actually analyzed this relationship, her emotions would not be dissociated from her story.

D. I agree that, while Smiley has analyzed the father-daughter relationship, Ginny has not. In order to recover, as Herman says in Trauma and Recovery, *a victim must tell her story —complete with accompanying affect.*

As previously stated, Smiley does not achieve the overthrow of the Father's Story. Instead, she continues this traditional story by disallowing any resemblance of a community of women for Ginny and Rose to seek support, comfort, or shelter.

Allison's own experience allows her to achieve a literary realism that other authors could not achieve. Her realistic portrayal of the actual abuse is incredibly graphic and violent, but, at the same time, Bone is not passive in her response to the incestuous violation. Smiley's brief portrayal of the incest deals primarily with the breasts of Ginny and Rose; therefore, Smiley remains well within the boundaries of what is acceptable to the institutional powers that be.

D: That's an interesting point. Smiley may have decided to protect her readers by not depicting the abuse in graphic terms. But if children are expected to bear this trauma, why shouldn't readers be expected to have the courage to at least read about it? But does Allison pay a price for expecting readers to bear witness?

R: Unfortunately, yes. She is not as acceptable either to a mass audience or to the academic community.

The abuse begins in the hospital parking lot, immediately following the stillborn death of her mother and Daddy Glen's baby. Daddy Glen's (her stepfather) abuse of Bone at the time is brief yet haunting. In the scene following the abuse, Bone states the following:

> I remembered those moments in the hospital parking lot like a bad dream, hazy and shadowed. When Daddy Glen looked at me, I saw no sign that he ever thought about it at all. Maybe it had not happened. Maybe he really did love us. I wanted him to love us. I wanted to be able to love him. (51–52)

Allison illustrates the disbelief that is associated with incest without romanticizing it or becoming melodramatic. She simply shows how far a child's need for love extends. It is her ability to depict this need–without trivializing it or giving authority, respect, or sympathy to the father–which enables her to revise the incest narrative. Again, this depiction of Bone stands in sharp opposition to Smiley's Rose who never recognizes that it was not "seduction"; it was rape.

Allison continues to show the realities of the destruction of self that incest ultimately carries with it. Repeatedly throughout the novel we hear Bone, as well as her mother and stepfather, assign the responsibility of Bone's abuse to Bone herself. This is an accurate depiction of the internalization of sexual abuse. Although Bone does express denial of the abuse and/or her stepfather's responsibility for it, in the end she places the responsibility upon him. In this way it becomes a redefinition of the traditional incest narrative. After her aunts and uncles learn of the physical abuse

Chapter 7

Bone was subjected to by Daddy Glen, her mother moves Bone, her sister, and herself into an apartment. After a series of self-destructive mental conversations, Bone answers the question of responsibility in this way:

> What was it I had done? Why had he always hated me? Maybe I was a bad girl, evil, nasty, willful, stupid, ugly– everything he said. Maybe I was, but it didn't matter. I hated him.... No, it did not matter whether I had screamed or not. It had all been the way he wanted it. It had nothing to do with me or anything I had done. It was an animal thing, just him using me. (252–53)

In this passage Allison completely deconstructs the traditional incest narrative; she holds the father accountable for his actions against the daughter, without excusing him through senility or a divine transformation. Allison vilifies Daddy Glen and allows Bone the authority to condemn him. By contrast, Smiley lets Larry Cook off the hook by making him go mad.

D: Yes, again, we see the influence of Shakespeare's plot: because Lear goes mad, Larry Cook does too. Allison is freer to tell the truth about incest because she is not burdened with Lear's story.

R: That's almost a cop-out to me. If Smiley could not be true to the daughter's experience of incest due to the constraints of revisioning King Lear, *she should have chosen a different way to tell the story.*

There is another aspect of *Bastard Out of Carolina* which I have yet to discuss: the symbolism of the dredging hook and chain that Bone finds at the river. The hook actually becomes a power-filled phallic symbol for Bone–a phallus that she controls and can use with, not against, her body. Her late-night Woolworth's raid is not only a gesture of defiance but also a movement of raw power. With the hook (phallus) Bone obtains the control to overcome adversity. The fact that she uses the hook to go up and over into the building, while not allowing her male cousin to enter the same way, illustrates her control of this male phallic symbol; possession of the hook allows her to "rise with the trash."

D: But doesn't Allison's use of phallic symbolism make her guilty of claiming to speak in the father's voice, according to his law?

R: The difference is that Bone is in control of the hook; she makes it a part of herself. She possesses the phallus.

D: But why not use some sort of woman-identified image? For example, Smiley links the maternal womb, the power of birth and regeneration, to images of the water—water lying beneath the surface of the prairie. In fact, since Bone recovers the hook, not from any man, but from the water, perhaps this is not simply a "phallic" hook?

R: It is both things at once. Since the phallic hook causes her pain, she must control it; at the same time, she combines this power with the strength represented by her aunt Raylene.

By contrast, Smiley's most powerful imagery troubles me. When Ginny fantasizes herself a sow in order to achieve sexual pleasure with her husband, this scene not only invokes the hog farming plot, which destroys the family's farm, the word conjures up powerful images of filth, stupidity, and obesity. Linking these adjectives to the character of Ginny further taints her incest story, biasing the reader against such a "slovenly" creature.

D: I had some trouble with this imagery too. Why not have Ginny associate her sexual arousal with horses, for example. A farm girl might well have enjoyed horseback riding in an erotic way, and horses aren't loaded with ugly connotations as pigs are. But maybe Smiley is suggesting that, in Ginny's mind, sex is ugly, piggish.

R: I agree; however, Ginny's associatons with this image are not fully developed.

Unlike the ending of *A Thousand Acres*, Bone is not alone at the end of *Bastard*. Bone has the love, support, and understanding of her Aunt Raylene. This is a very important final statement. Allison emphasizes the importance of community, a sense of belonging. She knows that the trauma of incest cannot be healed without others supporting the victim. Unlike Smiley, Allison replaces the American myth of individualism with the always important perspective of interconnectedness. Allison's own experience allows her to achieve a literary realism that other authors, including Smiley, have not achieved.

Conclusion

The importance of the revisioning of the incest narrative crosses the boundaries of literary goals. Incest victims/survivors need to hear their stories told; they need the validation of their own voices. It is through such talented writers as Dorothy Allison that these women can and will hear their own stories and voices. However, before works such as *Bastard Out of Carolina* will be accepted into the literary canon, a major overhauling of both our canon and our culture must take place. If the canon continues to exclude any incest narrative that does not center on the father's story, this is detrimental not only to the millions of incest victims/survivors but also to daughters of the future. The literary canon has the power to shape and reshape American norms and values; therefore, it is the responsibility of institutions controlling the canon to incorporate works that expose the injustices of our culture.

D: Given the current backlash against the daughter's incest narrative, it seems unlikely this change will occur any time soon. But we must continue the effort to choose texts that represent the incest victim's point of view and, in our classrooms, to address sexual abuse in ways that support survivors. I am curious as to why, from out of the nine novels we read—novels by Kathy Acker, Dorothy Allison, Margaret Atwood, Russell Banks, Carolivia Herron, Toni Morrison, Joyce Carol Oates, and Jane Smiley—you chose to analyze Allison and Smiley. What criteria did you have in mind?

R: The reason I chose to analyze A Thousand Acres *and* Bastard Out of Carolina *is that my objections to Smiley's representation of father-daughter incest, particularly in light of the critical acclaim she had received, sparked our initial discussion. I chose Allison's novel because, in my view, it is the best—the most accurate and honest. With astounding insight, Allison captures the world of an incest victim with painful honesty. Along with Morrison's* The Bluest Eye, *Allison's* Bastard *deserves a place in the college literature curriculum because of its integrity, honesty, and brilliance. Once I too become a literature instructor—that is, if my goal is realized—I will evaluate these novels in terms of the writer's authority, imagination, and experience. Experience—that is, the writer's actual experience with incest as a child—definitely adds to the authority of a work. Imagination is a powerful tool; however, some experiences seem almost beyond the imagination. (Something for which, I believe, we should be thankful.) The survivor has a greater authority and higher stake in writing the incest narrative in a manner that challenges the archaic patriarchal world view. Therefore, if I were to teach an incest narrative, I would strive to include only those that draw upon autobiographical experiences.*

D: Here we disagree. Neither Morrison nor Oates is a survivor, but both depict father-daughter incest with accuracy, as well as sympathy for the victim. I also think that, since father-daughter incest occurs in all social classes, as well as in different races, it is important to teach narratives which illustrate these differences. It is also helpful to hear a range of narrative voices—even those that may be repulsive to us. For example, Kathy

Acker's narrator in Blood and Guts in High School *speaks with such flat affect that the novel seems, at moments, akin to pornography. Yet Acker's satire of* The Scarlet Letter, *along with your evocative phrase, "The Scarlet Letter I," has changed how I read Hawthorne's novel: I now regard Hester's marriage to Chillingsworth as a kind of father-daughter incest. However, I wouldn't teach Acker's novel to undergraduates. Have you considered what narratives you would teach, and at what level?*

R: I do not believe incest narratives belong in a 100-level course, unless the option is discussed with the students first. I doubt that most would choose to read and discuss incest narratives. In my rather uninformed opinion these narratives belong in at least a 200-level, preferably in upper-level seminar courses.

D: I have met student resistance to the study of these narratives—such as The Bluest Eye—*even in courses at the 300-level, where one expects mostly juniors and seniors. It is, however, most often nonmajors whose objections are the strongest; they want "happy endings." Students who take courses in women's literature seem a bit more receptive, but it depends on their backgrounds. Politically conservative students, those who believe in Father Rule, often refuse to discuss such a taboo topic.*

R: I have yet to solve the problem of student backgrounds. It would be extremely unprofessional and highly intrusive to ask students for a show of hands as to who is a survivor of incest. Shame remains a powerful inhibitor.

D: I agree. It is important to be supportive of survivors; therefore, I would never force them to "come out" in my classroom. For one thing, I could not assure them that their peers would be understanding or supportive.

R: Exactly. I have often not voiced my experience for the simple reason that I fear my classmates and the instructor will not believe my story, as so many have not. To compound matters, when I was in your seminar, the male students (and some of the females) were highly uncomfortable during the discussion of incest in Smiley's A Thousand Acres. *In fact, every time the subject surfaced, they made every attempt to silence it. It was as if they went running to the door to keep some horrible, hideous, devouring, fatal monster or plague out of the classroom.*

D: Perhaps because the dynamics of classroom discussions are so complex, I was not as aware of student fear and resistance. However, male students who analyzed A Thousand Acres *in their final papers placed little emphasis on the father's incestuous acts; in fact, they positioned themselves as defenders of Shakespeare, often by criticizing Smiley's revision of* King Lear. *However, whenever I bring up the issue of sexual violence against women, including incest, I can expect at least a few students to accuse me of "male bashing" —not to my face, but in course evaluations. What irony: to speak of the violence done to women by men is often regarded—by students of both genders—as a form of verbal violence against men. For that reason, even though I state my feminist positions openly, I strive to encourage debate among students. I want male students to feel that their ideas are welcome while, at the same time, I try to raise the consciousness of males— with the help of feminist students.*

R: Unfortunately, with so few feminist students at Iowa State, we get very tired. As a feminist in your seminar, I was aware that many of the students— having failed to put an end to the discussion of incest—tended to argue the father's position, reinforcing my decision not to self-disclose. Another factor is that—because the classroom is not a therapy session—students and instructors fear to divulge personal information.

D: Quite right. In my view, if a female teacher discloses a history of sexual abuse, some students might infer that she lacks detachment and neutrality, just as many students assume that a feminist teacher cannot judge the work of male students with fairness. That is why I share my personal history only in the privacy of my office, and only when a student chooses to "come out" to me about her own abuse.

R: Unlike you, when I teach incest narratives, I plan to be as straightforward in the classroom as possible. I am an incest survivor, and it affects me in every aspect of my life, including professionally. I believe students need to know that their instructors are human beings with a past, present, and future. I hope that by divulging such personal information, students who are survivors will be more secure in discussing their own experiences both inside and outside the classroom. It is also possible that students who are not survivors will be more open to discussing the incest narrative and not try to shove it under the bed—as has happened so many times in my classes. I agree wholeheartedly with those who argue that the classroom is not the place for therapy, but it is necessary to examine how we, as readers, are affected by incest narratives.

D: I have mixed feelings. On the one hand, a teacher's self-disclosure in the classroom may actually save a student's life. For example, according to Lynn Bloom in "Teaching College English as a Woman," her personal revelation—she told students how she had resisted rape while discussing Oates's "Where are you going, where have you been?"—encouraged a student to fight off a rapist. On the other hand, self-disclosure might lead to a woman professor's loss of authority since stories that arouse emotions are suspect in the academy. In most classrooms, emotional topics are presented from a distanced, intellectualized perspective. Women's Studies courses have bad reputations—critics accuse them of lacking intellectual rigor—because personal revelations, along with emotions, have been allowed. However, I agree with Jane Tompkins that "an epistemology which excludes emotions from the process of attaining knowledge radically undercuts women's epistemic authority" ("Me and My Shadow" 123). That is why I share my history only in the privacy of my office, primarily to reassure survivors of incest that they are not alone. Unfortunately, I did not find this support until after the advent of the women's movement, during my doctoral program.

R: One reason that, as a teacher, I will disclose in the classroom is to demonstrate support for survivors. Even today such support is not widely available. In most of my classes, the instructor is held out to be revered as a deity, a profound sage within the field of literature and we, as students, have no new insights to offer. Our only function is to listen, mouths agape, to their amazing words of wisdom. Because authority within the classroom is rarely shared, students are placed in a subservient position. Some professors make it seem as if a discussion is occurring when, in fact, it is not.

D: I suppose some of us do have the habit of falling in love with our own voices. At the same time, students bring political views to the classroom that play a powerful part in how I conduct discussions. Given the hostility of many students toward feminism, I avoid employing an authoritarian voice, recognizing that some students will automatically infer that I am hostile toward male students. When you begin teaching, you will probably constantly monitor student responses, as I do.

R: I will begin a teaching assistantship in the fall of 1996, and, as a result, I have already experienced certain institutional constraints. This past May, a former professor informed me that another of my professors, after reading my autobiographical essays on the World Wide Web, suggested that I consider taking them off before I begin teaching. Although I do not want to believe that this was an attempt to silence me, I cannot help but feel it was.

D: Since harassment of female instructors in introductory composition classes has been a real problem, it may have been an attempt to protect you.

R: Understanding the context in which this advice was offered helps me to accept it as protective. The shame involved with incest does not disappear; I fight the battle on a daily basis. In this case, I chose to let my essays remain on the Web page.

D: I respect your decision to leave the essay on the Web. In this instance you had multiple audiences to consider. Because you will soon be a teaching assistant and a graduate student, you have to monitor how both your students and professors react to your disclosure. I often ask myself, as I'm sure you do: "If I speak out, what will the consequences be? Can I handle it?" As you say, this is a choice that must be made again and again. Each time

I write an essay on incest in literature, I must decide whether or not to risk self-disclosure. Personal disclosure remains a taboo for many of my colleagues, whether in the classroom or in an academic paper. In fact, whenever I write autobiographically, I anticipate some readers saying, "You should be ashamed of yourself," just as they mocked Jane Tompkins for describing herself, in "Me and My Shadow," as trying to decide whether or not to go to the bathroom. These readers missed Tompkins's point: that the intellect is embodied. We forget this at our peril. As we have seen, because theories may cover up and thereby perpetuate the abuse of women, women must insist upon the right to name and theorize their own experiences.

R: That is why I plan to write my thesis on the topic of incest narratives, but I do so with some reservation. Will I be labeled...a male-bashing, man-hating, angry woman with nothing but a chip on my shoulder? Will I even be able to find employment with a thesis on such a volatile topic? These fears are, I believe, symptomatic of explicit or implicit institutional constraints. My only hope is that the field continues on its course of becoming more inclusive and nonjudgmental.

D: I hope so too, but the political climate is becoming increasingly hostile toward women. Since your immediate goal is to teach in a community college, you might risk it. However, you must consider the fact that, during a job interview, you are likely to be asked to discuss your thesis. Nevertheless, if you find a teaching position, women students will surely benefit from your knowledge and support. As you point out, the decision to speak or write autobiographically must be made again and again. As each situation arises, we must ask: What is the nature of the constraint? What are the risks of speaking openly? Who benefits from my silence? Who benefits when I speak out?

CHAPTER 8

What Do Survivors Need?
To Make Ourselves Visible,
To Make Ourselves Heard

Girls and women have more difficulty

than boys and men in asserting their authority

or considering themselves as authorities.

–Mary Field Belenky et al.

If there is a single thing I have learned . . .

in the age of women's studies

it is the importance of remembering, retelling,

offering our own narratives

which so frequently run counter to official versions

of reality.

–Elizabeth Alexander

AS ILLUSTRATED IN THE PREVIOUS CHAPTER, Laura Randolph, a survivor of childhood sexual abuse, felt isolated in my classroom during a discussion of *A Thousand Acres,* a story of father-daughter incest. She noticed that other students became "highly uncomfortable during the discussion of incest," and she felt they "made every attempt to silence it," as if "to keep some horrible, hideous, devouring, fatal monster or plague out of the classroom." Now, as a result of these disclosures from Laura, I must reevaluate my pedagogy: was I right to remain silent? Or did I, in effect, abandon a young incest survivor? Did my own silence enforce the silence of other young women who, like Laura, have been sexually abused as children? Should I have made my connection to other survivors visible? As I have already explained, I have not overcome the powerful taboo against bringing personal (and emotional) issues into the classroom. I fear that, if I become emotional, I might lose my "professional" composure, my authority. For that reason, disclosing my personal history in the classroom remains far more difficult for me than writing about it.[38] However, because Laura plans to disclose her own history of abuse in the classroom in order, as she says, "to demonstrate support for survivors," I must reconsider my own silence. If I had spoken out, afterward inviting student survivors to voice their personal experiences, would such a pedagogy have been more effective? Would this approach–the sharing

191

of personal experiences–provide support for survivors, as well as better instruction for other students?

Initially, because I am committed to mentoring survivors of sexual violence, I decided that I must overcome my fears and "come out" in the classroom. However, after struggling with this difficult question for more than six months, I have concluded that it is not wise for a teacher, at least not for this teacher, to disclose father-daughter incest in the classroom. Out of concern that Laura might feel abandoned if I disagreed with her in such a public forum, I talked to her about it. She acknowledged that she had, intially, struggled with feelings of abandonment, but she had concluded that her personal feelings were less important than the larger good of our project: making child sexual abuse known to others. Hence, after carefully scrutinizing my position–was I simply afraid, I asked myself, or did I have valid reasons for silence?– I concluded that a teacher's self-disclosure on this topic would be likely to inhibit discussion. Because most students would not be prepared to discuss such a taboo topic, they would, like the teachers in middle school classrooms (see chapter 5), resort to a range of denial tactics; for example, they might either over-sympathize with the victimizer or over-identify with the victim. My point is that most students, like most teachers, have not been trained to listen in nonjudgmental ways to stories of father-daughter incest. For that reason, it is best to maintain the focus on the text, at least in a literature classroom. This focus on the text, rather than on personal stories, is valuable because it allows us, both teachers and students, to place emotion-laden topics at a distance where they can be more effectively analyzed. Personal confession, especially by a teacher, would inappropriately shift the focus of discussion from the text to the teacher. In short, English classrooms should not become therapy sessions.

For similar reasons, students should not assume that the literature classroom is a safe space in which to tell personal stories, especially such taboo stories as father-daughter incest. Even in women's studies classrooms, survivors cannot be certain that their teachers or peers have the training–for it is not simply a matter of listening with compassion–to hear their stories. Frances Maher and Mary Kay Tetreault illustrate my point in *The Feminist Classroom* when a feminist teacher dismisses the topic of father-daughter incest with the comment, "Thank you for sharing that" (120). Although the course is called "Women in Groups," and although only women are enrolled, the teacher, while making a supportive comment, does not effectively integrate her student's confession, "I was incested by my father while I was growing up and I never told anybody for, like, six years" (120), into her discussion of women and lying. One would think that such a context–a feminist classroom addressing the question, "Why do women lie?"–would be an ideal situation for a student to reveal the truth about childhood sexual abuse. In fact, the student goes on to explain that she has not told the truth about her personal life because, as she says, "I held a lot of shame" (120). Fortunately, according to Maher and Tetreault, the teacher had "created a supportive climate for these revelations" (121); therefore, two students at least make an effort to support the incest survivor. One student remarks that "most of the things that I lie about have affected me so hard personally that it's hard to share," and another says, "I am also an incest survivor and I appreciate you sharing that" (120). But such personal revelations would not be considered acceptable in most classrooms.

Another major problem, as Anneliese Kramer-Dahl reminds us, is that notions of "experience" and "voice," if "left untheorized," can be "highly problematic" (252). As Kramer-Dahl reports, in her classroom, where the emphasis was on multicultural texts and the experiences of minority students, "they 'one downed' each other on the oppression scale"; "minority students viewed themselves as the ones with superior 'insider-knowledge' of more 'authentically' experienced oppressions, relegating the white students to marginal observer-status, with no legitimate contributions of their own to offer" (253). I wonder: if I had encouraged personal disclosures from survivors of father-daughter incest, would they have similarly "one downed" each other on the abuse scale, while also claiming that their experience made them more expert—more authentic, more authoritative—interpreters of Jane Smiley's *A Thousand Acres?* I think this is a likely outcome. The problem, according to Kramer-Dahl, is that for students "experience is understood as a transparent window on reality, not, as poststructuralist work on language and subjectivity insists, the product of our insertion into particular practices and discourses" (252–53). For that reason, it is important to explain to students that personal experience alone cannot be a basis for their authority; students must understand, as Kramer-Dahl insists, how their discourse is inserted into "particular practices and discourses." For example, when analyzing father-daughter incest, students should be informed that, prior to the second wave of the women's movement, survivors of childhood father-daughter incest would not have been believed. Only when inserted into feminist practices and discourses did the daughter's confession become credible enough to challenge the pervasive Freudian view that daughters, or hysterics, lie.[39] Students also need to know that, while we may understand our experiences—including experiences of bodily violation, such as rape or torture—only through language, it does not follow, as some poststructuralists suggest, that such experiences exist only in language. As Herman explains in *Trauma and Recovery*, memories of traumatic experiences do not take linguistic form; they may be repressed, in which case the trauma may be expressed through bodily symptoms (hysteria). Indeed, as I explain in chapter 1, recovery takes place only when the trauma, along with accompanying affect, is translated into language, into narrative. Furthermore, although I agree that the survivor has a "higher stake in writing the incest narrative in a manner that challenges the archaic patriarchal world view," as Laura argues, I would add this qualification: that all survivors of sexual violence, not only survivors of father-daughter incest, have a high stake in challenging the patriarchal world view. Having experienced the long-term effects of violence, many survivors—at least those who acquire a feminist consciousness—become aware of the need to change a society that perpetuates violence against what is "foreign" or "weak." Some poststructuralists, charging that this is an "essentialist" argument, would dismiss it, but I hope that most feminists, including those who identify themselves as poststructuralists, would question this too-hasty dismissal of claims based on bodily experiences.

Because of the current efforts to discredit survivor discourse—some of which come from poststructuralists—Laura and I are in complete agreement on one point: that we must decide "on a daily basis," as Laura emphasizes, whether to speak out or remain silent about our personal experiences of childhood sexual abuse. Such caution is certainly justified in the current political climate, which Susan Faludi accurately describes as a period of backlash against feminist issues, both in the classroom and beyond. By the spring of 1994, resistance to incest stories had intensified dramatically, as evident in news reports. For example, on "Sixty Minutes" (17 April 1994), Morley Safer reported on a number of legal suits which were dropped by patients who later acknowledged that they were not remembering the experience, but responding to suggestions by their therapists. One month later, NBC (10 May 1994) reported that Gary Romana was suing the therapists who had assisted his daughter in remembering paternal sexual abuse. During the same month, *The New York Times Review of Books* (15 May 1994) published a front-page review called, "The Monster in the Mists," with the subtitle: "Are long-buried memories of child abuse reliable? Three new books tackle a difficult issue" (1). Only one of the books, Lenore Terr's *Unchained Memories: True Stories of Traumatic*

Memories, Lost and Found, argues, though not to the complete satisfaction of the reviewer, that repressed memories of childhood
trauma may turn out to be valid.

Janet Jacobs, a researcher in the field of child sexual abuse,
suggests that the public may be suffering in the 1990s from what
she calls "trauma overload." She explains, "As revelations of sexual criminal behavior are met with doubt and disbelief, strong
emotional reactions...are fueled by the sheer magnitude of the
problem" (x). The sheer magnitude of the problem became apparent in the spring of 1994. Within a single two-month period, the
same period in which "Sixty Minutes" and NBC presented news
reports on the topic, the daytime soap, "Days of Our Lives," ran
an incest story, while the April issue of *NEA Today,* published a column by an expert on sexual abuse. "Try not to communicate any
disbelief," Dr. Brian Abbott advised teachers, "because what's
most devastating to a child is disbelief or inaction" (13).[40] A special
program, "Break the Silence: Kids Against Child Abuse," Abbott
announced, would air on network television in May. But intense
public interest in the topic had already begun to create resistance.
For example, despite the fact that Holly Romana's father was
found guilty of incest, a different jury awarded him damages when
he sued his daughter's therapists for malpractice, charging them
with "implanting" memories of paternal sexual abuse in his daughter's mind. Even though Holly's therapists, along with her mother
and sisters, believed her, jurors felt that, because of the methods
the psychiatrist had used, they could not determine "beyond a reasonable doubt" whether Holly was remembering actual experiences of childhood sexual abuse or whether her therapists had
"implanted" them—in which case Holly was not reporting on
memories, but fantasizing abuse.

This method of discrediting the daughter's story has a familiar ring: almost one hundred years ago, Freud decided that his
female patients had fantasized episodes of paternal sexual abuse.

Are we about to enter another period of denial? According to Herman, the history of psychological investigations of trauma follows just such a pattern: a period of "active investigation" followed by a period of "oblivion" (*Trauma and Recovery* 7). "Though the field has in fact an abundant and rich tradition," she says, "it has been periodically forgotten and must be periodically reclaimed" (7). What is the reason for such "episodic amnesia" in the history of the study of trauma? Neither changes in fashion nor loss of interest can account for such a pattern, according to Herman; the answer is that traumatic events force bystanders to take sides. Herman explains that it costs the bystander very little to take the side of the victimizer, the perpetrator of incest; however, taking the side of the victim requires the bystander to become an active witness. If this demand, that bystanders "share the pain" (7), becomes too intense, the public may resist in a variety of ways, for example: by trivializing the topic; by calling for a return to "family values," often a strategy for propping up father rule; by promulgating theories which, as Alice Miller points out in *Thou Shalt Not Be Aware*, deny or obfuscate the problem; by attempting to silence those who employ personal disclosures of abuse in the classroom or in academic writing; by attempting to destroy the bonds among women.

How, given this resistance to survivor stories, is it possible for literature professors to continue to support young survivors? My answer to this question is pragmatic: we cannot expect literature teachers to become experts on the topic of father-daughter incest; however, now that many teachers have some knowledge of feminist criticism of the traditional canon, we can, as I explain below, build on this critique. Second, we must promote feminist theories of the family romance that not only challenge the Oedipal paradigm, but also provide frameworks for changing a family system that perpetuates violence. Third, we must demand that literature courses in the public school curriculum (grades 1 through 12) include narratives written by and about women: stories in which women, such as mothers and daughters, are central, as well as stories of father-daughter incest. Fourth, we must continue to critique the pedagogies we employ in our literature classrooms from grade school to graduate school, as well as the pedagogies employed by the media, the courts, the church, and the healing professions. The discourses of these institutions—by mirroring the gender imbalance in my home and by their silence about incest—taught me that my sister was to blame for what my father did to her. Millions of other survivors, including my younger sisters, have been similarly scapegoated—forced to bear the shame and suffering that belongs, rightfully, to adults who perpetuate an unjust status quo. Finally, women and girls must continue to make visible their strong bonds in order to assure that survivors are heard.

My first argument is that the traditional canon, which promotes father-daughter incest through its model of heterosexual relations, must be challenged in middle school and high school classrooms. As explained in previous chapters, and as feminists have been arguing for some time, the traditional canon perpetuates a violent and incestuous model of masculinity. Teachers should also inform students that there are racial differences in depictions of father-daughter incest.[41] As Janet Jacobs explains, experiences of abuse differ in some ways for women of different races, primarily because "racial stereotyping within the dominant culture frequently leads to minimizing the importance of victimization among women of color" (6). There are also differences in the severity of the trauma: only a therapist can help some victims, such as those who suffer from multiple personality disorders; however, some survivors may appear to be functioning well in the classroom (as I once did) when, in fact, their imaginations and intelligence may have been severely constricted by the trauma of abuse. Literature teachers should at least be aware that students suffering from self-doubt or shame—those who tend to be quieter, those who use "feminine" speech and apologize for work which turns out to be quite good—may be survivors of sexual violence, including incest.

To some extent, most women suffer from the effects of this "pedagogy of shame," as Sandra Bartky calls it. Women, she argues, are "formed within an interlocking grid of social ensembles—school, family, church, workplace, media—that teach us to serve and to please" (225). However, as long as the trauma remains a secret, the burden of shame is usually more severe for victims of sexual abuse. This burden, along with the inability to trust authority figures, interferes with a survivor's ability to learn. Ronnie Janoff-Bulman explains why this is so. After investigating the effects of different kinds of trauma, both unintentional (such as floods or fires) or intentional (traumas involving perpetrators), Janoff-Bulman concluded that "the most extreme, devastating effects of negative life events on children are likely to be those that involve victimization by the very people who are looked to for protection and safety. . . . In the most severe instances, the child has no one to turn to for care and protection" (86). Nevertheless, while acknowledging that my argument derives in part from an intense need for affiliation, I believe it is important to recognize that father-daughter incest differs only in degree from other forms of sexual violence. As I have explained, one long-lasting consequence of childhood sexual abuse is the pain of emotional exile from the human community, especially from other women. Had I failed to acknowledge my own traumatic past—identifying only my more severely abused sisters as survivors—I would not have been able to transform my constricted survivor self, the voice that told me to "freeze" when I tried to speak or write, into my ideal author-self.

But is it possible to find a framework—a psychosocial theory—that will allow for differences in experiences while, at the same time, enabling survivors to identify their commonalties? For an answer to this question, I turn to psychologist Ellyn Kaschak. She says that because "the changes instigated by the women's movement of the 1970s have failed to alter the Oedipus-Antigone relationship, whereby one [gender] subsumes the other, the generation of women currently coming of age is not really being offered qualitatively new roles" (163). Even feminist psychologists such as Nancy Chodorow, who emphasizes the importance of the pre-oedipal phase for daughters, Kaschak argues, continue to employ an oedipal model which not only silences the mother, but leaves intact a theory requiring daughters *to see themselves through paternal eyes.* If we are to move beyond an oedipal psychology, Kaschak asserts, we must take into account the perspectives of both mothers and daughters,[42] points of view missing or subsumed in Freud's conception of the Oedipus complex. To demonstrate this point, Kaschak explains that Freud's interpretation of Sophocles' trilogy focused on a single play, "Oedipus Rex," while ignoring two plays in which daughters play important roles. In the pivotal play, "Antigone" (the play written first but performed last), the daughter's part is central, while in the second play, "Oedipus at Colonus," Antigone and her sister, Ismene, serve as eyes for their blind father.

Freud's theory not only ignores the daughter's part, as Kaschak points out, it also ignores the fact that in two plays in the trilogy, Oedipus is a father, not a son. In short, "The father of psychology all but ignored the psychology of fathers" (Kaschak 60), and because of this significant blind spot, the father's sexual desire for his daughter has been denied by psychoanalysts for almost a century. Now that feminists have "conclusively established and documented the prevalence of molestation by fathers and other adult male relatives" (59), Kaschak emphasizes, a new model of female development must be formulated. She proposes a feminist model, named "Antigone," in which daughters refuse to see with paternal eyes. Rather than viewing herself through the eyes of a father or the eyes of an indeterminate male, the daughter must reintegrate aspects of the self which have been fragmented by the male gaze. To do so, she must overthrow the patriarchal injunction, "Away from the mother." This injunction, as Joyce Carol Oates points out in an analysis of *King Lear*, is dangerous not only for daughters, but for society as a whole: "The patriarch's unspoken imperative, *Away from the unconscious, away from the mother*, is dangerous precisely because it is unspoken, unarticulated, kept below the threshold of consciousness itself" ("Is This the Promised End?" 75). However, if the father insists on being the major character in his daughter's life story, often at the exact psychological moment she wishes to make him a minor character, how is she to resolve this developmental dilemma?

In short, how can Antigone say no to her father's demands, while meeting her own needs for love and connection? That is, how can a girl create a mature self without being labeled "selfish"? For incested daughters, most of whom have been molested while in elementary school, this problem is especially severe. As Jacobs explains, the father's incestuous demands are internalized by the child, distorting her development. Teachers should watch for behaviors such as shame, shyness, chronic fatigue, and a lack of boundaries. Elementary teachers must, of course, report suspected cases of child abuse, and they should also support efforts to teach children that they have the right to say no to sexual touching by adults, including their own parents.[43] But what Kaschak calls the "Antigone" crisis usually occurs between the ages of ten and thirteen, just as girls enter puberty. Unfortunately, as documented by Carol Gilligan, Lyn Mikel Brown, Peggy Orenstein, and others,[44] it is just at this moment that girls are usually strikingly absent from most school curricula. At the same time, their presence increases in advertisements which teach them "denial of self and feeding of others" (Bordo 131). The crisis does, however, differ for girls of different classes and races, as Jill Taylor et al. illustrates in *Voice into*

Silence. For example, working-class girls, black or white, do not feel "the pressure to meet idealized images of femininity" as do girls from more privileged classes (42). Raised to be strong and resilient as well as nurturant, working-class girls are less concerned about hurting people's feelings and more capable of fighting back, verbally and physically. Nevertheless, Kashack's argument–that girls will achieve more fully integrated identities through visible affiliation with women–appears to hold true for all girls, regardless of race or class.

This brings me to my third point: that literature teachers in our public schools must provide students with opportunities, not only to read and discuss father-daughter incest narratives, but also to read and discuss narratives in which female relationships are central. Unfortunately, the literature curricula of most high schools have changed very little during the past thirty years, a lack of change that holds true across the nation, according to Arthur Applebee's *Literature in the Secondary School* (1993). As I know from my own observations of high school English classrooms in North Dakota, Minnesota, and Iowa during the late 1980s and early 1990s,[45] changes in the literature canon have not reached our public schools despite the availability of works such as Liz Whaley and Liz Dodge's *Weaving in the Women* (1993) which argue for the inclusion of women's writing in junior high and high school literature curricula. If we listen to the testimony of feminist literary critics, women learn to plot their lives–they become authors of their lives–by reading novels and autobiographies by and about women. Nevertheless, traditional language arts curricula continue to deny young women opportunities to imagine, discuss, and analyze their narrative options. As Joanne Frye points out, traditional plots are inequitable: "The paradigmatic plots based in the qualities of strength, autonomy, and aspiration seem reserved for male protagonists; the paradigmatic plots based specifically in female experience seem to confine women in domesticity and apparent passivity" (1). To counter the gender constraints of traditional plots, we must do more than simply add women's writing to the curriculum; we must choose at least some narratives that actively and explicitly revision old plots. By comparing plots and counterplots, students of both genders will learn a wider range of narrative options.

Unfortunately, most young women see no connection between their middle school or high school English classes and their own lives. For example, the eleventh-grade girls I interviewed at Minot High School in 1993 saw no relationship between their lives—past, present, or future—and the readings assigned in their English classes. Although every girl planned to have both a career and a family, not one could recall having read a story in which a woman resolves this common conflict.[46] Unfortunately, as Kim Chernin argues, we have raised the expectations of girls without, at the same time, providing the support which will enable them to fulfill their dreams. According to Chernin, daughters face a dilemma which society as a whole has not resolved: how is the daughter "to become the mother without taking on her sacrifice?" (200). As Belenky, Gilligan, Orenstein, and others have documented, the absence of women from the curriculum has a very negative effect upon young women who are struggling to resolve such major developmental dilemmas. Yet the relationship problems that young women confront are important to all of us. As Gilligan points out, "The problem girls face is also a problem in the world at this time: the need to find ways of making connection in the face of difference" (*Making Connections* 10). Girls often acquire such knowledge—the knowledge of how to find and maintain social relations—during adolescent experimentation.

For example, as depicted in Margaret Atwood's *Cat's Eye*, at about the age of eleven or twelve, girls often encounter painful problems of inclusion/exclusion. In an essay called "Women as Image-Makers," I argue that Atwood's *kunstlerromane*, narrated by a woman attending a retrospective exhibit of her paintings, might be taught to high school students along with works by such visual artists as Claude Breeze, Helen Lundeberg, Fred Marcellino, and Joyce Wieland. As I explain below, since girls often lose their voices just at the moment they become objects of the male gaze, it is important to challenge the ways in which they are silenced by their increasing visibility in male-created art or in the mass media. Once objectified in this way, girls begin to "forget" their struggles to maintain relationships with other girls. Such knowledge is easy for girls to forget since it is not represented in the curriculum. As a result, girls often pretend—as I once did—not to know what they know. As Carol Gilligan observes, girls frequently begin their observations with the phrase, "I don't know" (*Making Connections* 14). To affirm the value of what young women know about themselves and their relationships, teachers of literature should actively encourage students to engage in feminist critiques of the verbal and visual arts. In this way, English teachers can effectively assist girls to remain confident and audible about their experiences, rather than undermining their perceptions. Pedagogies that invite students to critique depictions of women should also prompt more students to reflect upon their own experiences.

This brings me to my fourth point: we must not only make women visible in the literature curriculum, but revise some of our classroom practices to increase the self-confidence of girls. Although I do not advocate the sharing of personal experiences during classroom discussions, teachers can provide students with opportunities to write about such experiences. Autobiographical assignments should, however, always be optional, and teachers should identify the audience in advance, specifying whether a student's personal narrative will be read only by the teacher, by peers, or by both. Such information will enable most victims to decide whether it is safe to reveal the secret of sexual trauma. For example, a victim may decide to disclose an experience of sexual abuse in a journal she expects will be read only by a teacher, especially if she perceives her teacher to be sympathetic and nonjudgmental. Teachers should always follow up on such self-disclosures, never challenging the veracity of the story, but calmly offering nonjudgmental support. If a victim has not yet received therapeutic help, the teacher should also recommend a feminist therapist. Another reason that I prefer written over oral disclosures is that, while free of immediate concern for all students, teachers have more time to reflect on how to help. In general, teachers can support young women by striving to become more attentive listeners and by scrutinizing their own attitudes and classroom practices. Most of us must become more aware of how our pedagogies are gendered and, therefore, often inequitable.

While many of us have become aware that teachers—male and female—tend to call on boys more often than girls, tend to ask boys more complex questions and wait longer for them to answer, we may not be aware, as Brown and Gilligan demonstrate in *Meeting at the Crossroads,* that white middle-class women sometimes teach girls to avoid open conflict. This problem is not as severe for working-class girls, according to Taylor et al.; nonetheless, working-class girls also move from "voice" into "silence" during their middle school years, partly because they are absent in the curriculum, but also because of their increasing isolation from other women and girls. According to different studies by Brown et al. and Taylor et al., a major problem for many girls at this age, regardless of class or race, is that few adults listen to them. To further complicate matters, Gilligan points out, "As girls themselves say clearly, they will speak only when they feel that someone will listen and will not leave in the fact of conflict or disagreement. Thus the fate of girls' knowledge and girls' education becomes tied to the fate of their relationships" ("Teaching Shakespeare's Sister" 24). However, many girls feel isolated at this age and, as a consequence, they become vulnerable, as I was, to society's belief in a sacrificial morality for women:

the belief that women should give up their own dreams in order to maintain relationships, even destructive relationships.

As a result of societal pedagogies—such as advertising images which teach young women to shrink their bodies, appetites, and desires if they wish to be considered desirable—young women must struggle to maintain egalitarian connections. Tragically, however, they are often forced to maintain connections by sacrificing their own identities. For example, Gilligan found in many young women

> a willingness often to sacrifice oneself for others in the hope that if one cared for others one would be loved and cared for by them: the central problem—feeling abandoned by others or feeling one should abandon oneself for others—was a problem of disconnection, and often led to desperate actions, desperate efforts at connection, which was one way in which some women spoke about their pregnancies. With their bodies women can create connection by having a child who will be with them and love them. (*Making Connections* 8–9)

However, rather than listening to girls, rather than trying to understand the reasons for teenage pregnancy, our society is currently making scapegoats of these young women. Instead, both male and female students should be given opportunities to read narratives which offer alternatives to female self-sacrifice. Many contemporary novels offer such alternatives; see, for example, novels by Dorothy Allison, Margaret Atwood, Angela Carter, Sandra Cisneros, Margaret Drabble, Louise Erdrich, Marilyn French, Jamaica Kincaid, Doris Lessing, Sue Miller, Toni Morrison, Gloria Naylor, Joyce Carol Oates, Grace Paley, Jane Smiley, Faye Weldon, and many others.

Another pedagogical problem that educators have only begun to address is the disabling effects of sexual harassment—by both male teachers and students—on young women.[47] Sexual harassment, whether verbal or physical, is a method of intimidation, a method of teaching young women to be silent and invisible. To illustrate my point, I want to tell a story of verbal harassment at a local middle school, a story which ended, not with the victimization of young women, but with their triumph—that is: they dared to become both visible and audible. When told by local feminists, this story is usually called the "hooters/cocks" debate, despite the fact that when it was reported in our local and state newspapers the term *cocks* was usually replaced by the term *rooster*. Two girls, Erin Rollenhagen and Sarah Hegland, both eighth graders at Ames Middle School at the time of the conflict in April of 1994, are the heroes of this feminist story. It began when these brave young women, both raised by feminist mothers,[48] decided to protest against the sexist T-shirts being worn to school by some eighth-grade boys. The front sides of these shirts, advertising the new Hooters restaurant which had recently opened in Des Moines, Iowa (just thirty-five miles from Ames), pictured an owl, placed near the double-Os (implying breasts) in the word *Hooters*. On the back of the shirts was the sexually suggestive slogan, "More than a mouthful."

Since authorities at Ames Middle School did not voice any objections to the Hooters T-shirts, Erin and Sarah launched an imaginative protest, with the full knowledge and support of their parents. They designed T-shirts which, on the front, portrayed a rooster's head, its beak penetrating the "C" in the word *Cocks*, and on the back, the slogan, "Nothin' to crow about!" The principal at Ames Middle School, John Kinley, responded by telling the twelve girls who wore the shirts that they must either turn their shirts inside-out or face suspension. Having anticipated this response, Erin and Sarah agreed to the principal's demands, on condition that he would sponsor a forum on sexual harassment and first amendment rights of students. The *Des Moines Register* began its story: "Ames Middle School students will discuss freedom of speech and sexual harassment next week after four students were sent home on Tuesday wearing homemade T-shirts satirizing popular 'Hooters' shirts" (22 April 1994: 1M). Assistant superintendent Ralph Farrar was quoted in the story as explaining that "school policy forbids students from wearing anything that is disruptive or that makes it difficult for students to learn. A sexual harassment policy also forbids anything that is sexually demeaning" (1M).

What the superintendent did not say was that prior to the publicity resulting from the "Cocks" protest school officials had not objected to the Hooters T-shirts, which certainly constituted sexual harassment since it would interfere with the concentration of girls. Through their tolerance of the Hooters shirts, school officials supported the sexism of young men while abandoning young women. As I learned during my interview with Erin and Sarah, they had carefully and intelligently planned their protest: they had decided, for example, that their goal was not to interfere with young men's freedom of speech but to make the point that their language, which objectified the female body, was offensive; they had also decided that if the principal demanded it, they would not defy him but rather obediently turn their Cocks shirts inside-out— on condition that the school sponsor a forum on the topic. The principal accepted this condition. According to Sarah and Erin, their experience in "Mock Trials" helped them succeed in this negotiation: because of their understanding of due process, they "went by the rules," they said, contacting the right people and "talking rather than throwing stones." They also acknowledged that their background in "Mock Trials" made them comfortable with open conflict. It gave them confidence, they said, when their team defeated a team that was "90 percent male." "Conflict is good," Sarah said, "it teaches you to think more." Erin agreed, commenting that "conflict draws you out of your ideologies."

The outcome of their intelligent and witty protest was a

highly publicized and well-attended forum which took place on
April 26, 1994. Most of the middle school students attended the
forum, not out of concern about sexual harassment, according to
Erin and Sarah, but because of an interest in their right to free
speech. Arranged by the principal, the forum spent most of its
time addressing first amendent rights rather than sexual harassment; only one adult member of the forum, Professor Jane Vallier,
who teaches a course in gender and language at Iowa State, shifted
the focus of the debate to the issue of sexual harassment. Yet, as
the President of the American Civil Liberties Union pointed out in
an excellent opening speech, it is usually a hotly contested topic–
as, for example, the Vietnam War–which generates controversy
over first amendment rights. Since I attended this forum, I had the
good fortune to see just how effectively–even eloquently–Erin
and Sarah debated the issues of free speech and sexual harassment. How I wished, as I sat listening to them, that I had been
encouraged to participate in public debate and had been supported in my efforts to resist verbal harassment by young men.
"Are some guys put off," I asked, "by your intelligence?" Erin
answered that "most guys are behind us by two years, but they'll
catch up when they're twenty." Although I did not ask them to
explain why males are so far behind, they suggested that pedagogies–beyond family and school–have an effect. "Pretty Woman"
was a good movie, Sarah said, but she "hated it." She explained,
"People like it when the male hero rescues the girl, but it's not so
exciting when the girl rescues the guy." Such attitudes, they
agreed, "are hard on smart girls," but the guys in their group
accept their intelligence. "There are guys," they said, "but not
enough of them."

After the panel presentation, when the audience was invited
to take the microphone, one young woman–a supporter of Erin
and Sarah's–complained about a teacher who had tried to discourage her from speaking out with the comment, "I hope you're

not involved in this conflict." Professor Vallier responded that this teacher had no right to interfere in the young woman's participation in public debate. Sarah and Erin said the teacher probably thought Ma Ling should "sit by and look pretty, and not say anything." Ma Ling is "smart and female," they agreed, and so she is being told "not just to 'shut up and look pretty,' but to 'shut up and look sexy.'" Why? Because "guys want girls to be dependent," they said. Had they, I asked, studied issues of gender and language in their English classes? They had not. Had they studied any women writers? No, they said. In fact, their English teacher announced–after the prefatory comment, "I don't mean to offend anyone"–that he hadn't found any good women writers. He probably hadn't studied any women writers in college, they agreed. Their history teacher was better on gender issues, they said. Ironically, these young women had been forced to educate school authorities on the issue of sexual harassment. Even though the principal doesn't yet "fully understand the issues," Erin said, "once he gets over being mad, he'll think about it." She had probably shocked Mr. Kinley, Erin said, because before the debate she had been "good and invisible."

The "hooters/cocks" debate may seem far removed from the issue of father-daughter incest; however, whether the abuse is physical or verbal, both are attempts to silence women by objectifying their bodies. To varying degrees, then, all women share this problem. Therefore, to make my fifth and final point: women and girls must refuse to remain "good and invisible," but must continue to make themselves visible–in a manner that assures they will be heard. I begin with the example of Emma Goldman who, when she courageously spoke against conscription for World War I, was harassed by crowds who yelled, "Strip her naked" (Chernin 32, quoted in Kaschak 85). Kaschak asks, "Would a man be threatened this way by a crowd of women? How does this come to be a way both to humiliate and silence a strong and visible woman?" and she answers: "It reminds her of her place: a woman's body" (85). The crowd attempted to silence Goldman's intelligent public voice by reminding her of her place—as a muted body—in a patriarchal society. Goldman spoke alone; however, Erin and Sarah enlisted the help of other girls, and this gave strength to their protest. Such a use of collective feminist strength is also evident in the petition signed by 166 survivors of child-hood sexual abuse published in *Ms.* magazine in 1987. Describing themselves as "among the one in five females who have been sex-ually abused before we reached the age of 13," they demanded "that teachers and health workers, lawmakers and law enforcers, family members and friends—all those who love children and are entrusted with their care—encourage past survivors and present victims to speak out to create realistic and compassionate protec-tion for children" (*Ms.* 88). Although I do not consider the class-room the best public place for self-disclosures, I hope that, in other public forums, I am helping "to create realistic and compas-sionate protection" for survivors by making visible my connec-tions to them.[49]

It often takes great courage to risk visibility. A survivor of childhood sexual abuse, a graduate student at Iowa State in 1994, illustrates my point. For years, without knowing why, this young woman had tried to remain invisible.[50] With the return of repressed memories, she finally learned why: the perpetrator, a man who had molested her when she was only four or five years old, had promised to find her wherever she went. With the help of a therapist, she recalled that the abuse had taken place dur-ing her family's brief stay in the perpetrator's home. She some-times managed to outwit the perpetrator by hiding, but finally he had broken into the bathroom, a hiding place, and, in a rage at her resistance, had thrown her against a wall, knocking her out. At this point her father discovered the abuse and removed her from danger; unfortunately, he also cautioned her not to tell her mother, who was suffering from severe mental illness. As a result, the young woman repressed all memory of the abuse until, during a state of hyperarousal triggered by the stress of an upcoming exam, she saw the perpetrator's shadow silhouetted in her doorway. Finally, she understood her intense desire for invisibility. Unfortunately, unaware that she was hiding from the perpetrator, she had for many years severely constricted her life choices: she had, for example, stayed "safely" at home while attending a large university where she could remain anonymous and invisible.

Many women share, to some degree, this survivor's desire for invisibility. For example, when Susan Faludi's publicist asked her, "Isn't it wonderful that so many people want to hear what you have to say about women's rights?" Faludi answered, "About as wonderful as walking down the street with no clothes on" ("Speak for Yourself" 10). Some might find it surprising that Faludi, the well-known author of *Backlash*, would fear public speaking; however, she explains that "like many female writers with strong convictions but weak stomachs for confrontation, I write so forcefully because I speak so tentatively. One form of self-expression has overcompensated for the weakness of the other, like a blind person who develops a hypersensitive ear" ("Speak for Yourself" 10). Faludi's shift from the visual, "walking down the street with no clothes on," to the auditory, "like a blind person who develops a hypersensitive ear," makes my point: the danger of public speaking is that visibility makes one vulnerable, threatening the loss of the writer's authorial ear and voice. Once again: objectifying women, making spectacles of them, is a strategy for denying them public voices, for taking away their authority. Of course, Faludi is a professional writer who has greater authority than an unknown survivor of childhood sexual abuse who, invited to appear on a talk show, may be treated as a victim who lacks expertise on the long-term effects of the trauma.

Nevertheless, Faludi's anxieties about public speaking–about having no clothes on–should be located on a continuum with other women who resist the power of the male gaze in order to speak out in public. For example, when my older sister was asked to speak on the topic of chemical dependency and childhood sexual abuse to an audience of health-care professionals, she began with these words: "My name is Una Fay, and I speak to you tonight as an incest survivor and as a professional in the drug and alcohol addiction field. As the survivor of sexual abuse, I find it scary to stand before you tonight and tell my story. I feel naked in front of you, as vulnerable as a child. But I also have a healthy adult operating in me and have chosen to read to you from my writing since it feels safer" (1). Before presenting this public address, my sister called me, and I fully supported her decision to risk self-disclosure but, following the advice of Alcoff and Gray, I recommended that she maintain a professional persona and voice. In other words, I encouraged her to take her clothes off in public in order, paradoxically, to assert her authority as a professional health-care worker: "Make nakedness powerful by immediately putting on your professional clothes," I suggested.

Other feminists–including those who, like Faludi, are professional writers–also use the image of nakedness, or exposure, to express anxiety, not about public speaking but about writing personal narratives. In "Reticence and Resistance: A Conversation," Shirley Geok-lin Lim (SGL), Valerie Miner (VM), and Judith Barrington (JB) discuss the risks, for themselves and their families, of writing memoirs.

VM: I could never have written this book before my mother died, because I'm telling so many things that she would consider absolutely horrible. In telling about my grandmother's abortion, about my mother working in a dance hall when she was twelve, I think that I have a kind of a political commitment, and I certainly think that they're part of a wonderfully rich human story that's filled with emotion, and so I'm not going to not tell them. But in a way I do feel it's a form of betrayal to tell them. [Here the notion of betrayal, or exposure, is applied to one's personal relationships, one's family. While I understand Miner's reluctance to speak out about members of her family, I agree with her political commitment: our violent society will not change unless women speak out, despite the risks.]

JB: I'm struck by how much discomfort all three of us express with the taking on of the memoir. And the word Valerie used—betrayal—the sense of betrayal, I think is constantly there, whether people are alive or dead. I often wonder if there are gender-specific aspects to these feelings. Do we as women struggle with this aspect of the memoir, the need to be loyal to family members and to protect people from the consequences of our telling our truths? [Incest victims certainly struggle with this issue: Do I save myself and other victims, or do I protect my family? It is possible that I chose to write autobiographical criticism, rather than a memoir, primarily because my family is less likely to read a genre employed primarily by academics.]

SGL: It's important for women to start being brave about having a public voice. In having a public voice, you're setting yourself up for people to throw things at you, accuse you, to be seen as a traitor. The words expose and exposure have a sense of shamefulness—not only in the sense of being naked but of stripping yourself naked. Lots of women have refused that, and I don't blame them. [Again, the word naked is used to suggest feelings of exposure and shame. Women have been taught to feel shame when, in fact, their oppressors should feel it.]

JB: Yet I know that as a reader I can look at a woman who is not afraid to say "I" and put herself center stage, and it can be the most empowering and inspiring thing to read—though it can also be the most embarrassing and horrible thing to read. [Yes, as I know from writing Authoring a Life, *placing the "I" at center stage is both empowering and embarrassing.]*

SGL: But women have to begin to take that risk, and I think the memoir is one way. The honest memoir, the one that the writer really struggles with, is the one place where women are doing it.

Memoir is not the only genre in which women are taking such risks. I prefer mixed-genre writing, as I have practiced it in *Authoring a Life*. As I explain in "I Stand Here Naked, or Best Dressed in Theory: On Feminist Refashionings of Academic Discourse," I find it difficult to make personal revelations, to stand "naked" in a public forum, unless, at the same time, I quickly clothe myself in theory. However, when I submitted "I Stand Here Naked" to an academic journal, some readers objected to my use of metaphors: naked/dressed. One reader, who noticed that "autobiography is positioned against theory in the metaphor that gets played with in the title," while the essay itself argued that "autobiography, for this writer, is the synthesis of the personal and the theoretical," did not recognize that the intent of my essay was to undo the binary opposition of the title. Apparently, my title was misleading since another reader, voicing a similar objection, said that "the trope that guides the discussion seems unexamined." When yet another reader complained, "the essay relies on a fairly reductive binary between 'autobiography'/'theory,' 'clothed'/'unclothed,' 'unsafe'/'safe' without challenging or complicating that rather tired and monological distinction," I realized that readers did not understand my essay as a delibrate effort to challenge the binary opposition of my title, naked/dressed.

My point was that, as an academic writer, I have the right to take my clothes off and put them back on—like a feminist strip-tease artist—while, at the same time, resisting objectification. Based on these mostly "friendly" criticisms, I recognize that my title should probably have been revised as follows: "I Stand Here Naked, *and* Best Dressed in Theory." The impossibility of this stance, in a material sense, would serve to emphasize its linguistic or imaginative necessity. However, the criticism of yet another reader, who argued that "the title [is] too coy or flippant for its subject," indicated that I would have to explain why this metaphor—and not some other—is a suitable one for this mixed-genre form of writing which includes both personal revelations and theoretical analysis. Here is my argument: the voices of women are not heard as authoritative—and they find it much more difficult to speak with authority, especially in public—precisely *because they are seen* through the male gaze. Being seen, or made a spectacle of, actually makes a woman "invisible"— that is, invisible as a human being—and this invisibility takes away a woman's voice. Childhood sexual abuse is one of the most dramatic examples of this method of silencing women: At the very moment my father transformed my sisters into objects, he took away their voices by turning a deaf ear to their cries. This point, while not original, bears repeating.

Rather than attempting to be "flippant," "coy," or "original," I am using the metaphors, naked/dressed, in an effort to make visible my bonds with other women—a bond I acknowledge in my writing but not (as yet) in the classroom. As I have illustrated, many women employ the metaphor of nakedness to describe their anxieties about public speaking or the writing of memoirs; I suggest, therefore, that this metaphor is one way that women writers announce their membership in a gendered-speech community. As Ted Cohen explains, "A figurative use [of language] can be inaccessible to all but those who share information about one another's knowledge, beliefs, intentions, attitudes" (7). To fully understand your metaphor, the reader must be a member of your community in order to "penetrate your remark, so to speak, in order to explore you yourself, in order to grasp the import" (Cohen 7). I rejoice in such communal metaphors. I happily acknowledge that my use of the phrase naked/ dressed is not original; instead, this metaphor celebrates a communal model of authorship: I speak and write with authority only when I imagine my voice/body not as a solo but as part of a feminist choir, a chorus of strip-tease artists. I imagine us singing, shaking up an astonished crowd, as, rhythmically, collectively, we take off our robes and put them on again: naked/dressed, naked/dressed, naked/dressed. In this way, we proclaim the sacredness of women's bodies, women's voices.[51]

Afterword

In the summer of 1996, on the day I finished the first draft of *Authoring a Life,* I was cleaning up my files when I discovered a poem I had written in 1976, shortly after my father's death. I was not aware that I had promised, twenty years before, to tell my story, nor was I aware that I had decided on a title. Memory works in strange ways. Why did I wait so long to tell this story? The answer is that I waited until I had achieved some degree of professional authority through my membership in a professional community. Significantly, however, it was at the time of my father's death that I resolved to begin the struggle to "author" my life. I am not alone in waiting for the perpetrator's death before revealing his crimes. Other survivors of childhood sexual abuse have told me that they been unable to tell their stories or, in some instances, even remember their traumas, until the death of their violators. It appears, then, that my father's early death–a death brought about, I am certain, by his terrible guilt–gave me a second chance at life at the age of thirty-five. At my father's funeral, I wrote in the guest register, "I am my father's daughter." I wrote this poem a few days later.

I AM MY FATHER'S DAUGHTER

As my father lay dying,
A man I thought I hated
I discovered in his suffering body,
What love is.

He told me what he'd given my
brothers and sisters,

And said he'd given me nothing.
But in the telling I heard his
Trust in me.

He left me a legacy: a story to tell.
And so I will become a story teller.
My father authored me. I am now
authorized to become, at last,
author of my own life.

Even though I hate what he did to my sisters, I loved my father. I love my mother too: she did the best she could—she kept us fed and clothed under extremely difficult circumstances—often with creativity, resiliance, and even humor. *Authoring a Life* was written, not out of hatred, but out of love: in support of all those who continue to struggle, through language and action, to overcome the damaging effects of father-daughter incest. At present, in 1997, I feel that I have won this struggle. I am no longer paralyzed with fear when I speak in public, and I no longer find writing a physically painful activity. In fact, I have come to enjoy both writing and, though to a lesser degree, speaking in public. What a distance I have traveled since the National Women's Studies Association in 1986 when I gave a panel presentation, along with two of my sisters, on father-daughter incest! We called our presentation, "Three Sisters." Because I could not have spoken out in public about our family secret without their courageous support, I think of my sisters as among my collaborators in *Authoring a Life*. For that reason, I want to give each of them an opportunity to speak for themselves. "How," I asked, "do you help young survivors in your professional lives?" My older sister, Una Fay Rystedt, a chemical dependency counsellor, will respond to this question first, followed by our younger sister, Che Che Luckini, a special education teacher.

220

Una Fay: I realize that as a child, a young girl, and even as an adult in my thirties, I had little idea of my basic human rights, particularly my right to be heard. I found my voice in writing when I went back to undergraduate study in my forties. I now understand that because of the alcoholism, incest, and other dysfunctions within my family of origin, I did not trust my feelings, did not trust others, and lived with the unspoken rule: Don't talk. In my professional role as an addiction counsellor, I claim my right to be heard and to mentor other women who survive incest and their own chemical dependence. I affirm them by listening with empathy to their stories. I believe their stories. I assure them they did not deserve to be sexually violated and that they are not to blame; it isn't their fault. I teach them their basic human rights through lectures, group therapy, and individual therapy.

I offer skills-building classes to help them develop awareness of the need to communicate more effectively, and give them the tools to set boundaries assertively. I teach them about feelings—to own them—and about behaviors they may engage in to avoid or suppress painful feelings. I also seek out reputable therapists to refer these women to when they complete chemical dependency treatment. I find the personal support I need in Twelve-Step self-help groups, and I also offer sponsorship to those seeking recovery from chemical dependency and sexual abuse. I teach them by modeling healthy behaviors in both my professional and personal life. In all these ways, I know I make a difference in my life and in the lives of others.

Che Che: In preparing my response to your question, "How, through your work, do you help young survivors?," I've thought a lot about the many children who have come into my classroom. In twenty-seven years of teaching those who have learning disabilities, I've known that they, too, have gone through their own personal traumas. For those dealing with various forms of abuse, my first goal, when getting acquainted, was to respect their grief. Since most were unable to freely discuss their lives, we focused on how we would change our treatment of each other in our lives. We talked about choices. *But most of all, I* trusted *them to have the courage to face reality. Privately, and then in small groups, we practiced scripts of positive state-*

ments, or, as my students sometimes translate, how to "deal with bossy people who don't respect us."

As I traced back to the times before I began teaching, I realized I needed to know how this attitude developed. Was it my idea or was the seed planted by someone else? All of a sudden I knew my statement in the Afterword wasn't so much how I've touched others as rain nourishes the plant, but how my rascal of a sister, dear Brenda, had been fiercely supportive of my potential. I recall, when in my junior year in high school, she came home for a brief visit and asked about my choice of colleges. She was angry that not one person in my life had encouraged me to consider higher education—not even me! Her fury worked for good: she forced my dad to fill out financial aide forms despite his paranoia that the IRS would use this information against him. For all she's done for me then, and since, I will always love her!

Brenda: I'm so glad to know, Che Che, that I provided a small measure of support as you struggled to leave home. To "author a life," as your story and Una Fay's demonstrate, means to assume responsibility for directing the course of one's life—personally, professionally, politically. In Getting Personal *Nancy K. Miller defines the term more narrowly, as giving yourself permission to write. However, giving one's self permission to write does not automatically confer authority, especially if you are a woman. Historically, as any number of feminists have argued, the act of authorship itself has been defined as masculine. Yet, for me, as for most feminists, an author is someone, male or female, with authority, someone who expects to be heard, not simply because she is speaking about her experience, but because she has reflected on it. Her "objectivity" has been achieved, not by ignoring her emotions, but by analyzing them.*

But, finally, an author is someone who has the authority to speak because of the existence of "authorizing" communities of which she is a member—in particular, the feminist community, but also professional communities. By valuing a survivor's story, even to the point of publishing it, these communities invest her point of view with some measure of authority.

An author, then, is someone who expects her words to be read or heard. She does not assume that others will always agree with her, but she hopes that her words have the power, the authority, to affect the minds of readers, especially those actively engaged in in the struggle to author their own lives.

NOTES

1. By now it is well known that Freud at first believed his patients, both female and male, who told him they had been sexually abused as children. A number of critics have since speculated about why Freud changed his mind. See, for example, Julia Kristeva's *Desire in Language*, Geoffrey Masson's *Assault on Truth*, and Alice Miller's *Thou Shalt Not Be Aware*.

2. Once, I recall, my father did go for help, or so I inferred (and my sister has since confirmed my inference). While I waited in a room outside a priest's study (I was nine or ten years old), entertaining myself by looking at a nativity set carved in wood, my father took my older sister inside to talk to the priest. The priest may have assumed, since my father had confessed his sin, that he would never sexually abuse my sister again. The priest was wrong, tragically wrong. My father, who was a Lutheran, not a Catholic, probably wanted the confidentiality of the Catholic confessional, but he may also have wanted someone to stop him. He didn't find that help.

3. However, a number of recent novels have portrayed the mother's part with some degree of sympathy: Dorothy Allison's *Bastard Out of Carolina*, Carolivia Herron's *Thereafter Johnnie*, Gayl Jones's *Corregidora,* and Joyce Carol Oates's *You Must Remember This.* The maternal story is also being investigated by feminist psychologists and sociologists; for example, see Janis Tyler Johnson's *Mothers of Incest Survivors,* which challenges the assumption that "all mothers know," and Janet Liebman Jacobs' *Victimized Daughters,* which describes the ways in which the incestuous father disrupts the daughter's relationship with her mother.

4. It takes a minimum of two to create a speech community, a speaker and a listener, a writer and a reader. Furthermore, since each of us must both listen and speak if communication is to occur, "We must all," according to Mikhail Bakhtin, "become authors" (Holquist 66).

5. Citing Chesler's blunt argument, Herman says, "Women are encouraged to commit incest as a way of life.... As opposed to marrying

our fathers, we marry men like our fathers...men who are older than us, have more money than us, more power than us, are taller than us" (quoted in *Father-Daughter Incest* 57–58).

6. Despite Jung's formulation of the concept of the shadow, he did not recognize the shadow of patriarchal power. Following Freud, Jung believed that most of his female patients had fantasized these traumatic events. See, for example, Jung's *Critique of Psychoanalysis*, in which he concludes that "we are thus obliged to assume that many traumata in early infancy are of a purely fantastic nature, mere fantasies in fact, while others do have objective reality" (13). Later, when a patient struggles to relate how her father had stood by her bed "in an obscene attitude," Jung persists in his belief, despite the patient's "wild lamentations about how dreadful it was," that "nothing is less probable than that the father really did this" (91).

7. For example, in a review of Harriet Lerner's *The Dance of Deception*, Judith S. Antrobus, who describes Lerner's style as "self-confessional" because she uses "examples from her own experience" (28), says, "I suppose she does this to make you feel at home; the implication is that she knows how you feel because she's been there.... Yet I felt manipulated by Lerner's confessional style. What begins as a confession often ends up as self-congratulation" (28). Antrobus objects whether Lerner attributes her success "to luck" or describes it as "fame and glory" (28). To ascribe her success to luck is "a typical female disclaimer," according to Antrobus, while calling it fame and glory "seems over-inflated...and belies her stated modesty" (28). As judged by Antrobus, Lerner is damned if she's modest and damned if she's immodest.

8. David Bleich has recognized the importance of emotions, particularly in our studies of reading, at least since the publication of *Readings and Feelings: An Introduction to Subjective Criticism* (1975). However, as Bleich himself acknowledges, *Readings and Feelings* did not address the complex problem of the social identity of readers—such as their gender, race, class, and ethnicity—an issue central in Bleich's *The Double Perspective: Language Literacy and Social Relations* (1988).

9. As Ellyn Kaschak explains, "Memories are stored everywhere, not just in our minds. Or, better said, the mind's realm is not confined to the brain. Intelligence exists at all levels of experience" (49).

10. Linda Alcoff and Laura Gray give numerous examples of television talk shows, from "Phil Donahue" to "Sally Jessy Raphael," which deny the power of theoretical analysis to survivors of sexual violence. Alcoff and Gray describe a formulaic pattern of presentation which opens with emotional "confessions" by survivors—"The host of the show makes sure to ask questions that are sufficiiently probing to get the survivors to cry on screen"—after which "the inevitable expert shows up; almost invariably a white man or woman with a middle-class and professional appearance, who, with a sympathetic but dispassionate air, explains to the audience the nature, symptoms, and possible therapies for such crimes of violence" (277). Through the use of this pattern, "survivors are reduced to victims, represented as pathetic objects who can only recount their experiences as if these are transparent, and who offer pitiable instantiations of the universal truth the experts reveal" (277). Their numerous examples include ABC's "The Home show," cohosted by Gary Collins and Dana Fleming, September 10, 1990; "Sally Jessie Raphael," January 21, 1991; "Geraldo," November 14, 1989; and "Oprah Winfrey," April 14, 1988. Geraldo Rivera, whose shows "are often organized around having survivors, rather than perpetrators explain and defend themselves" (277), is the worst, while Oprah Winfrey, who does not allow women "to be put in the position of having to defend the truth of their stories or their own actions" and "does not always defer to an expert but presents herself as a survivor/expert" (278), is the best.

11. I have had difficulty dating this traumatic event. Initially, I placed it much earlier; however, based on my memory of the specific bedroom into which my father carried me (we lived in a number of different houses while I was in grade school), I have revised the date: it must have taken place in 1952, when I was eleven. However, I was only seven when I became aware that my father was molesting my sister. "You girls should go to sleep," he said the first time he got into our bed—on my sister's side. The next day I made plans for leaving home: I packed a small bag and hid it behind the furnace which was adjacent to the bedroom I shared with my sister. During the night, while everyone else slept, I planned to gather my provisions—some sandwiches and my photo-developing kit—and leave. Despite my good intentions, I slept through the night. When I

retrieved my bag, I discovered that heat from the furnace had melted both the butter and my photo-developing kit. Suitable punishment, I decided (turning my anger inward): since I had failed to wake up, my favorite Christmas present—the photo-developing kit—had been destroyed.

12. *The Bluest Eye* is sometimes taught in high school literature classes, but is more commonly taught in college literature classrooms. As David Bleich illustrates, teaching this novel presents a challenge since it may elicit racist/sexist responses from students.

13. Fortunately, feminist scholars have criticized Freud's conclusions in this case study. See, for example, *In Dora's Case: Freud–Hysteria–Feminism*, edited by Charles Berheimer and Clare Kahane, and *Father Knows Best* by Robin Tolmach Lakoff, and James C. Coyne.

14. As Alice Miller says, "In order for Freud to take his patients' accounts seriously in the face of resistance from the public, he would have had to be free from the strictures of the patriarchal family, from the demands of the Fourth Commandment, and from the guilt feelings caused by his introjected parents. Since that kind of freedom was totally impossible at the time, perhaps Freud had no choice but to interpret what his patients told him as fantasies and to construct a theory that would spare adults from reproach and would allow him to trace his patients' symptoms back to the repression of their own infantile sexual wishes" (*Thou Shalt Not Be Aware* 113). As my anger has abated, I have come to accept this humane account of Freud's betrayal of his patients.

15. With the exception of "Lysistrada," which I did not read until my first year in college, I do not recall reading a single story about the collective power of women. I was thrilled when the women in "Lysistrada" refused to have intercourse with their husbands to force them to stop making war. However, most of the comedies I was assigned in college taught me quite a different lesson: that women had one role in life, to marry. Young women have been, and continue to be, denied opportunties to read the kind of stories that would allow them to examine their assumptions about family relations and create new maps for the future.

16. When I asked my son for his permission to write about the divorce, he responded, with characteristic generosity and trust, "Oh, Mom, You go right ahead."

17. I considered the possibility of discussing these disagreements among feminists without mentioning names, a strategy that Diane Price Herndl follows ("On the Margins of Discourse" 204–25). Based on the recommendation of Shari Benstock, Price Herndl follows the practice of not "naming names" because of the possibility that "the space which has been opened for feminist criticism may be merely a carnival provided by institutional authority–an event staged to allow feminists to drown out their own voices and thereby return to silence" ("The Dilemmas of a Feminine Dialogic" 20). I have rejected this solution for two reasons: first, Jane Gallop had already commented openly upon Koppelman Cornillon's attack on Oates; therefore, my references to the debate could be easily traced; second, despite the dangers, I don't think the feminist community should pretend to be a monologic site. Open controversy is best.

18. I have contributed essays to collections edited by the following, all of whom I thank: *The Critical Reception to Ann Beattie*, ed. Jaye Berman Montresor; *Anxious Power*, ed. S. E. Sweeny and Carol J. Singley; *The Intimate Critique*, ed. Olivia Frey, Diane Freedman, and Francis Murphy Zauhar; *Misogyny in Literature*, ed. Katherine Ackley; *Feminism, Bakhtin and the Dailogic*, ed. Dale Bauer and Susan Jaret McKinstry; *Where Are You Going, Where Have You Been?* ed. Elaine Showalter; *Telling Tales*, ed. Barbara Lounsberry; *Creating Safe Space*, ed. Tomoko Kuribayashi and Julie Tharp; *Integrating Visual and Verbal Literacies*, ed. Will Garrett-Pett and Donald Lawrence.

19. I became a "schoolaholic" in an attempt to protect myself from abuse and to create an acceptable social persona. This strategy, which enabled me to survive for many years, finally resulted in such psychic self-division that it threatened my ability to function as a professional (see chapter 1).

20. Even as I write these words, I grieve for my sisters who, for years, found no one to listen, no one to help.

21. As Herman writes, "The image of the Seductive Daughter is part of the literary and religious tradition. It is found in the biblical story of Lot, a man who managed to impregnate both his daughters while apparently maintaining complete innocence of the matter" (36). The

story of Lot is, of course, written from the paternal perspective; we don't know what his daughters actually felt or experienced.

22. Herman provides this information based on studies by Kinsey (1953), Gagnon (1965), Landis (1956), and Finkelhorn (1978). See especially 7–21.

23. See Dickinson and Leming 394–96.

24. Such sensitivity to power inequities is not surprising in authors Hadley [and] Irwin who have frequently demonstrated their understanding of the effects of social injustice, both racism and sexism, in novels such as *We Are Mesquakie, We Are One; I Be Somebody;* and *The Lilith Summer.* I was saddened when my friend and colleague, Lee Hadley, died. Like Joyce Carol Oates, Lee Hadley was not afraid to explore the dark side of human nature.

25. This CBS "After School Special" did not appear in all cities; Minneapolis, Minnesota, for example, chose not to show the movie, whereas it did appear in Ames, Iowa.

26. In the most severe cases of sexual abuse, which often begin in early childhood, psychological splitting may occur to such an extent that neither personality is aware of the other. In especially brutal repetitions of childhood sexual abuse, as the general public knows from seeing movies such as "Sybil," multiple personalities may result. In Abby's case, although the abuse continued for many years, she does not describe it as physically brutal; in other words, we do not hear that she was beaten, although she was a prisoner of her father's wishes, as my sisters were.

27. The term *seduction* is, of course, a euphemism for rape, for one must take into account the father's power over his daughters. In the course of her research Herman discovered "a vastly elaborated intellectual tradition which served the purpose of suppressing the truth about incest, a tradition which, like so many others, originates in the works of Freud" (9–10).

28. As Herman explains, the greatest difference between the families of incestuous fathers and seductive fathers–that is, between those whose behavior was sexually motivated but "did not involve physical contact or a requirement for secrecy"–was the strength of the mothers. Daughters who grew up in the households of seductive fathers described

their mothers as "healthier, more assertive, more competent, more socially active, and less isolated than the mothers in incestuous families" (112).

29. Benjamin emphasizes the importance of strong, healthy mothers—mothers capable of setting boundaries for their own benefit, not just for their children—for the healthy maturation of both daughters and sons.

30. I learned this lesson—that fathers do not stop with one victim—through painful personal experience. For information on this problem, see Herman and Miller. Also see Bass and Davis whose chapter headings provide a thumbnail sketch of the recovery process for incest survivors: "Recognizing the Damage," "Coping: Honoring What You Did to Survive," "The Emergency Stage," "Remembering," "Breaking Silence," "Understanding That It Wasn't Your Fault," "The Child Within," "Anger: The Backbone of Healing," "Your Body," and others—all relevant to Abby's recovery, and to mine.

31. I make this cautionary comment because, after observing a young teacher skillfully lead a discussion of the movie based on *Abby, My Love*, I heard almost every student express anger toward the father, followed by the suggestion that he should be harshly punished, imprisoned and electrocuted, for example. Such responses, while understandable, would undoubtedly have made Abby herself, had she been in the classroom, decide not to tell her story out of the fear that she would be responsible for her father's death. As Maya Angelou records in her autobiography, after abuse by her stepfather, she testified against her abusive stepfather in court. Following his violent death, Angelou was mute for at least a year, a child's response to feelings of guilt. No matter how great a daughter's own suffering, she often feels responsible for the suffering of the incestuous father.

32. I am happy to report that, since earning tenure in 1992, I have had my own office.

33. In 1993, two years after I drafted this chapter, a new English department chair allowed me to redefine my teaching responsibilities. I now teach courses in literature and women's studies, along with a graduate-level pedagogy course designed primarily for those who plan to teach English at the college level. I requested this redefinition of my

job because, lacking the institutional authority to effect changes–in particular, changes in institutional hierarchies which create distrust between teachers in secondary schools and higher education–I found this teaching assignment increasingly stressful. One of our greatest educational challenges, as participants in the 1988 Right to Literacy Conference discovered, is how to "best reach out to schools and communities to affect the teaching of reading and writing." They explain, "Time and time again, commission members circled around this question, producing voluminous notes on the need for university-school-community collaboration but settling on few concrete ways to allow for such collaboration" (Lunsford et al. 1).

34. Each time I teach this course, I challenge the canon: in the fall of 1996, for example, I opened with the debate over *Huckleberry Finn*, using a collection of critical essays edited by Gerald Graff, followed by a study of Chicano/a narratives. Afterward, students worked in teams to develop syllabi for a college-level course called "U.S. Multicultural Literatures."

35. More recent additions to this canon include Alice Walker's *The Color Purple* (Harcourt Brace Jovanovich 1982), Jane Smiley's *A Thousand Acres* (Knopf 1991), Dorothy Allison's *Bastard Out of Carolina* (Penguin 1992), Margaret Atwood's *The Robber Bride* (Bantam 1993), Marilyn French's *Our Father* (Ballantine 1994), Sapphire's *Push* (Knopf 1996), and Sally Patterson Tubach's *Memoirs of a Terrorist* (State University of New York Press 1996). A collection edited by Karen Jacobsen McLennan, *Nature's Ban: Women's Incest Literature* (Northeastern University Press), also appeared in 1996.

36. For an example of an attempt at trivialization, see Roiphe's "Making the Incest Scene" in which she looks forward to the day when publishers declare, *"I've heard enough about incest"* (71). As long as incest continues, to declare that we have "heard enough" about it is tantamount to abandoning children to abusive parents.

37. See, for example, Michael Yapko's *Suggestions of Abuse* and Mark Pendergrast's *Victims of Memory*. While these books address important issues, they may also lead some readers to conclude that women's stories of abuse should be regarded with suspicion.

38. Although I have never disclosed my personal history in the classroom, I have briefly acknowledged it in two public forums within the academy: in the fall of 1991, during a discussion which followed my paper on father-daughter incest in *Abby, My Love*, presented at the Midwest Modern Language Association, and again, in the spring of 1991, during discussion which followed my invited talk, "Daughters in Peril in Late Twentieth-Century America: Toni Morrison's *The Bluest Eye* and Joyce Carol Oates's *You Must Remember This*" at Women's History Week, University of Texas-Arlington.

39. Within such a sociopolitical context, a daughter's story of incest may function as a theoretical discourse even when it is not explicitly theoretical. As Joanne Pagano claims, "To write autobiographically is...to theorize as well" ("Moral Fictions" 195). But students should understand that it is the existence of a feminist community—which theorizes that the personal is political—that has made it possible for survivors to continue to speak out; therefore, if young women fail to support the feminist movement, they may lose many rights they take for granted.

40. Dr. Abbott offers concise advice to teachers on what to do if they suspect that a child is being abused. Such abuse most often begins in elementary school.

41. What theory of father-daughter incest can accomodate the experiences of African American women? I examine this problem more fully in "Whose Daughter Is Johnnie? Revisionary Myth-making in Carolivia Herron's *Thereafter Johnnie.*"

42. I make the same argument, along with my coeditor, in the introduction to *Narrating Mothers: Theorizing Maternal Subjectivities;* Marianne Hirsch points out this silencing of mothers in psychoanalytic models of the family in *The Mother/Daughter Plot: Narrative, Psychoanalysis, Feminism.*

43. Unfortunately, according to a graduate student at Iowa State University, a survivor of childhood sexual abuse who works with a local CAPE organization (Child Abuse Protection Education), many schools do not welcome educators who warn children about the dangers of sexual abuse. CAPE, which presents skits designed to educate children about their right to say no, has met resistance from elementary school

principals despite the fact that its members are prepared to intervene if a child shows symptoms of abuse or requests help. As a result of such resistance, CAPE may change its focus from "child abuse" to "child safety" (interview, Iowa State University, 27 April 1994).

44. For further information about research on this topic, see Debra L. Schultz's *Risk, Resiliency, and Resistance: Current Research on Adolescent Girls.* National Council for Research on Women, 1991. Write: The Sara Delano Roosevelt Memorial House, 47–49 East 65th Street, New York, New York 10021.

45. From 1987 through 1993, I observed student teachers in literature classrooms from grades seven through twelve in Iowa. In the fall of 1993, to research this problem, I returned to high schools in North Dakota and Minnesota where I had been a student or high school teacher.

46. Between 27 and 29 September 1993, I interviewed fifteen girls, most in the eleventh grade, at the "Magic City" campus of Minot High School in Minot, North Dakota. I opened each interview by asking the young woman to define "conflict," preferably with an example from her own life. I followed up by asking if she had ever read about women's conflicts. A few students mentioned young adult romances, especially the Sweet Valley High series, but not one could recall having been assigned a narrative centered on the conflicts of women in a literature class. However, since the eleventh-grade English classes were reading *The Scarlet Letter*, I began to probe: could they see any similarities between Hester's conflicts and those of women today? Only one young woman saw any similarities and, remarkably, she did not mention the problem of teen pregnancy. I concluded each interview by asking how the young woman imagined her life fifteen years from now: every girl planned to have both career and marriage, although no one planned to have more than two children. My thanks to Principal Richard J. Olthoff for his support, and to Marcy Blikre, counsellor, for helping to arrange these interviews, as well as members of the English department who allowed me to observe their classes.

47. For a brief introduction to this topic, including strategies for intervention, as well as a short bibliography, see "Flirting or Hurting" by Stephanie Weiss.

48. During the audio-taped interview I conducted with Erin Rollenhagen and Sarah Hegland on 10 May 1994, they credited their mothers, more than anyone else, for their resistance to the sexist Hooters T-shirts. For more on the topic of feminist mothers and their daughters, see Rose Glickman's *Daughters of Feminists: Young Women with Feminist Mothers Talk About Their Lives.* Significantly, not one daughter of a feminist mother reported sexual abuse by a family member.

49. Signers of the petition also asked readers to "call to account and treat the victimizers, including those within our own families, help the adults now suffering the effects of sexual abuse, and identify and neutralize the root causes of child sexual abuse" (*Ms.* 88).

50. I taped an interview with this graduate student, who chose to remain anonymous, on 17 May 1994. I find it helpful to talk to other surviviors since, by comparing experiences and recurring symptoms, I am able to analyze how the trauma of childhood sexual abuse continues to affect my perceptions and coping behaviors.

51. In a short story called "Naked," Joyce Carol Oates transforms a woman's shame, after she is attacked and undressed by a pack of children, into a powerful form of knowledge. *"I do what I want to do"* (Oates's italics 238), the unnamed woman thinks as she stands naked in the darkness, deciding when and how to reenter her own home. This story suggests that invisibility may be a source of power, that the experience of nakedness may be potentially transformative.

WORKS CITED

Abbott, Brian, M.D. "Child Abuse: Information about Health Factors That Affect the Way Students Learn." *NEA Today* 12, 8 (April 1994): 4–5.

Alcoff, Linda, and Laura Gray. "Survivor Discourse: Transgression or Recuperation." *Signs* 18, 2 (Winter 1993): 260–90.

Alexander, Elizabeth. "The Anxiety of Authority." *The Women's Review of Books* (February 1994): 7.

Allison, Dorothy. *Bastard Out of Carolina.* 1992. New York: Plume, 1993.

Angelou, Maya. *I Know Why the Caged Bird Sings.* New York: Random House, 1970.

Antrobus, Judith S. "In Praise of Honesty." *The Women's Review of Books* 11, 2 (November 1993): 28–29.

Applebee, Arthur N. *Tradition and Reform in the Teaching of English: A History.* Urbana, Ill.: National Council of Teachers of English, 1974.

Armstrong, Louise. *Rocking the Cradle of Sexual Politics.* Reading, Mass.: Addison-Wesley, 1994.

Atwood, Margaret. *Cat's Eye.* 1988. New York: Doubleday, 1989.

——. *The Handmaid's Tale.* New York: Fawcett Crest, 1985.

Bakhtin, Mikhail. *The Dialogic Imagination.* Austin: University of Texas Press, 1981.

——. *Speech Genres and Other Late Essays.* Trans. V. McGee. Austin: University of Texas Press, 1986.

Barthes, Roland. "The Death of the Author." *Image, Music, Text.* Ed. and trans. Stephen Heath. New York: Hill and Wange, 1977.

Bass, Ellen, and Laura Davis. *The Courage to Heal.* New York: Harper & Row, 1988.

Bartky, Sandra Lee. "The Pedagogy of Shame." *Feminisms and Pedagogies of Everyday Life.* Ed. Carmen Luke. Albany: State University of New York Press, 1996, 225–41.

Baym, Nina. "The Madwoman and Her Languages: Why I Don't Do Feminist Literary Theory." *Tulsa Studies in Women's Literature* 3 (Fall 1984): 45–59.

Belenky, Mary Field, Blythe McVicker Clinchy, Nancy Rule Goldberger, and Jill Mattuck Tarule. *Women's Ways of Knowing: The Development of Self, Voice, and Mind.* New York: Basic, 1986.

Bender, Eileen Teper. *Joyce Carol Oates, Artist in Residence.* Bloomington: Indiana University Press, 1987.

Benjamin, Jessica. *The Bonds of Love: Psychoanalysis, Feminism, and the Problem of Domination.* New York: Pantheon, 1988.

Bennett, William. "Course Descriptions." *Education Week* (13 January 1988): 28.

Benstock, Shari. "On the Margins of Discourse." *PMLA* 98 (1982): 204–25.

Bernheimer, Charles, and Claire Kahane, eds. *In Dora's Case: Freud–Hysteria–Feminism.* New York: Columbia University Press, 1985.

Bleich, David. "Literacy and Citizenship." *The Right to Literacy.* Ed. Andrea A. Lunsford, Helen Moglen, and James Slevin. New York: Modern Language Association, 1990, 163–69.

——. "Sexism and Racism in Literary Responses to Morrison's *The Bluest Eye.*" *Iowa English Bulletin* 37 (1989): 1–23.

——. *The Double Perspective: Language, Literacy, and Social Relations.* New York: Oxford University Press, 1988.

——. *Readings and Feelings: An Introduction to Subjective Criticism.* Urbana: NCTE, 1975.

Bloom, Lynn Z. "Teaching College English as a Woman." *College English* 54, 7 (November 1992): 818–25.

Blume, E. Sue. *Secret Survivors: Uncovering Incest and Its Aftereffects in Women.* New York: Ballantine Books, 1990.

Boose, Lynda E. "The Father's House and the Daughter in It: The Structures of Western Culture's Daughter-Father Relationship." *Daughters and Fathers.* Ed. Lynda E. Boose and Betty Flowers. Baltimore, Md.: Johns Hopkins University Press, 1989, 19–74.

Bordo, Susan. "Hunger as Ideology." *Feminisms and Pedagogies of Everyday Life.* Ed. Carmen Luke. Albany: State University of New York Press, 1996, 119–46.

Brown, Lyn Mikel, and Carol Gilligan. *Meeting at the Crossroads: Women's Psychology and Girls' Development.* New York: Ballantine, 1992.

Brownmiller, Susan. Introduction: *The Best-Kept Secret: Sexual Abuse of Children,* by Florence Howe. New York: McGraw-Hill, 1980, viii–ix.

Carlson, Susan, and Faye Whitaker. "Interview: Jane Smiley." Unpublished Paper. 11 May 1993.

Chell, Cara. "Untricking the Eye: Joyce Carol Oates and the Feminist Ghost Story." *Arizona Quarterly* 41, 1 (Spring 1985): 5–23.

Chernin, Kim. *The Hungry Self: Women, Eating, Identity.* New York: Harper & Row, 1985.

Chodorow, Nancy, and Susan Contratto. "The Fantasy of the Perfect Mother." In *Rethinking the Family.* Ed. Barrie Thorne and Marilyn Yalom. New York: Longman, 1982, 54–73.

Cixous, Helene. "The Laugh of the Medusa." *New French Feminisms.* Ed. Elaine Marks and Isabelle de Courtivron. New York: Schocken, 1981, 245–64.

Clark, Katrina, and Holquist, Michael. *Mikhail Bakhtin.* Cambridge, Mass.: Harvard University Press, 1984.

Cohen, Ted. "Metaphor and the Cultivation of Intimacy." *On Metaphor.* Ed. Sheldon Sacks. Chicago: University of Chicago Press, 1979, 1–10.

Culbertson, Roberta. "Embodied Memory, Transcendence, and Telling: Recounting Trauma, Re-establishing the Self." *New Literary History* 26 (1995): 169–95.

Creighton, Joanne V. *Joyce Carol Oates: Novels of the Middle Years.* New York: Twayne, 1992.

Daly, Brenda. "Women as Image-Makers: An Integrated Approach to Teaching the Visual and Verbal Arts, with Margaret Atwood, Claude Breeze, Helen Lundeberg, Fred Marcellino, and Joyce Wieland." *Verbal and Visual Literacies.* Ed. Will Garrett-Pett and Donald Lawrence. Toronto: Inkshed Publications, 1997, 106–29.

——. "I Stand Here Naked, and Best Dressed in Theory: Feminist Refashionings of Academic Discourse." Ed. Julie Tharp and Tomoko Kuribayashi. *Creating Safe Space: Violence and Women's Writing.* Albany: State University of New York Press, 1997, 11–26.

——. "Whose Daughter Is Johnnie? Revisionary Myth-making in

Carolivia Herron's *Thereafter Johnnie.*" *Callaloo: A Journal of African American and African Arts and Letters* 18, 2 (1995): 473–91.

——. "An Unfilmable Conclusion: Joyce Carol Oates at the Movies." *Journal of Popular Culture* 23, 3 (Winter 1989): 101–14. Rpt. in *Where Are You Going, Where Have You Been?* Ed. Elaine Showalter. Newark, N.J.: Rutgers University Press, 1994, 145–62.

——. "My Friend, Joyce Carol Oates." Diane Freedman, Olivia Frey, and Frances Murphy Zauhar, eds. *The Intimate Critique: Autobiographical Literary Criticism.* Durham, N.C.: Duke University Press, 1993, 163–73.

——. "'How do we [not] become these people who victimize us?' Anxious Power in the Early Fiction of Joyce Carol Oates." *Anxious Power: Reading, Writing, and Ambivalence in Narrative by Women.* Ed. Carol J. Singley and Susan Elizabeth Sweeney. Albany: State University of New York Press, 1993, 220–33.

——. "Tragic Revelations: Father-Daughter Incest in Smiley's *A Thousand Acres* and Herron's *Thereafter Johnnie.*" Unpublished paper, presented at the Midwest Modern Language Association, November 1993.

——. "Father-Daughter Incest in Hadley Irwin's *Abby, My Love*: Repairing the Effects of Childhood Sexual Abuse During the Adolescent Years." *Children's Literature Quarterly* 17, 3 (Fall 1992): 5–11.

——. "Teaching Alice Walker's *Meridian*: Civil Rights According to Mothers." *Narrating Mothers: Theorizing Maternal Subjectivities.* Knoxville: University of Tennessee Press, 1991, 239–587.

——. "Of Bread and Shadows, Beginnings." *There Lies a Fair Land: An Anthology of Norwegian-American Writings.* Ed. John Solensten. Minneapolis: New Rivers, 1985, 146–53.

——. "I VIVIDLY REMEMBER, pretty well: A Witness Against Her Self." *Hurricane Alice: University of Minnesota Feminist Review* (Fall/Winter 1983): 1–4.

Daly, Brenda, and Maureen T. Reddy. *Narrating Mothers: Theorizing Maternal Subjectivies.* Knoxville: University of Tennessee Press, 1991.

Dickinson, George E., and Michael R. Leming. *Understanding Families: Diversity, Continuity and Change.* Boston: Allyn and Bacon, 1991.

"Divided Memories." PBS (4 April 1995).

Dostoevsky, Fyodor. *Crime and Punishment.* Trans. Constance Garnett. New York: Harper & Brothers, 1927.

Faludi, Susan. "Speak for Yourself." *The New York Times Magazine* (26 January 1992) (Section 6): 10.

——. *Backlash: The Undeclared War against American Women.* New York: Crown, 1991.

Felman, Shoshona, and Dori Laub, M.D. *Testimony: Crises of Witnessing in Literature, Psychoanalysis, and History.* New York: Routledge, 1992.

Fetterley, Judith. "'Not in the Least American': Nineteenth-Century Literary Regionalism." *College English* 56, 8 (December 1994): 877–95.

——. *The Resisting Reader: A Feminist Approach to American Fiction.* Bloomington: Indiana University Press, 1978.

Finke, Laurie. "The Rhetoric of Marginality: Why I Do Feminist Theory." *Tulsa Studies in Women's Literature* 5, 2 (Fall 1986): 251–72.

Flynn, Elizabeth A., and Patrocinio P. Schweickart, eds. *Gender and Reading: Essays on Readers, Texts, and Contexts.* Baltimore: Johns Hopkins University Press, 1986.

Forward, Susan, and Craig Buck. *Betrayal of Innocence: Incest and Its Devestation.* New York: Penguin, 1992.

Foucault, Michel. "What Is an Author?" (1969). *The Critical Tradition: Classic Texts and Contemporary Trends.* Ed. David H. Richter. New York: St. Martin's, 1989, 978–89.

Freedman, Diane, Olivia Frey, and Frances Murphy Zauhar, eds. *The Intimate Critique: Autobiographical Literary Criticism.* Durham, N.C.: Duke University Press, 1993.

Friedman, Ellen G. *Joyce Carol Oates.* New York: Frederick Ungar, 1980.

Fromm, Erich. *Escape from Freedom.* New York: Holt, Rinehart & Winston, 1964.

Froula, Christine. "The Daughter's Seduction: Sexual Violence and Literary History." *Daughters and Fathers.* Eds. Lynda E. Boose and Betty S. Flowers. Baltimore, Md.: Johns Hopkins University Press, 1989, 111–35.

Frye, Joanne. *Living Stories, Telling Lives: Women and the Novel in Contemporary Experience.* Ann Arbor: University of Michigan Press, 1986.

Frye, Northrop. *The Secular Scripture: A Study of the Structure of Romance.* 1976. Cambridge, Mass.: Harvard University Press, 1978.

———. *The Educated Imagination.* Bloomington: Indiana University Press, 1968.

Fuss, Diana. *Essentially Speaking: Feminism, Nature and Difference.* New York: Routledge, 1989.

Gallop, Jane. *Around 1981: Academic Feminist Literary Theory.* New York: Routledge, 1992.

———. "The Father's Seduction." *Daughters and Fathers.* Eds. Lynda E. Boose and Betty S. Flowers. Baltimore, Md.: Johns Hopkins University Press, 1989, 97–110.

———. *Reading Lacan.* Ithaca, N.Y.: Cornell University Press, 1985.

———. *The Daughter's Seduction: Feminism and Psychoanalysis.* Ithaca, N.Y.: Cornell University Press, 1982.

Gallop, Jane, Marianne Hirsch, and Nancy Miller. "Criticizing Feminist Criticism." *Conflicts in Feminism.* Ed. Marianne Hirsch and Evelyn Fox Keller. New York: Routledge, 1990, 349–69.

Gates, Henry Louis, Jr. "Introduction: Tell Me Sir, … What Is 'Black Literature'?" *PMLA* 105, 1 (January 1991): 11–12.

———. "Murder She Wrote." Review of *Because It Is Bitter, and Because It Is My Heart." The Nation* (2 July 1990): 27–29.

———. "Whose Canon Is It, Anyway?" *New York Times Review of Books* (26 February 1989): 1, 44–45.

Gilbert, Sandra M. "Life's Empty Pack: Notes toward a Literary Daughter-onomy." *Daughters and Fathers.* Eds. Lynda E. Boose and Betty S. Flowers. Baltimore, Md.: Johns Hopkins University Press, 1989, 256–77.

Gilligan, Carol. "Teaching Shakespeare's Sister: Notes from the Underground of Female Adolescence." Preface to *Making Connections: The Relational Worlds of Adolescent Girls at Emma Willard School.* Cambridge, Mass.: Harvard University Press, 1990, 6–27.

Gilligan, Carol, Nona P. Lyons, and Trudy J. Hanmer, eds. *Making Connections: The Relational Worlds of Adolescent Girls at Emma Willard School.* Cambridge, Mass.: Harvard University Press, 1990.

Glass, James M. *Shattered Selves: Multiple Personality in a Postmodern World.* Ithaca, N.Y.: Cornell University Press, 1993.

Glickman, Rose. *Daughters of Feminists: Young Women with Feminist Mothers Talk about Their Lives.* New York: St. Martin's, 1993.

Goldstein, Kenneth M., and Sheldon Blackman. "Goodlad Tests His Vision of Teacher Education." NCTE's *The Council Chronicle* 1, 3 (February 1992): 1, 15.

——. *Cognitive Style: Five Approaches and Relevant Research.* New York: Wiley, 1978.

Graff, Gerald. "Organizing the Conflicts in the Curriculum." *M/MLA* 25, 1 (Spring 1992): 63–76.

Greene, Gayle. *Changing the Story: Feminist Fiction and the Tradition.* Bloomington: Indiana University Press, 1991.

Hawthorne, Nathaniel. *The Scarlet Letter* (1850). Ed. Ross C. Murfin. Boston: St. Martin's, 1991.

Heller, Scott. "Experience and Expertise Meet in New Brand of Scholarship." *The Chronicle of Higher Education* (6 May 1992): A7–A9.

Herman, Judith Lewis. *Trauma and Recovery.* New York: Basic, 1992.

Herman, Judith Lewis, with Lisa Hirschman. *Father-Daughter Incest.* Cambridge, Mass.: Harvard University Press, 1981.

Herndl, Diane Price. "The Dilemmas of a Feminine Dialogic." *Feminism, Bakhtin, and the Dialogic.* Ed. Dale M. Bauer and S. Jaret McKinstry. Albany: State University of New York Press, 1991, 7–24.

Hirsch, Marianne. *The Mother/Daughter Plot: Narrative, Psychoanalysis, Feminism.* Bloomington: Indiana University Press, 1989.

Holquist, Michael. "Answering as Authoring: Mikhail Bakhtin's Trans-Linguistics." *Bakhtin: Essays and Dialogics on His Work.* Ed. Gary Saul Morson. Chicago: University of Chicago Press, 1986, 59–71.

hooks, bell. *Talking Back: Thinking Feminist, Thinking Black.* Boston: South End, 1989.

Irigaray, Luce. *This Sex Which Is Not One.* Trans. C. Porter with C. Burke. Ithaca, N.Y.: Cornell University Press, 1985.

Irwin, Hadley. *Abby, My Love.* Boston: Atheneum, 1985.

———. *I Be Somebody.* New York: Atheneum, 1984.

———. *We Are Mesquakie, We Are One.* New York: Feminist Press, 1981.

———. *The Lilith Summer.* New York: Feminist Press, 1979.

Jacobs, Janet Liebman. *Victimized Daughters: Incest and the Development of the Female Self.* New York: Routledge, 1994.

Janoff-Bulman, Ronnie. *Shattered Assumptions: Toward a New Psychology of Trauma.* New York: Free Press, 1992.

Jehlen, Myra. "Archimedes and the Paradox of Feminist Criticism." *Feminist Theory: A Critique of Ideology.* Ed. Nannerl O. Keohane, Michelle Z. Rosaldo, and Barbara G. Gelpi. Chicago: University of Chicago Press, 1981, 1982, 189–215.

Johnson, Janis Tyler. *Mothers of Incest Survivors: Another Side of the Story.* Bloomington: Indiana University Press, 1992.

Juhasz, Suzanne. *Reading from the Heart: Women, Literature, and the Search for True Love.* New York: Viking, 1994.

Jung, Carl G. *Critique of Psychoanalysis.* Princeton, N.J.: Princeton University Press, 1975.

Kaschak, Ellyn. *Engendered Lives: A New Psychology of Women's Experience.* New York: Basic, 1992.

Kennard, Jean E. "Ourself Behind Ourself: A Theory for Lesbian Readers. *Gender and Reading: Essays on Readers, Texts, and Contexts.* Eds. Elizabeth A. Flynn and Patrocinio P. Schweickart. Baltimore, Md.: Johns Hopkins University Press, 1986, 63–80.

Kramer-Dahl, Anneliese. "Reconsidering the Notions of Voice and Experience in Critical Pedagogy." *Feminisms and Pedagogies of Everyday Life.* Ed. Carmen Luke. Albany: State University of New York Press, 1996, 242–62.

Kristeva, Julia. *Desire in Language: A Semiotic Approach to Literature and Art.* Ed. Leon S. Roudiez. Trans. Thomas Gora, Alice Jardine, and Leon S. Roudiez. New York: Columbia University Press, 1980.

Lakoff, Robin Tolmach. *Language and Women's Place.* 1975. New York: Harper & Row, 1989.

Lakoff, Robin Tolmach, and James C. Coyne. *Father Knows Best: The Use and Abuse of Power in Freud's* Case of Dora. New York: Teachers College Press, 1993.

Lanser, Susan Sniader. *Fictions of Authority: Women Writers and Narrative Voice.* Ithaca, N.Y.: Cornell University Press, 1992.

Laplanche, Jean. *Life and Death in Psychoanalysis.* Trans. by Jeffrey Mehlman. Baltimore, Md.: Johns Hopkins University Press, 1976.

Lauter, Paul. *Canons and Contexts.* New York: Oxford University Press, 1991.

"Levy Fails Though School Bans Jane Smiley's Book." *Iowa State Daily* 23 Feb. 1994:1.

Lim, Shirley Geok-lin, Valerie Miner, and Judith Barrington. "Reticence and Resistance: A Conversation." *The Women's Review of Books* 13, 10/11 (July 1996): 24–25.

Lunsford, Andrea A., Helene Moglen, and James Slevin, eds. *The Right to Literacy.* New York: Modern Language Association, 1990.

Maher, Frances A., and Mary Kay Tompson Tetreault. *The Feminist Classroom.* New York: Basic, 1994.

Masson, Jeffrey Moussaieff. *The Assault on Truth: Freud's Suppression of the Seduction Theory.* New York: Farrar, Straus, and Giroux, 1984.

Michie, Helena. *Sororophobia: Differences among Women in Literature and Culture.* New York: Oxford University Press, 1992.

Miller, Alice. *Thou Shalt Not Be Aware: Society's Betrayal of the Child.* New York: Farrar, Straus, and Giroux, 1984.

———. *The Drama of the Gifted Child.* New York: Basic, 1981.

Miller, Nancy K. "Changing the Subject: Authorship, Writing, and the Reader." *Feminist Studies/Critical Studies.* Ed. Teresa de Lauretis. Bloomington: Indiana University Press, 1986, 102–20.

———. *Getting Personal: Feminist Occasions and Other Autobiographical Acts.* New York: Routledge, 1991.

Miller, Richard E. "The Central Nervous System." *College English* 58, 3 (March 1996): 265–86.

Moffett, James. *Storm in the Mountains: A Case Study of Censorship, Conflict, and Consciousness.* Carbondale: Southern Illinois University Press, 1988.

Morgan, Robin, ed. *Sisterhood is Powerful: An Anthology of Writings from the Women's Liberation Movement.* New York: Vintage, 1970.

Oates, Joyce Carol. "Naked." *Heat and Other Stories.* New York: E. P. Dutton, 1991. 123–38.

——. *Marya, A Life.* New York: E. P. Dutton, 1988.

——. Reply to Joanna Russ. *Women's Review of Books* 11, 10 (July 1985).

——. "Stories That Define Me." *New York Times Book Review* (July 11, 1982): 1,15.

——. "Why Is Your Writing So Violent?" *New York Times Book Review* (29 March 1981): 15, 35.

——. "Where are you going, where have you been?" *Where are you going, where have you been? Stories of Young America.* Greenwich, Conn.: Fawcett, 1974.

——. *The Edge of Impossibility: Tragic Forms in Literature.* New York: Vanguard, 1972.

——. *A Garden of Earthly Delights.* New York: Vanguard, 1966.

Orenstein, Peggy. *School Girls: Young Women, Self-Esteem, and the Confidence Gap.* New York: Doubleday, 1994.

Pagano, Jo Anne. "Moral Fictions: The Dilemma of Theory and Practice." *Stories Lives Tell: Narrative and Dialogue in Education.* Ed. Carol Witherell and Nel Nodding. New York: Teachers College Press, 1991, 193–206.

——. *Exiles and Communities: Teaching in the Patriarchal Wilderness.* Albany: State University of New York Press, 1990.

Patai, Daphne. "Point of View." *The Chronicle of Higher Education* (23 February 1994): 52–53.

Pendergrast, Mark. *Victims of Memory: Incest Accusations and Shattered Lives.* Hinesburg, Vt.: Upper Access, 1995.

"The Pied Piper of Tucson." *Life* (March 4, 1966): 18.

Pipher, Mary. *Reviving Ophelia: Saving the Selves of Adolescent Girls.* New York: Ballantine, 1995.

Pratt, Annis, with Andrea Loewenstein. "Love and Friendship between Women." *Archetypal Patterns in Women's Fiction.* Bloomington: Indiana University Press, 1981.

Radway, Janice A. *Reading the Romance: Women, Patriarchy and Popular Culture.* Chapel Hill: University of North Carolina Press, 1984.

Rich, Adrienne. *Of Woman Born: Motherhood as Experience and Institution.* New York: W. W. Norton, 1976.

Roiphe, Katie. "Making the Incest Scene." *Harper's Magazine* (November 1995): 65, 68–71.

Rokeach, Milton, et al. *The Open and Closed Mind.* New York: Basic, 1960.

Ruddick, Sara. *Maternal Thinking: Toward a Politics of Peace.* Boston: Beacon, 1989.

——. "Preservative Love and Military Destructiveness: Some Reflections on Mothering and Peace." *Mothering: Essays in Feminist Theory.* Ed. Joyce Trebilcot. Totowa, N.J.: Rowman and Allanheld, 1984, 231–61.

Rush, Florence. *The Best-Kept Secret: Sexual Abuse of Children.* New York: McGraw-Hill, 1980.

Russ, Joanna. Letter to the Editor. *Women's Review of Books* 2, 9 (June 1985).

Russell, Diana E. H. *The Secret Trauma: Incest in the Lives of Girls and Women.* New York: Basic, 1986.

Rystedt, Una Fay. "I Speak to You Tonight as an Incest Survivor." Unpublished paper. Presented at Trinity Hospital Open Forum, Minot, North Dakota, 17 March 1994.

Sage, Lorna. *Women in the House of Fiction: Post-War Women Novelists.* New York: Routledge, 1992.

Schultz, Debra L. *Risk, Resiliency, and Resistance: Current Research on Adolescent Girls.* New York: National Council for Research on Women, 1991.

Schuster, Charles. "The Ideology of Illiteracy: A Bakhtinian Perspective." *The Right to Literacy.* Ed. Andrea A. Lunsford, Helen Moglen, and James Slevin. New York: Modern Language Association, 1990, 225–32.

Showalter, Elaine. "Joyce Carol Oates: A Portrait." *Ms.* (March 1986): 44–50. Rpt. *Joyce Carol Oates.* Ed. Harold Bloom. New York: Chelsea House Publishers, 1987, 137–42.

——. "Women Who Write Are Women." *The New York Times Book Review* (16 December 1984): 1, 31–33.

Singley, Carol J., and Susan Elizabeth Sweeney, eds. *Anxious Power: Reading, Writing and Ambivalence in Narrative by Women.* Albany: State University of New York Press, 1993.

Smiley, Jane. *A Thousand Acres.* New York: Alfred Knopf, 1992.

Sprengnether, Madelon. Respondent to the Session, "Telling the Truth of the Body: Rereading Literary Representations of Father-Daughter Incest and Domestic Violence." Modern Language Association, Washington, D.C. 29 December 1989.

Stimpson, Catharine. "President's Column." *MLA Newsletter* 22, 1 (Spring 1990): 2.

Stowe, Harriet Beecher. *Uncle Tom's Cabin* (1851–52). New York: Bantam, 1981.

Straus, Nina Pelikan. "Why Did I Say 'Women!'? Raskolnikov Reimagined." *Diacritics* 23, 1 (Spring 1993): 54–65.

Tappan, Mark B., and Lyn Mikel Brown. "Stories Told and Lessons Learned: Toward a Narrative Approach to Moral Development and Moral Education." *Stories Lives Tell: Narrative and Dialogue in Education.* Ed. Carol Witherell and Nel Noddings. New York: Teachers College Press, 1991, 171–92.

Taylor, Jill McLean, Carol Gilligan, and Amy M. Sullivan. *Between Voice and Silence: Women and Girls, Race and Relationship.* Cambridge, Mass.: Harvard University Press, 1995.

Terr, Lenore. *Unchained Memories: True Stories of Traumatic Memories, Lost and Found.* New York: Basic, 1994.

Tharp, Julie, and Tomoko Kuribayashi, eds. *Creating Safe Space: Violence and Women's Writing.* Albany: State University of New York Press, 1997.

Tompkins, Jane. "Me and My Shadow." *New Literary History* 19 (1987): 169–78.

——. *Sensational Designs: The Cultural Work of American Fiction, 1790–1860.* New York: Oxford University Press, 1985.

Wagner, Linda, ed. *Critical Essays on Joyce Carol Oates.* Boston: G. K. Hall, 1979.

Wall, Cheryl. "Feminist Literary Criticism and the Author." *Critical Inquiry* 16, 3 (Spring 1990): 551–71.

"We Are Survivors." *Ms.* (July/August 1987): 88–89.

Weiss, Stephanie. "Flirting or Hurting: Sexual Harassment in the Schools." *NEA Today* 12, 8 (April 1994): 4–5.

Welch, Robert. *The Blue Book of the John Birch Society.* Belmont, Mass.: Western Islands, 1961.

Wesley, Marilyn C. *Refusal and Transgression in Joyce Carol Oates's Fiction.* Westport, Conn.: Greenwood, 1993.

Whaley, Liz, and Liz Dodge. *Weaving in the Women: Transforming the High School English Curriculum.* Portsmouth, N.H.: Boynton/Cook, 1993.

Wilson, Harriet E. *Our Nig* (1859). New York: Random House, 1983.

Witherell, Carol, and Nel Noddings, eds. *Stories Lives Tell: Narrative and Dialogue in Education.* New York: Teachers College Press, 1991.

Woodiwiss, Kathleen E. *The Flame and the Flower.* New York: Avon, 1972.

Yapko, Michael D. *Suggestions of Abuse: True and False Memories of Childhood Sexual Trauma.* New York: Simon and Schuster, 1994.

Zimmerman, Bonnie. "Feminist Fiction and the Postmodern Challenge." *Post-Modern Fiction: A Bio-Bibliographical Guide.* Ed. Larry McCaffery. New York: Greenwood, 1986, 175–88.

Zinker, Joseph. *Creative Process in Gestalt Therapy.* New York: Random House, 1977.

INDEX

abandoned: cars in Oates's fiction, 88;
  by husband, 67; by sister, 40; by
  teacher, 191, 192
Abbott, Dr. Brian, 196, 233n 40
Abby, My Love, 31, 103, 231n 31, 233n
  38
ABC's "The Home Show," 227n 10
abortion, 66, 67, 69, 213
abuse, sexual: ix, x, 4, 6, 17, 216; bear
  in silence, 35; cycle of, 177; disclosure in classroom, 191; fantasy of,
  16, 36, 196; inhibited ability to
  speak or write, 5; molestation, 29;
  in *A Thousand Acres,* 168; of Woolf,
  11
academic: agnosis, 123; papers, 135;
  resistance fighter, 138; woman, 132
Acker, Kathy, 183, 184
Ackley, Katherine, 229n 18
advertisements, pedagogies of, 201
African American, 141, 142, 143, 233n
  41
agency, claim through writing, 14
agnosis, 123, 143, 145, 146
agoraphobia, of mother, 56
Alcoff, Linda, and Laura Gray, 20, 21,
  213, 227n 10
Alexander, Elizabeth, 189
Allison, Dorothy, 159–88, 206, 225n
  1, 232n 35
ambivalence, 118, 119, 121, 122
"American Canon Debate," 158
American Civil Liberties Union,
  President of, 209
Ames Middle School, 207, 208
amnesia, episodic, of public, 197
Angelou, Maya, 6, 34, 156, 231n 31
anger: 34, 35, 110, 120, 122, 131; of
  authors, 172, 173; displaced, 147; as

madness, 35; madness inherited, 37;
  may surface in classroom, 122
Anna O., first patient of Freud, 121
anthologies, feminist, 77
Antigone, 200, 201
Antrobus, Judith S., 226n 7
anxiety, 5, 20, 93, 107, 146
Anxious Power, 128, 229n 18
Anzaldua, Gloria, 20
Applebee, Arthur, 202
"Archimedes and the Paradox of
  Feminist Criticism," 86
Armstrong, Louise, x
Around 1981, 95
art, visual and verbal, 204
ashamed, survivors of incest, 162
Assault on Truth, 225n 1
assumptions shattered, 36
Atwood, Margaret, 144, 183, 203, 206,
  232n 35
author: xii, 4, 222, 223; dead 5; death
  of, birth of, 1; fluid, 22; god-the
  father, 6; learn through reading,
  202; might become, 8, 74; must
  become, 6, 14; of my life, 72, 219,
  220, 222, 223; requires listener or
  reader, 14; survival of, 95
authoring: collaborative, 152; of
  father, 151; a new kind of, 70; of an
  other, 152; of self, 15, 23, 152
authoritarian, views of father, 146
authority: 4; adolescent lack of, 128;
  assert in public, 213, 216; and
  authorship, xi; in classroom, 187;
  comes from membership in communities, feminist and professional,
  222; daughter deprived of, 163; of
  father, 137; of father, challenged by
  daughter's story, 157; of father-rule,

251

Froula, Christine, 82, 155, 157, 169
Frye, Joanne, 202
Frye, Northrop, 42

Gabler, Mel, and Norma Gabler, 144
Gallop, Jane, 20, 81, 82, 95, 169, 229n 17
Garden of Earthly Delights, A, 8, 85, 86, 88
Garner, Shirley Nelson, 133
Garrett-Pett, Will, and Donald Lawrence, 229n 18
Gates, Henry Louis, Jr., 96, 131, 143
gaze, male, 201, 204, 213
gender: blindness, 149; of censor, 150; and language, 210; -neutral, 150; of one subsumed by other, 200; training, 19; stereotypes, 115
Gender and Reading, 142
Geok-lin Lim, Shirley, 213–15
"Geraldo," 227n 10
Gilbert, Sandra M., 161, 165
Gilligan, Carol, 31, 97, 98, 201, 203
girls: absent from curricula, 201, 203; All American, 31; as competitors, 31; need visible affiliation with women, 202; desired dependency of, 210; exclusion of and by, 31, 203; good vs. bad, 8, 9, 14, 31; how to become mothers, 203; loss of voice of, 204; objectified in art and media, 204; protest by, 208; taught to avoid conflict, 205; taught to shrink, 206; triumph of, 206; visible and audible, 206; vulnerable to sacrifical morality of, 206; working class, 202, 205
Glass, James, 12, 17, 18
Glickman, Rose, 235n 48
God, patriarchal, 163
Goldman, Emma, 210, 211
Goldstein and Blackman, 147
Goldwater, Barry, 145

good vs. bad: 90; daughters, 8, 9, 14, 40, 45; girls, 8, 9, 14, 31
Goodlad, John, 129, 130
Graff, E. J., 175
Graff, Gerald, 143, 232n 34
grammar, 143
Gray, Laura, 20, 21, 213, 227n 10
Greene, Gayle, 96
grief, grieving, 12; of father, 28
Griffin, Susan, 20
guilt: 4, 35, 36, 63; induced by maternal fantasy of perfection, 66
Guinivere, 43

Hadley, Lee, 103, 230n 24
Hamlet, 37
Handmaid's Tale, The, 144
harassment, sexual, 206, 207, 208, 209
Hawthorne, Nathaniel, 184
heal, healing: xi, 118, 119
Hegland, Sarah, 207, 208, 209, 210, 235n 48
Heidi story, 145, 146
helplessness: daughter reduces feelings of, 41; learned, 36, 63, 64; engendered by revelations of abuse, 69
Hemenway, Robert, 160
Herman, Judith Lewis, 3, 9, 10, 11, 14, 36, 41, 45, 72, 82, 106, 155, 163, 178, 194, 197, 225,n 5, 229n 21, 230n 21, 230n 27, 230n 28, 231n 30
hermaphrodite, 92
Herndl, Diane Price, 229n 17
heroine, 63
Herron, Carolivia, 183, 225n 1, 233n 41
hierarchy, 140, 147
Hirsch, Marianne, 63, 71, 95, 233n 42
honor student(s), 31, 32
hooks, bell, 20
"hooters"/"cocks" debate, 207, 208, 210
Hooters Restaurant, 207